An Introduction to Programming with IDL

An Introduction to Programming with IDL

Interactive Data Language

Kenneth P. Bowman

Department of Atmospheric Sciences

Texas A&M University

ELSEVIER

AMSTERDAM · BOSTON · HEIDELBERG · LONDON
NEW YORK · OXFORD · PARIS · SAN DIEGO
SAN FRANCISCO · SINGAPORE · SYDNEY · TOKYO

Academic Press is an imprint of Elsevier

Acquisitions Editor: Jennifer Helé
Project Manager: Jeff Freeland
Marketing Manager: Linda Beattie
Cover Art Direction: Cate Rickard Barr
Interior Design: Julio Esperas
Composition: CEPHA Imaging Pvt. Ltd.
Cover Printer: Phoenix Color Corp.
Interior Printer: The Maple-Vail Book Manufacturing Group

Academic Press is an imprint of Elsevier
30 Corporate Drive, Suite 400, Burlington, MA 01803, USA
525 B Street, Suite 1900, San Diego, California 92101-4495, USA
84 Theobald's Road, London WC1X 8RR, UK

Library of Congress Cataloging-in-Publication Data
Application submitted

British Library Cataloguing-in-Publication Data
A catalogue record for this book is available from the British Library.

ISBN 13: 978-0-12-088559-6
ISBN 10: 0-12-088559-X

For information on all Elsevier Academic Press Publications
visit our Web site at www.books.elsevier.com

Printed in the United States of America
05 06 07 08 09 10   9 8 7 6 5 4 3 2 1

Contents

Preface

*It is a trite but true Observation, that Examples work
more forcibly on the Mind than Precepts.*

—Henry Fielding, *Joseph Andrews*

Students in undergraduate science and engineering programs typically take one semester of computer programming, often using Fortran or C or, more recently, Java or C++. Although these languages are all used to write scientific software, in one or two semesters it is difficult for students to develop the skills needed to write useful programs. Students who go on to graduate school are frequently unprepared to begin writing, or even using, scientific software.

Interactive Data Language (IDL) is a high-level language designed specifically for scientific programming and data analysis. In addition to a complete set of basic programming tools (numerical types, strings, arrays, structures, pointers, etc.), it includes a wide range of graphical functions and device drivers. A major advantage of IDL compared to traditional programming languages is that beginners can begin writing programs and plotting graphs after only a few hours of use. Although not covered in this book, IDL also makes it easy to create programs with point-and-click graphical user interfaces and to develop programs using an object-oriented style. IDL is available on Microsoft Windows and Unix-derived operating systems, including popular commercial versions of Unix, Linux, and Apple's Mac OS X. With a little planning, IDL programs can be moved easily between platforms.

This book is intended to be used in an introductory computer programming course for science and engineering students at either the undergraduate or graduate level. Students can learn IDL quickly enough that it can be taught as part of a topical course, either as a separate "lab" section or as an integral part of the course. It does not assume that students have experience with another programming language, although occasional comparisons are made with Fortran or C to help students who are familiar with those languages adjust to IDL syntax and programming style.

The goal of this book is to teach beginners enough about programming, and give them enough practical experience, that they can write useful programs for courses in their discipline or for their research. This book introduces students to the following concepts:

- Variables and data structures
    - Variable assignment and expression evaluation
    - When to use integers and floating-point numbers
    - Underflow and overflow
    - Round-off error
    - Infinities and Not-a-Numbers
    - Arrays and IDL array syntax
    - Data structures

- Input and output
    - When and how to use text files, binary files, and scientific file formats, such as netCDF
    - Trade-offs among speed, portability, simplicity, and transparency

- Procedures and functions
    - How procedures and functions work
    - Positional arguments
    - Keyword arguments

- Programming style
    - Writing readable programs
    - Modularizing programs

- Graphics
    - Making good graphs: line graphs, contour graphs, and maps
    - Generating printed output

- Typical applications
    - Basic statistics and pseudorandom numbers
    - Interpolation
    - Fast Fourier transforms

You will notice that this list contains some relatively fundamental concepts, such as integer and floating-point arithmetic, and some very practical topics, such as how to plot a map or print a graph. In keeping with the quotation at the beginning of this preface, these concepts are taught primarily through examples. The example programs and data sets used in this book are all available via the World Wide Web (see Chapter 3 for details).

Acknowledgments

Many people assisted with the preparation of this book; my apologies to anyone I may have overlooked. My thanks go first to the students in my classes at Texas A&M University for whom I wrote this book. They used earlier versions when it was only a set of class notes and helped track down numerous errors along the way. The people of Research Systems, Inc., the developers of IDL, have been very supportive of this effort, particularly Karl Nichols, who encouraged me when I first approached RSI for help. Much of the final draft of the book was completed while I was a visitor to the Atmospheric Chemistry Division (ACD) at the National Center for Atmospheric Research (NCAR), which is funded by the National Science Foundation. My thanks to my host, Bill Randel, and an outstanding group of colleagues and friends, Andrew Gettelman, Doug Kinnison, Steve Massie, Dan Marsh, Laura Pan, and many others, as well as to ACD and NCAR, for providing such an excellent environment in which to work. I would like to thank all of the contributors to the Usenet newsgroup `comp.lang.idl-pvwave`, where zealous, convivial, and sometimes perplexing discussions of IDL go on every day. Over the years I have learned much of what I know about IDL from the generous assistance of its participants. It is, in my experience, a unique group of online compatriots, many of whom have met only electronically. Finally, thanks to my family, Jean Ann and Ellie, for putting up with all the time away from them needed to write a book.

Part I

IDL BASICS

1

Introduction

1.1 What Is IDL?

IDL is a computer software system that is produced and sold by Research Systems Inc. of Boulder, Colorado. IDL is an acronym for *Interactive Data Language*.[1] IDL consists of both an interactive programming environment and a programming language. It is used in a wide range of science and engineering disciplines for processing and analyzing numerical and image data. It draws features from many other programming languages, including Fortran, C, BASIC, and APL, but it differs from each of those languages in important ways.

The most important difference between IDL and many of the languages used for data analysis is that it is truly interactive. Within the IDL environment (or *interpreter*), it is possible to type a command and see the results immediately. This is quite different from Fortran and C, two languages that are often used to write scientific data analysis software. To create a Fortran program, a programmer must first create a file (or multiple files) containing the Fortran program (also called the *source code*). This is done with a *text editor*, which is a word-processing program suited for writing computer programs. The Fortran program consists of statements in the Fortran language. The Fortran program is then *compiled* into a form that the computer can understand and execute. The compiled program is referred to as the *object code*. The object code is then *linked* with any other precompiled programs (*libraries*) that are needed. The object code can then be executed. If an error (or *bug*) is found in the program, it can be corrected, recompiled, relinked, and then re-executed. Although much of this process can be automated (using a utility program called *make*, for example), it can be rather time-consuming to write and debug a Fortran program.

Compiled languages like Fortran and C do have some advantages over interactive or interpreted languages. For one thing, compilers can often organize the object code so that it executes very quickly. This is called *optimization*. As a result, compiled languages can usually execute a program faster than the equivalent program written in an interactive language. Large computer

---

1   Not to be confused with another type of software called *Interface Definition Language* that has the same acronym.

models that have heavy computational requirements are usually written in Fortran or C.

Many modern desktop computers and workstations have more than one central processing unit (CPU). For some types of operations, IDL can make use of a small number of CPUs (probably in the range of two to eight CPUs) using a technique called multithreading. Large-scale scientific computers, on the other hand, often have hundreds or even thousands of CPUs. IDL is not designed to make use of those *massively parallel* computers. Therefore, when developing for high-performance, highly parallel computers, programmers generally use advanced *parallel* Fortran and C compilers.

Why use IDL, then? There are several good reasons. One is that you can take a quick look at a data set without going to the trouble of writing an entire program for that purpose. Using IDL it is often possible to browse through a large data set with only a few IDL commands. Even complex graphs can usually be plotted with only a few lines of IDL. A second reason to use IDL is that the "programmer's loop" of write-compile-execute-debug can be done very quickly without the use of special software known as a debugger. (IDL *is* the debugger.) Third, IDL contains a *large* number of built-in functions for statistics, graphics, linear algebra, and the like. Finally, it is remarkably easy to write self-contained programs in IDL with truly *interactive* interfaces, including menus, buttons, windows, dialog boxes, and graphics. In the author's experience, the combination of these factors makes it possible to write better, more flexible programs much faster than using Fortran or C. If you have experience with other programming languages, some of the other advantages of IDL will become more apparent as you use it.

The most recent version of IDL runs under a variety of operating systems, including the most commonly used versions of Unix, Linux, Mac OS X, and Windows. (This book was developed and tested with IDL Version 6.1.) Visit the Research Systems web site (see Section 1.2) for current information on the platforms supported. With a modest amount of care, IDL programs can be written that will run on all supported systems. IDL programs are thus quite *portable*.

Recent versions of IDL also include extensive *object-oriented programming* features. However, object-oriented programming is not covered in this book.

1.2   IDL Resources

Information about IDL is available from the Research Systems web site:

```
http://rsinc.com
```

Among other things, you can download an almost fully functional demo version of IDL from the web site and install it on your computer. Without purchasing a license, the demo version will run for 7 minutes before automatically exiting.

RSI also sells a student version of IDL. If you qualify, you can purchase the student version for your personal computer at a reduced price. At the present time, the student version of IDL is a fully functional copy of the next-to-last release of IDL.

Another useful source of IDL information is the Usenet newsgroup `comp.lang.idl-pvwave`. (PV-WAVE is a data analysis and visualization package based on IDL that is produced and sold by Visual Numerics, Inc. At one time IDL and PV-WAVE were identical, but the two products have diverged over the years. The basic syntax and functionality remain the same, however.) Do not go to the newsgroup `comp.lang.idl`, which concerns the Interface Definition Language mentioned earlier. If you are not familiar with Usenet or newsgroups, ask your local system administrator for help. `Comp.lang.idl-pvwave` is a bulletin board for the exchange of questions and answers about IDL. Newcomers to `comp.lang.idl-pvwave` are encouraged to read the newsgroup for at least a few days before posting questions in order to learn the Usenet rules of etiquette. The volume of traffic in `comp.lang.idl-pvwave` is generally low. If you are spending a lot of time programming in IDL, it will be worth your time to read the newsgroup on a daily basis.

1.3   The IDL Software System

The heart of the IDL software system is the interpreter, which translates IDL statements into instructions that the computer can understand and execute. You can use IDL in its simplest form by simply typing `idl` at the system prompt in a terminal window. IDL must be installed on your computer and located where your user environment can find it. (On a computer running Windows, you double-click the IDL icon, which starts the full IDL Development Environment, which is discussed below.) A snapshot of IDL running in a terminal window is shown in Figure 1.1. When using IDL in a terminal window, you can enter commands and execute them or you can run more complex programs stored in files. This approach to running IDL is referred to as the *command-line environment*. To create and save programs, you will need to use a separate program mentioned earlier, a *text editor*. Basics of using the command-line environment are covered in Chapter 3.

In addition to the command-line interpreter, IDL has *device drivers*, which are software packages that allow IDL to display graphics on different types of graphic devices. On Microsoft Windows systems, IDL uses the standard Windows graphics functions to display graphics windows. On Unix and Mac OS X systems, a software package called *X-Windows* is used to display graphical output on the screen. X-Windows is a separate software package that must be running at the same time as IDL. If you are using this book in a class, your instructor will show you how to start IDL and X-Windows on your computer.

IDL also includes a device driver for creating PostScript output. This is the preferred method for creating printed graphical output, although other

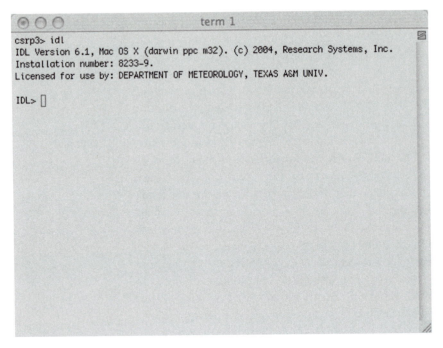

FIGURE 1.1   IDL running at the command line in a terminal window. (Screen capture)

options are available. Creating printed output in IDL will be covered in several different chapters in Part IV of this book.

Recent versions of IDL include a complete software *Development Environment* (IDLDE) that can be used to run and edit IDL programs and to display graphics. To start IDLDE you enter `idlde` at the command line instead of `idl`. On Mac OS X and Unix systems, the IDL Development Environment uses X-Windows. On Windows systems, you double-click the IDL icon. A snapshot of the IDL Development Environment running on a Mac OS X system is shown in Figure 1.2. *With newer versions of Windows, it is not possible to use the command-line version of IDL. When you start IDL on Windows systems it will automatically use the Development Environment version.*

The Development Environment provides windows for editing programs, entering commands, viewing text output, viewing graphics, debugging, and managing program files. On Unix, Linux, and OS X systems, the Development Environment uses the X-Windows system to display all of the necessary windows.

Although it is possible to use the Development Environment on any system on which IDL runs (Unix, Linux, OS X, or Windows), this book does not make specific reference to DE functions. There are several reasons for this. First, the DE on X-Windows systems is somewhat clunky compared to the Windows version. As a result, there is less incentive to use the DE on non-Windows systems. Second, the DE has a complicated interface with many menus, buttons, and settings. It takes up a great deal of screen space, and many of the functions are of little use to beginning programmers. This

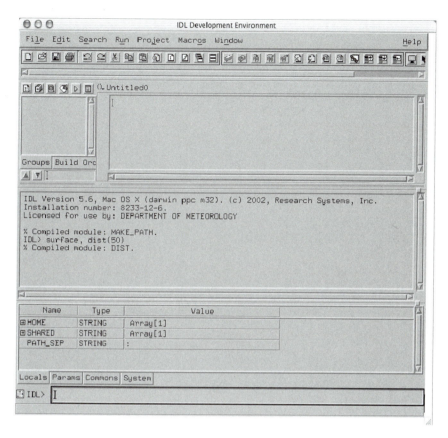

FIGURE 1.2   The IDL Development Environment. (Screen capture)

book concentrates on the IDL language, not on the Development Environment. Third, it is not necessary to use the DE to learn IDL. To keep this book from growing even longer than it is, material on the DE has been omitted. Fourth, at the author's institution we have Unix labs and Mac labs, but no PC (Windows) labs, and we customarily do not use the DE. Fifth, many users prefer a different text editor to the one included in the DE. (Unix and Mac OS X users can find a very nice emacs mode for IDL. Search comp.lang.idl-pvwave for references to emacs.) Finally, this is largely a matter of personal taste, so if you find that you prefer to use the Development Environment, please do so. Microsoft Windows users will, of course, have to use the DE.

IDL Manuals and Books

This chapter describes some of the features of this book, the parts of the IDL user manuals that you are most likely to use, and a few of the third-party books that are available on IDL programming.

2.1 Features of This Book

2.1.1 Example Programs and Data

Because IDL is an interactive language, many of the programming examples in this book can be executed by typing the commands at the IDL prompt. Here is a one-line example:

```
IDL> print, 'Hello, world.'
Hello, world.
```

   This sort of example appears in the book exactly as it would appear on your computer terminal if you executed the same commands. As you work through this book, it is a good idea to have an IDL session open on your computer so that you can try the examples and experiment on your own.

   Sequences of IDL commands that are too long to enter at the command line can be saved in *program files*. These files can be executed in different ways (more on this later). IDL program files have the suffix ".pro", for example, animate.pro or surface1.pro. All of the example programs and data files used in this book are available at

```
http://idl.Tamu.edu
```

You should download those files to your computer and place them in your IDL search path. Details of how to do that are in Chapter 3 and on the web site. A list of the program files and short descriptions of each program are included in B, organized by topic.

2.1.2 Figures and Illustrations

Most of the figures in this book were created using IDL. The programs that created each figure are included with the example programs. Furthermore, each figure caption includes the name of the IDL procedure that generated the figure. The source is either *screen capture* (a snapshot of the actual computer screen), the program name (for example, LINEGRAPH1), or *not IDL* (if the figure was not created with IDL).

In order to keep the programming examples in this book short and clear, and also include good graphics, multiple versions of some programs are included. For example, surface1.pro plots a wiremesh-type surface plot on the computer screen. A longer version of the same program, surface1_ps.pro creates a more detailed plot (including labels, for example) and can optionally save the graphics output to a PostScript file. The PostScript file created by surface1_ps.pro was used to make Figure 18.4. Both versions of the program are included with the example programs.

2.2   IDL Documentation from Research Systems

All told, RSI provides thousands of pages of documentation divided among many different manuals. Although the sheer size of the IDL manuals can be daunting, the online files provided by RSI usually make it easy to find what you need.

The IDL manuals are included with the IDL software in the form of Portable Document Format (PDF) files. These files can be viewed with the free Adobe Acrobat Reader software (and with some third-party software). The manuals consist of a number of volumes ("books"). Each volume is in a separate PDF file. The files are located in the /help directory of the IDL distribution. On a Unix or OS X system, the files are typically found in /usr/local/rsi/idl_6.1/help (for IDL version 6.1). You may need to ask your system manager for the location of the files on your computer.

To accommodate older operating systems that do not allow long file names, the PDF files have somewhat obscure names like getstart.pdf, datamine.pdf, and onlguide.pdf. For convenience I generally create a link (also called a shortcut or alias) to the file onlguide.pdf so that I can open it easily. This file has links to all of the other RSI documentation. You should not move or rename any of the PDF files. If you do, Acrobat Reader may not be able to follow the links from one book to another.

The complete IDL documentation can be accessed from the *Online Guide* (onlguide.pdf). While working through this book, the two manuals that you will use most often are:

IDL Reference Guide   This volume has descriptions of the hundreds of built-in IDL procedures and functions. Once you learn basic IDL syntax, you will find yourself referring to this volume much more often than any of the others. To find a description of a procedure or function, click on *IDL Reference Guide*, then **IDL Commands**, then **Alphabetical List of Routines**. This provides quick access to each procedure definition.

Scientific Data Formats   This manual contains descriptions of the procedures and functions used to read and write netCDF, CDF, and HDF data files. These files are commonly used in science and engineering to store scientific data. Reading and writing netCDF files is covered in Chapters 13 and 14.

The PDF files contain embedded links to make it easy to find related material. For example, click your way to the description of the BYTE function in *IDL Reference Guide*. On the first page you will see a link to the section of *Building IDL Applications* that describes type-conversion functions. At the bottom of the next page are links to the reference pages for the other type-conversion functions in *IDL Reference Guide* (these include DOUBLE, FLOAT, LONG, and others).

To find documentation for a particular topic, you can use the following:

IDL Master Index As the name indicates, this is a combined index to all of the volumes of manuals.

IDL Quick Reference This contains a list of all the IDL procedures and functions sorted into categories, such as **Array Creation** or **Color Table Manipulation**.

As you learn more about IDL, or to learn details of a particular topic, you can refer to:

Using IDL This is a reasonably good introduction to IDL for experienced programmers. It is difficult for beginners, though.

Building IDL Applications This is a typical computer-language reference manual. It contains descriptions of IDL syntax, data types, input and output methods, and more.

Image Processing in IDL As the name indicates, this volume covers image display and analysis techniques, as well as the use of color in IDL.

The IDL manuals, like most computer manuals, make it easy to find something *if you already know its name*. On the other hand, if you are trying to find a procedure to search an ordered list of numbers, how would you know that it is called VALUE_LOCATE? (The sort function is called SORT, but the search function is called VALUE_LOCATE. As you can see, some procedure names are not as obvious as one might hope!) For that you must use the *Master Index* or *IDL Quick Reference*.

Throughout the rest of the book, there will be marginal notes like this example to point you to particular parts of the IDL documentation.

See the VALUE_LOCATE function in *IDL Reference Guide*.

2.3 Other IDL Books

There are a number of books available on IDL that are not produced by RSI. Two of these may be of interest to experienced programmers who are new to IDL.

The first is *Practical IDL Programming*, by Liam E. Gumley (Gumley, 2002). This book covers a large part of the IDL language and toolkits. It has many examples, and is a good choice for a reference book to follow this one. Like this book, *Practical IDL Programming* does not cover how to use IDL objects. Liam Gumley maintains a web site at `http://www.gumley.com` with information about the book and some very useful sample programs.

The second book is *IDL Programming Techniques, Second Edition* by David W. Fanning (Fanning, 2002). This is also a relatively comprehensive look at IDL, and is particularly strong in the area of graphics output. It includes substantial material on writing programs with graphical user interfaces (widget interfaces). Finally, it introduces the ideas of object-oriented programming and shows how to write basic object-oriented programs in IDL. David Fanning has an extensive web site of IDL-related material (`http://www.dfanning.com`) with a wide variety of useful IDL programs, as well as very helpful explanations of some of the more obscure corners of the language.

Interactive IDL

This chapter is a quick introduction to using IDL for interactive calculations. The goal of this chapter is to get you started using IDL, entering interactive commands, and plotting graphs.

3.1 IDL Commands

The following IDL procedures and functions are used in this chapter:

- PRINT procedure
- EXIT command
- .continue executive command (.c)
- HELP procedure
- FINDGEN function
- LINDGEN function
- PLOT procedure
- WINDOW procedure
- XSURFACE procedure

3.2 Setting Up IDL

To get the most from this chapter, you should be sitting at your computer with IDL running. You need to follow several steps before IDL will run correctly. These include:

1. Install and license IDL and set up the IDL environment so that the operating system can find the main IDL program and related files.

2. Set up your personal IDL directory and optionally install the example programs and data files from this book.

3. Set user preferences for IDL.

If you have problems with the initial installation and configuration, consult your system administrator or local computer guru for help.

3.2.1 Installing and Licensing IDL

If IDL is not already installed on your computer, follow the directions in the manual *Installing and Licensing IDL* on the IDL installation CD-ROM. Separate installation procedures are provided for Windows, Unix, and Mac OS X installations. If you do not have administrative privileges for your computer, you will need to ask your system administrator to install IDL.

On Unix systems, including Mac OS X, when a user types a command at the system prompt, the user's Unix *shell* program is responsible for finding the desired program and executing it. For Unix and Mac OS X users, instructions for setting up your shell so that it can find IDL are in the chapter Setting Up and Running IDL on UNIX/Macintosh in *Installing and Licensing IDL*.

On Windows systems, IDL is started by double-clicking the IDL icon.

3.2.2 Your Personal IDL Directory

Before using IDL you should create a directory in which to store your IDL program files. Within your home directory create a subdirectory called idl. Note the use of lowercase for the directory name.

All of the example programs and data files used in this book can be downloaded and run on your computer. To download the example programs and data, go to

```
http://idl.tamu.edu
```

Follow the links to the example programs and then select the appropriate download version for your computer. When uncompressed, the example programs and data require approximately 20 MB of disk space. Uncompress the downloaded file within your idl directory. The result is a subdirectory named bowman containing the example programs and data sets.

If you are new to IDL and have not already created a startup.pro file, copy the file startup.pro in the bowman subdirectory up one level to the idl directory.[1] If you do not wish to download the example programs and data sets, you should at least download the example startup.pro file and place it in your idl directory.

When you finish installing the example programs, the contents of your idl directory should look like this:

```
idl/
    bowman/
        add_arrays.pro

        .

        .
```

---

1   *Copying* the startup.pro file instead of *moving* it leaves the original file in the bowman directory. This can be a useful reference in the event you have problems after making changes to your startup.pro file.

```
        data/
        doc.html

          .

        image/

          .

          .

        ps/

          .

          .

        wx_ob__define.pro
    startup.pro
```

Dots indicate that items have been omitted from the list. A slash at the end of a name indicates that the item is a directory. The file `doc.html` contains descriptions of each of the example programs. You can view the file with any web browser. The `image` and `ps` directories contain images and PostScript files, respectively, created by the example programs.

You can create additional subdirectories within the `idl` directory to organize your program files. For example, you may want to create directories called `image` and `ps` within `idl` to hold image or PostScript output created by your own programs. When you create new directories, I recommend that you follow the Unix convention and use names that are entirely lowercase.

3.2.3 Setting IDL Preferences

User preferences are specified by the IDL *startup file*. This file contains IDL commands that are automatically executed when IDL is started. This section explains how to set up IDL to use the `startup.pro` file in your `idl` directory.[2] As you gain experience with IDL, you can customize the `startup.pro` file as needed.

Designating the Startup File

For Windows and IDLDE users, the location of the `startup.pro` file is set by using the **Preferences** menu item on the **File** menu. Select **Preferences** from the **File** menu and then click the **Startup** tab. Click the **Select Startup File...** button and then navigate to the `startup.pro` file. Select the `startup.pro` file and click **OK**.

For Unix and Mac OS X users running from the command line, the location of the startup file is contained in the user's shell variable IDL_STARTUP; c-shell and t-shell users should have something like this in their `.cshrc` or `.tcshrc` files:

```
setenv IDL_STARTUP ~/idl/startup.pro
```

---

2   The file does not have to be named `startup.pro`, but it is customary.

For Bourne shell and k-shell users, their `.profile` file should contain a line
like this:

```
export IDL_STARTUP=$HOME/idl/startup.pro
```

The tilde or `$HOME` indicates the user's home directory. These shell
commands set the user's shell environment variable `IDL_STARTUP` to
`~/idl/startup.pro`. This is how it looks on my computer. I can print my
home directory with

```
csrp3> echo ~
/Users/bowman
```

or

```
csrp3> echo $HOME
/Users/bowman
```

And I can print my `IDL_STARTUP` variable with

```
csrp3> echo $IDL_STARTUP
/Users/bowman/idl/startup.pro
```

My home directory is `/Users/bowman`, and my `IDL_STARTUP` variable is
set to `/Users/bowman/idl/startup.pro`. That file is executed each time
I start IDL.

Contents of the Example Startup File

The example `startup.pro` file that you downloaded above looks like
this:

```
;Set compiler options
COMPILE_OPT IDL2

;User's directory for IDL programs
!PATH = !PATH + ':' + EXPAND_PATH('+idl')

;Have IDL provide backing store
DEVICE, RETAIN = 2

;Path to example programs and data
DEFSYSV, '!Bowman', (FILE_SEARCH('idl/bowman/', $
   /FULLY_QUALIFY_PATH, /MARK_DIRECTORY))[0]

;Double precision degrees to radians
DEFSYSV, '!DDTOR',                 !DPI/180.0D0, 1
```

```
;Double precision radians to degrees
DEFSYSV, '!DRADEG',             180.0D0/!DPI, 1


;Speed of light in vacuum (m s^-1)
DEFSYSV, '!Speed_of_light',  299792458.0D0, 1
;Planck constant (J s)
DEFSYSV, '!Planck',            6.62606876D-34, 1
;Universal gas constant (J K^-1 kmol^-1)
DEFSYSV, '!Universal_gas',       8314.4720D0, 1
;Stefan-Boltzman constant (W m^-2 K^-4)
DEFSYSV, '!Stefan_Boltzmann',  5.670400D-08, 1
;Avogadro's number (molecules kmol^-1)
DEFSYSV, '!Avogadro',          6.02214199D+26, 1
;Gravitational constant (J K^-1)
DEFSYSV, '!Gravitation',          6.673D-11, 1
;Boltzmann's constant (N m^2 kg^-2)
DEFSYSV, '!Boltzmann',          1.3806503D-23, 1
```

The lines beginning with semicolons are *comments*.

The first three IDL commands in this file are the most important. The first is

```
COMPILE_OPT IDL2
```

which tells IDL to create 4-byte integers by default (LONGs) rather than 2-byte integers (INTs). It also tells IDL to require the use of square brackets, [and], rather than parentheses, (and), for array subscripts. Parentheses can be used only for function references, for example, SIN(x). More information on these topics can be found in Chapters 5 and 15, respectively.

The second IDL command is:

```
!PATH = !PATH + ':' + EXPAND_PATH('+idl')
```

This line adds your personal IDL directory idl to the IDL search path. The IDL search path is the list of directories that IDL searches when you enter a command at the IDL prompt. By adding your idl directory and its subdirectories to the search path, IDL can automatically find your programs and compile and run them. If you store IDL programs in locations outside the idl directory, IDL will not be able to find them automatically unless you add those directories to the search path.

The IDL search path is stored in the IDL *system variable* !PATH. The exclamation point is part of the variable name. Names of all IDL system variables begin with an exclamation point. System variables are *global variables* that can be accessed from within any IDL program or from the command line.

When you start IDL, !PATH is initially set so that IDL can find all of the built-in procedures and functions. Users should add their personal directories at the *end* of the search path, so that IDL finds built-in functions first.

The above command adds the user's idl directory to the search path. The +
sign tells the EXPAND_PATH function to find all of the subdirectories within
the idl directory (recursively). These are also added to the search path.

The third IDL command (DEVICE, RETAIN = 2) ensures that graphics
windows are redrawn when they are covered by other windows and then
uncovered. On Unix and Mac systems, this can also be accomplished by
changing your X-Windows settings.

The remaining lines in the startup.pro file define optional system variables by using the DEFSYSV command. The first example defines a system
variable !Bowman that contains that path to the example programs and data.
The remaining lines are primarily physical constants. Defining these constants as system variables, rather than entering them explicitly into each
program that uses them, ensures that consistent values are used throughout
your programs. As an example,

```
IDL> print, !planck
     6.6260688e-34
```

Because I use IDL in atmospheric science classes, my startup file includes a
number of physical constants, such as the speed of light. For brevity, some of
the constants included in the example startup file have been omitted from the
listing above. The point to remember is that the startup file is a good place to
define constants that you want to be sure have the same value in all of your
programs. This helps to ensure consistency in your numerical calculations.

3.3   Starting and Exiting IDL

Once the necessary environment variables have been set, the idl directory
has been created, and the startup.pro file has been designated, it's time to
start IDL.

IDL is started by entering idl at the system prompt or by double-clicking
the IDL icon in Windows. Most Unix commands are given in lowercase
letters. Unix is *case sensitive*, and unless special arrangements have been
made, typing IDL or Idl will result in an error message:

```
csrp3> IDL
IDL: Command not found.
```

Depending on other factors, the error message may be obscure:

```
csrp3> Idl
Idl: Permission denied.
```

Both of these error messages really mean "There is no executable file (program)
with *exactly* that name on this computer." If IDL does not start, and you get
an error message that you cannot decipher, ask your system administrator for
help or contact RSI.

When you start IDL, you should see something like this:

```
csrp3> idl
IDL Version 6.1, Mac OS X (darwin ppc m32). (c) 2004, Research Systems, Inc.
Installation number: 8233-12-6.
Licensed for use by: DEPARTMENT OF METEOROLOGY

IDL> print, 3 + 5
          8
IDL> quit
% Attempt to call undefined procedure/function: 'QUIT'.
% Execution halted at: $MAIN$
IDL> exit
csrp3>
```

In this case, IDL is running on a computer named `csrp3`. The Unix command-line prompt `csrp3>` includes the computer's name. Your command-line prompt will generally be different.

As it starts up, IDL prints the version number and the type of operating system on which it is running. In this case, it is Mac OS X, which is a Unix-based operating system. The next line is the license number, followed by the name of the licensee. After completing the start-up process, IDL displays the input prompt, `IDL>`. When you see this prompt you can enter IDL commands to do calculations or create graphics. Here we printed the result of the operation `3 + 5`.

As discussed earlier, if you are running on a Unix or Mac OS X system, you should also have X-Windows running so that you can display graphics. Once you have IDL running, you can test whether X-Windows is also running by entering `window` at the IDL prompt. It should open a new, empty graphics window. If you are using the IDL Development Environment (if, for example, you are running on a Windows computer), graphics windows should open automatically.

> See the `WINDOW` procedure in *IDL Reference Guide.*

To exit IDL and return to the command line, enter `exit` at the IDL prompt. As you can see above, IDL does not recognize the command `quit`. It prints an error message in response. Only `exit` will end the current IDL session.

3.4 Interrupting and Restarting IDL Calculations

Many IDL operations are very quick and are completed immediately after the command is entered. When working with large arrays of data or lengthy programs, however, some operations can require large amounts of time to complete (theoretically, as long as necessary). While IDL is performing calculations, the IDL prompt is not available to the user, and new commands cannot be executed. Depending on the type of IDL license, however, multiple IDL sessions can usually be started in separate terminal windows. This allows the user to work interactively while long calculations are done in a separate IDL session.

Sometimes it is necessary for the user to interrupt calculations in progress. For example, while testing a new program, the user may realize that the program contains an error (bug). Rather than wait for the program to complete (or crash), the calculation can be interrupted by pressing control-c on the keyboard. When this is done, IDL will stop execution as soon as it completes the currently executing IDL command (that is, the current line of the program). Because execution of a single line may take quite a lot of time, the program may still not be interrupted immediately. If you cannot wait for the current command to finish, the only option is to *kill* the IDL session by using features of the operating system (for example, the Unix kill command or the Mac OS X Activity Monitor).

To continue execution once it has been interrupted, enter .continue at the command line. (The dot is part of the command.) This can be abbreviated .c.

The .continue command is an example of an IDL *executive command*. IDL has a small set of executive commands that are used to compile IDL programs, control IDL sessions, and control IDL execution. A list of all of the IDL executive commands is given in Chapter 4 of Using IDL. To use this book, however, you will only need to know two executive commands. One is the .continue (.c) command just mentioned. The other is the .compile executive command, which, as the name indicates, is used to compile IDL programs. The .compile command can be abbreviated .com. (Programs can also be compiled with the .run command, which can be abbreviated .r. Chapter 15 contains more on compiling programs.)

3.5   Simple IDL Statements

It is a tradition in computer programming textbooks for the first example program to produce the greeting "Hello, world." In IDL, this is quite simple

```
IDL> print, 'Hello, world.'
Hello, world.
```

The PRINT command tells IDL to print in the terminal window the results of evaluating the *expressions* that follow the PRINT command. There can be more than one expression, separated by commas. In this case, there is only one expression, a *literal string* containing the phrase "Hello, world." The beginning and end of the string are indicated by the single quotation marks. Note that the quotation marks do not appear in the output, but the period, which is inside the quotes, does.

See the PRINT procedure in *IDL Reference Guide*.

In IDL you can use either single or double quotes to *delimit* a string (starting and ending quotes must match):

See *String Constants* in *Building IDL Applications*.

```
IDL> print, "Hello, world."
Hello, world.
```

This is handy for occasions when you want to include quotation marks (or an apostrophe) inside a string:

```
IDL> print, "Ken's world."
Ken's world.
```

Generally this book will use single quotes, except in cases where nested quotes (quotes within quotes) are needed.

IDL commands and variable names are *not* case sensitive. This means that

```
IDL> print, 'Hello, world.'
Hello, world.
```

and

```
IDL> PRINT, 'Hello, world.'
Hello, world.
```

produce exactly the same result. IDL does not care whether you type the PRINT command as print or as PRINT, or even as PrInT.

Literal strings, however, *are* case sensitive, so

```
IDL> print, 'Hello, world.'
Hello, world.
```

and

```
IDL> print, 'HELLO, WORLD.'
HELLO, WORLD.
```

give different results.

In this book, I use lowercase letters for IDL commands when entering them at the command line. This saves some effort when typing and is the way that people typically work when trying out short calculations interactively. When writing programs, however, I follow a strict rule of entering all IDL commands in uppercase. Generally, variable names will be lowercase. (Except for instances when upper case makes sense, such as writing T instead of t to represent temperature.) Using upper- and lowercase consistently makes it much easier to see the structure of a program. This, in turn, makes it easier to find errors in programs, which is an extremely important part of programming. Guidelines for writing readable programs and examples of good and bad programming style are given in A.

Let's move on and try some numerical calculations:

```
IDL> print, 3 + 5
       8
```

IDL generally does not care whether you include spaces or not, because it looks for commas to separate items in a list. So the following statements produce the same output:

```
IDL> print,3+5
       8
IDL> print,    3    +    5
       8
```

IDL may not care, but for humans there are big differences in the readability of the three versions of this simple statement. The human brain is very good at identifying patterns (and deviations from patterns) in visual material. Later on I will offer guidelines on how to lay out programs so as to make it as easy as possible to detect errors.

The command above tells IDL to evaluate the expression 3 + 5 and print the result. Obviously IDL knows about numbers, as well as strings, and how to carry out arithmetic operations. By the way, the following is also a valid IDL command

```
IDL> print, '3' + '5'
35
```

You can see from this that the + sign has two meanings in IDL. If the operands are numbers, then it means addition. If the operands are strings, it means concatenation (that is, stick the strings together). In this example, the 35 is actually a string, not a number.

See *String Concatenation* in *Building IDL Applications*.

Note that the results of the operations above (a number or a string) are printed and then discarded. They are not automatically stored for later use. In order to save results, you must assign the result to a variable (more on that shortly).

3.6   Getting Information

If you have *any* question about a particular expression or variable, there is a powerful, built-in facility to answer those questions, HELP:

See the HELP procedure in *IDL Reference Guide*.

```
IDL> help, 3 + 5
<Expression>    LONG      =           8
```

In this case, HELP tells us that 3 + 5 is an expression. It has a type of LONG and a value of 8. For comparison,

```
IDL> help, '3' + '5'
<Expression>    STRING    = '35'
```

You can *always* use HELP at the command line. It is usually the quickest and easiest way to sort out a complex operation, and it is essential for diagnosing errors in your program (debugging).

IDL can evaluate standard arithmetic expressions:

```
IDL> print, (3 + 5) * (2 + 4)^3
    1728
```

Note that parentheses are used in the traditional manner to indicate the order of operations. The ^ character indicates exponentiation.

3.7   Variables

In all of the examples so far, we have evaluated an expression and then simply printed the result. Obviously there are times when it is necessary to save the results of a calculation for later use. In IDL, as in many computer languages, this is done with the equal sign, as in:

See *Variables* in *Building IDL Applications*.

```
IDL> x = 3 + 5
IDL> help, x
X               LONG      =              8
IDL> print, x
          8
```

In the first statement above, the equal sign means "evaluate the expression on the right-hand side of the equal sign, store the result in computer memory, and use the name x to access the stored value." The thing named x is called a *variable* because the actual value assigned to that name can change. Note that this use of the equal sign is very different from the usual mathematical meaning of the equal sign. Typing "help, x" tells us that IDL has created a variable named x. The type of the variable x is LONG, and its value is 8.

The fundamental operation of assignment is one area in which IDL is different from many other computer languages. In many languages, the properties (type and size) of a variable must be defined before it is used. In IDL, on the other hand, if a variable does *not* exist, a new variable is *automatically created with properties that match those of the expression on the right-hand side*. Similarly, in some languages it is not possible to assign an expression of one type to a variable of another type. In IDL, on the other hand, if a variable already exists, assigning a new value to it causes the old value in memory to be destroyed and replaced with the value of the expression on the right-hand side, even if the type or structure of the variable is different. Here is an example:

```
IDL> x = 6.0
IDL> help, x
X               FLOAT     =         6.00000
IDL> x = 3 + 5
```

```
IDL> help, x
X               LONG      =           8
```

First, a variable named x is created and given the value of 6.0. The HELP command tells us that x is a floating-point variable. Executing the statement x = 3 + 5 destroys the old variable and replaces it with a LONG type variable with a value of 8.

This mutability of variables can be disconcerting to a Fortran or C programmer. It has both advantages and disadvantages. If you don't keep track of your variables, it is possible to make some very obscure mistakes. IDL will *not* tell you if you destroy an existing variable or change its type, size, or value. On the other hand, there are considerable advantages to being able to create variables on the fly. For one thing, the lengthy type declaration statements of Fortran and C are unnecessary. Programs are frequently much shorter in IDL than in Fortran or C. Partly as a result of this, IDL programs can usually be written much more quickly than equivalent Fortran or C programs.

As in any computer language, it is the responsibility of the programmer to keep track of variable names and types. It is important to pick variable names carefully so that their type and meaning are as obvious as possible. As a simple first step, you should try to follow the programming convention of using names that start with i, j, k, 1, m, or n for integers, and starting floating-point variable names with other letters. This is also consistent with general mathematical usage. Like most style rules, this one is not absolute, but you should have a good reason for breaking it.

3.8 Arrays

In addition to simple variables that have a single value (these are called *scalars*), IDL has powerful features for working with *arrays*. One-dimensional arrays are often referred to as *vectors*. Two-dimensional arrays can be used to store *matrices* for linear algebra calculations. An array is a multidimensional rectangular grid of values. IDL allows up to seven dimensions. The best way to understand arrays is to look at some examples.

See *Arrays* in *Building IDL Applications*.

The built-in IDL function FINDGEN produces an array of numbers in sequence starting at 0.0. (FINDGEN stands for Floating-point INDex GENerator.) The simplest arrays are one-dimensional.

See the FINDGEN function in *IDL Reference Guide*.

```
IDL> x = findgen(5)
IDL> print, x
      0.00000      1.00000      2.00000      3.00000      4.00000
```

In the first IDL statement, the constant 5 is the *argument* of the FINDGEN *function*. In the second statement, x is the argument of the PRINT *procedure*. Note that there is a difference in the notation or *syntax* for functions and procedures. Functions use parentheses around the argument list, whereas procedures use only commas. If the function or procedure has more than one argument, they are separated by commas. Functions and procedures are used somewhat differently, so don't try to use a function like a procedure, or vice versa. IDL will let you know if you do!

```
IDL> findgen(5)

findgen(5)
  ^
% Syntax error.
IDL> y = print, x

y = print, x
          ^
% Syntax error.
```

You can learn more about the array x that was created above by using HELP:

```
IDL> help, x
X                 FLOAT      = Array[5]
```

The result of the FINDGEN command is an array (list) of five numbers in sequence from 0.0 to 4.0. The "F" character at the beginning of the FINDGEN command indicates that the result should be a floating-point array of numbers. You can identify a floating-point number by the presence of a decimal point. This ability to automatically create arrays of numbers helps make IDL programs short and easy to read.

In IDL you can refer to any of the individual *elements* in an array using *subscripts. IDL subscripts start at 0, not 1.* If there are n elements in the array, the indices run from 0 to $n - 1$. (This is the same as in C, but is different from Fortran. In Fortran array indices run from 1 to n.)

```
IDL> print, x[0]
      0.00000
IDL> print, x[4]
      4.00000
```

Note that parentheses are used to specify arguments to the function FINDGEN, similar to standard mathematical notation, but square brackets are used for array subscripts. *You should always use square brackets for array subscripts.* For reasons too complicated to go into here, it is possible to use parentheses, but it is not a good idea.

If you try to access an array element that does not exist (such as a negative array index or an index that is too large), IDL prints an error message and stops execution:

```
IDL> print, x[-1]
% Attempt to subscript X with <LONG      (          -1)> is out of range.
```

```
% Execution halted at: $MAIN$
IDL> print, x[5]
% Attempt to subscript X with <LONG        (          5)> is out of range.
% Execution halted at: $MAIN$
```

There are functions like FINDGEN to generate sequences of each type of IDL variable. LINDGEN, for example, will generate an array of LONG integers:

See the LINDGEN function in *IDL Reference Guide.*

```
IDL> i = lindgen(4)
IDL> print, i
          0            1            2            3
```

To make a two-dimensional array, you specify the size of each dimension as arguments to FINDGEN. (Much more on arguments in Chapter 15.) This is a rectangular array with dimensions of size 3 and 4:

```
IDL> x = findgen(3, 4)
IDL> print, x
     0.00000      1.00000      2.00000
     3.00000      4.00000      5.00000
     6.00000      7.00000      8.00000
     9.00000      10.0000      11.0000
```

Note that this is different from an array with dimensions of size 4 and 3,

```
IDL> x = findgen(4, 3)
IDL> print, x
     0.00000      1.00000      2.00000      3.00000
     4.00000      5.00000      6.00000      7.00000
     8.00000      9.00000      10.0000      11.0000
```

although the values of the *elements* of the array are the same. The definition of the *shape* of the array is different in the two cases.

To access individual elements, you can use subscripts. Remember that indices start at 0:

```
IDL> print, x[2,1]
     6.00000
```

IDL will generally do an arithmetic operation on an entire array with a single statement:

```
IDL> x = findgen(5)
IDL> print, x
     0.00000      1.00000      2.00000      3.00000      4.00000
```

```
IDL> y = x^2
IDL> print, y
       0.00000        1.00000        4.00000        9.00000        16.0000
```

Most arithmetic operations on arrays can be written in IDL without the explicit use of *program loops*. These are referred to as *array expressions*. IDL programs can be written with explicit loops, like Fortran, but IDL almost always runs faster when you use array expressions instead.

3.9 Graphics

IDL has powerful built-in graphics capabilities. Here are some examples.
    Figure 3.1 shows the results of the following commands:

```
IDL> x = findgen(10)
IDL> y = x^2
IDL> window, xsize = 400, ysize = 400
IDL> plot, x, y
```

The WINDOW command is not required. IDL will automatically open a graphics window when one is needed. In this case the WINDOW command is used with the XSIZE and YSIZE keywords to ensure that the output window is square and the graphs have the same shape as the examples in the figures below. Feel free to experiment with windows of different shapes. In this case the PLOT

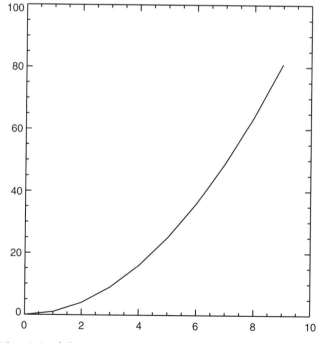

FIGURE 3.1   A simple line graph. (LINEGRAPH1)

command has two arrays as arguments, x and y. Each array has the same
number of elements—five in this case. The PLOT command plots each pair of
numbers on a standard two-dimensional graph, with x for the abscissa and y
for the ordinate, and connects the points with a solid line. As we will see later,
the appearance of graphs can be customized in many ways.

See the PLOT procedure
in *IDL Reference Guide*.

Note that the abscissa variable does not have to be named x and the
ordinate y. This form works just as well:

```
IDL> plot, y, x
```

The results are shown in Figure 3.2. Note that the two graphs are different!
It is not the *names* of the variables that matter, it is the *order* of the arguments
to the PLOT command. With PLOT, the first argument is always the abscissa
and the second the ordinate.

A quick note on an important built-in IDL convenience. The cursor (arrow)
keys on your keyboard can be used to retrieve and edit previously entered
commands. To make a quick change to the PLOT command, use the up arrow
to recall the command, then use the left arrow and the Delete key to replace
the 5 with a 10. Hit Enter or Return to execute the revised command.

```
IDL> plot, findgen(10)^2
```

or to replace the 2 with a 3

```
IDL> plot, findgen(10)^3
```

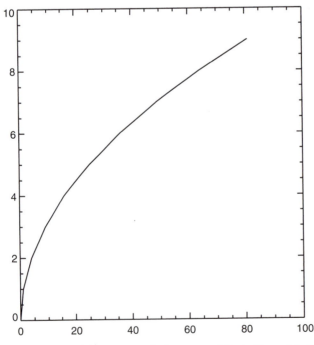

FIGURE 3.2   The order of the arguments is the reverse of that in Figure 3.1. (LINEGRAPH2)

The cursor keys can save you a great deal of typing when you are working interactively.

It is also possible to create interactive programs with a *graphical user interface* (abbreviated *GUI* and pronounced *gooey*) entirely in IDL. Here is an example that is provided by RSI as part of IDL:

See the XSURFACE procedure in *IDL Reference Guide*.

```
IDL> device, decomposed = 1
IDL> xsurface, dist(50)
% Compiled module: XREGISTERED.
% Compiled module: CW_PDMENU.
% Compiled module: XMANAGER.
```

The XSURFACE window is shown in Figure 3.3. Click the Done button when you are finished playing.

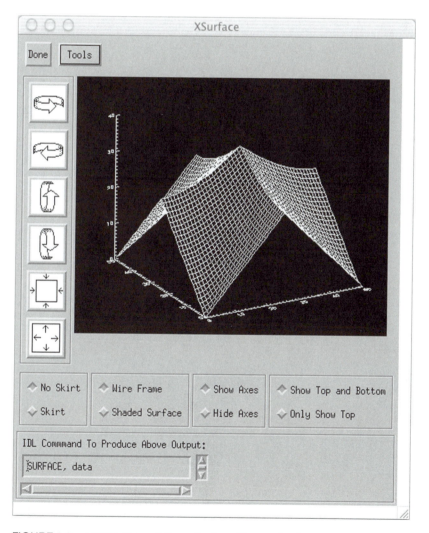

FIGURE 3.3   XSURFACE is an IDL application with a graphical user interface (GUI). (Screen capture)

3.10 Summary

In this chapter you learned how to start IDL, how to do simple calculations, and how to plot basic one- and two-dimensional graphs.

This chapter also described how to interrupt IDL calculations with `control-c` and restart them with `.c` (or `.continue`).

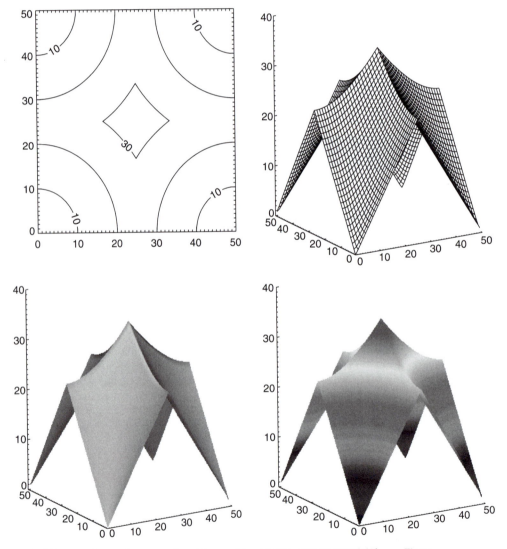

FIGURE 3.4   Some other types of graphics possible with IDL. (`MULTIGRAPH`) (Also see Figure 3.4 in color in the color plates section.)

3.11 Exercises

Enter the following commands at the IDL prompt. Use the HELP or PRINT command to learn the characteristics of the variables that you create.

1. b = bindgen(5)
   i = indgen(5)
   j = lindgen(5)
   a = dindgen(3, 3)
   c = cindgen(2, 2)

2. Try the following commands to see some of the other types of graphics that are possible with IDL.

```
IDL> !p.multi = [0, 2, 2]
IDL> z = dist(50)
IDL> contour, z, /follow
IDL> surface, z
IDL> shade_surf, z
IDL> device, decomposed = 0
IDL> loadct, 39
IDL> shade_surf, z, shades = bytscl(z)
IDL> !p.multi = 0
```

The results of the preceding commands are shown in Figure 3.4.

IDL Scripts (Batch Jobs)

This chapter covers how to create simple IDL *scripts*, which are referred to in the IDL documentation as *batch jobs*.

See *Executing Batch Jobs in IDL* in *Using IDL*.

4.1 IDL Commands and Notation

- `@script_name`

- `JOURNAL`

4.2 A Note on Files and File Names

Different operating systems have different requirements for file names. Some are case sensitive, some are not. Some require file name suffixes, some do not. In order to avoid some potential problems, particularly when moving programs between different computers, the following simple rules for naming files that contain IDL programs (procedures, functions, or scripts) should be followed:

- File names can contain letters, numerals, and the underscore character. Do not use any other characters (including spaces). Example: `my_prog.pro`, not `my prog.pro`.

- File names should start with a letter (not a number) and should be entirely lowercase. Example: `prog2.pro`, not `PROG2.pro`, `Prog2.pro`, or `2prog.pro`.

- File names should end with "`.pro`". This is the standard suffix for IDL files.

- Each file should contain only *one* procedure or function. The name of the file should exactly match the name of the procedure or function. *Internally, IDL is not case sensitive*, so a file named `my_prog.pro` would start with the statement

```
PRO MY_PROG
```

or

```
FUNCTION MY_PROG
```

depending on whether the file contains a procedure or a function.

Following these rules, and setting your IDL search path correctly, will allow IDL to automatically locate your IDL files.

4.3 Making a Script

Rather than repeatedly typing a sequence of IDL statements, you can save the statements in a *script* file and execute them with a single command. The IDL documentation refers to this as a *batch job*, although *script* seems to me to more accurately reflect current computer jargon.

Using your text editor, or the IDL Development Environment, create a file containing the following lines and save it in your `idl` directory as `log_plot.pro`:

```
n = 10
x = 1.0 + FINDGEN(n)
y = ALOG10(x)
PLOT, x, y
```

See the ALOG10 function in *IDL Reference Guide*.

To execute the script, simply type `@log_plot` at the IDL prompt. There is no space between the @ symbol and the file name. You should see a graph like that in Figure 4.1.

The `@log_plot` command tells IDL to do the following:

1. Search the directories in the IDL search path until a file named `log_plot.pro` is found.

2. Execute each line in the file `log_plot.pro` one line at a time.

If the script file does not exist, you will see an error message:

```
IDL> @log_plots
% Error opening file. File: log_plots
```

(The file we want is called `log_plot.pro`, not `log_plots.pro`.)

Using the text editor, we can clean up the `log_plot` script and add some comments. That way, when we look at the script again in a few months, we will have some clue as to what it does. We can also add some labels to the graph.

On each line of an IDL program or script, *everything to the right of a semicolon is treated as a comment and is ignored when the program is executed*. This makes it easy to add comments wherever necessary. Comments are an

See *Commenting Your IDL Code* in *Building IDL Applications*.

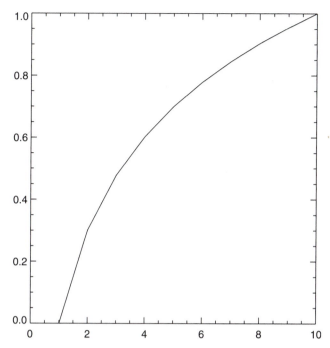

FIGURE 4.1   A line graph created by the script log_plot.pro. (LOG_PLOT_PS)

essential part of any computer program. You should get in the habit of adding comments *as you write each program.*

The updated script is saved as log_plot2.pro.

```
;  Script to plot log10(x)

n = 10                                     ;Number of points to plot
x = 1.0 + FINDGEN(n)                       ;Compute abscissa
y = ALOG10(x)                              ;Compute ordinate
PLOT, x, y, $                              ;Plot the graph
   TITLE  = 'Plot of base-10 logarithm of x', $
   XTITLE = 'x', $
   YTITLE = 'log10(x)'
```

When you type @log_plot2 at the IDL prompt, you should see a graph like that in Figure 4.2.

The PLOT command above uses several *keyword parameters*: TITLE, XTITLE, and YTITLE. These keywords are used to pass the various strings containing titles to the PLOT procedure. Because of the length of the titles, the PLOT command does not fit on a single line. In IDL the $ character is used to continue a command on the following line. Each line of the PLOT command has the *continuation character* ($), except the last. As the first line of the PLOT command demonstrates, you can place a comment on a line even if it is continued.

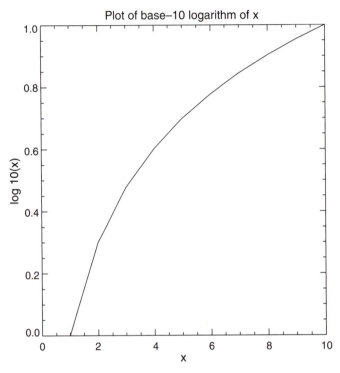

FIGURE 4.2   The new line graph created by the updated script log_plot2.pro.
(LOG_PLOT2_PS)

4.4 Journaling

If you know that you are going to be creating a script, you can save the statements you enter at the IDL prompt to a *journal file*. This is a plain text file that contains everything that you enter into IDL. Recording of statements, or *journaling*, is turned on and off with the JOURNAL command. The name of the journal file is specified in the first JOURNAL command. Here's an example:

See the JOURNAL procedure in *IDL Reference Guide*.

```
IDL> journal, 'exp_plot.pro'
IDL> x = -1.0 + 0.1*findgen(21)
IDL> y = exp(x)
IDL> plot, x, y
IDL> journal
```

Use your text editor to examine the file exp_plot.pro, which should be in your idl/bowman directory.

```
; IDL Version 5.6, Mac OS X (darwin ppc m32)
; Journal File for bowman@csrp3.local.
; Working directory: /Users/bowman
; Date: Sun May 18 08:31:39 2003
```

```
x = -1.0 + 0.1*findgen(21)
y = exp(x)
plot, x, y
```

The first few lines are comments inserted by IDL and can be deleted safely. (Note that the first character of the first four lines is a semicolon. Thus, all four of the lines are treated as comments.) The function EXP(x) computes e^x. This file can be modified with any text editor and executed like any other script file. When you execute the script by entering @exp_plot, you should see a graph like the one in Figure 4.3.

If you forget to turn on journaling, you can always copy and paste the contents of the terminal window into a text file. You will need to delete the IDL prompts and any IDL output, but it can save you from retyping the IDL statements.

4.5 Summary

This chapter has covered the basics of creating script files (batch jobs) with a text editor or by using the JOURNAL command.

Script files are a quick and convenient way to save a sequence of IDL statements for repeated execution. Scripts have some important limitations, however. First, each line in a script is executed one line at a time. It is not

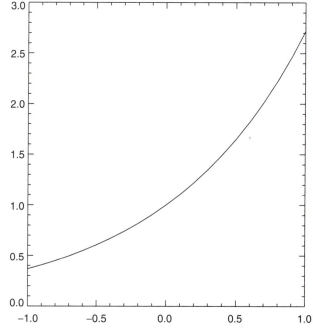

FIGURE 4.3   The line graph created by running the script exp_plot_ps.pro. (EXP_PLOT_PS)

possible to execute *blocks* of statements in a script.[1] Second, scripts don't accept arguments, so you can't easily change what a script does (the value of n in the `log_plot` script, for example) without changing the script itself.

We will see later that developing IDL procedures and functions is very easy, and that procedures and functions have a number of advantages over scripts. In fact, it is usually *very* easy to convert a script to a procedure.

- Scripts are good for
    - Developing and testing short sequences of IDL statements
    - Repeatedly executing short sequences of IDL statements that do not change often

- Scripts are *not* good for
    - Sequences of more than about 10 to 20 IDL statements
    - Anything that requires using blocks of IDL statements
    - Complex projects that require multiple scripts or nested scripts
    - Anything that can be done more easily with a procedure or function

4.6 Exercises

1. Write a script to print "So long, farewell, ..." and then exit IDL. (2 lines)

2. Write a script to plot the graph in Figure 3.1.

3. Write a script that uses the CD command to print the current directory. (2 lines)

---

1   This is not strictly true, but if you need to execute a block of statements, use a procedure or function.

Integer Constants and Variables

IDL has a variety of built-in ways to represent and store numbers. We will start by looking at how integers are represented. This chapter explains the basic properties and limitations of integer variable types. Chapter 6 describes floating-point numbers.

5.1 IDL Commands and Notation

- Integer constants: 15B, 15S, 15L, 15LL

- BYTE function

- INT function

- LONG function

- LONG64 function

- COMPILE_OPT statement

5.2 Decimal and Binary Notation

Integers are useful for keeping track of things that you can *count*; that is, things that logically cannot be divided into fractional parts. There are two limitations of integers that programmers need to be aware of at all times. The first is inherent in the mathematical concept of an integer (no fractional part). The second comes from the way integers are represented on computers (with a finite number of digits).

Normally we use familiar decimal notation to write numbers. Decimal notation uses 10 different symbols (the digits 0 through 9). Each position in a number is used to represent a power of 10. The rightmost position represents 1's (10^0), the next position to the left represents 10's (10^1), the next 100's (10^2), and so on. In principal it is possible to write a decimal number of any size by using enough digits. For a given number of digits, however, there is a limit to the magnitude of the largest number that can be written. For example, with 3 decimal digits it is possible to write a total of 1000 different decimal numbers from 0 to 999 (0 to $10^3 - 1$).

Internally, computers use binary notation to represent numbers. Binary notation uses only two different symbols, 0 and 1, instead of the 10 symbols used in the decimal system. Each "binary digit" is referred to as a *bit*. When writing an integer using binary notation, each position is used to represent a power of 2. The rightmost position represents 1's (2^0), the next position represents 2's (2^1), the next 4's (2^2), and so on. Examples of binary numbers are given in Table 5.1. As with decimal numbers, the largest number that can be represented depends on how many bits are used.

5.3 BYTE **Constants and Variables**

In all modern computers, computer memory is divided into *bytes*. Each byte is made up of 8 bits. Bytes can be grouped together to create larger numbers, but the smallest "chunk of bits" that can be accessed directly is one byte. The largest number that can be written using 8 bits is 255 ($2^8 - 1$). It is important to remember that although it is possible to write 256 (2^8) *different* numbers using 8 bits, because 0 is included the *largest* number that can be represented is 255, not 256.

IDL has a built-in ability to use 8-bit binary numbers, which are known, naturally enough, as BYTE constants and variables. Using the BYTE variable type you can store 8-bit numbers and do arithmetic with them. Because a byte contains 8 bits, you can think of it as representing numbers as shown in Table 5.2.[1]

See *Integer Constants* in *Building IDL Applications*.

A BYTE constant is written by adding the letter B to the end of a numerical constant. Note that because there cannot be a fractional part, there is no decimal point in an integer constant.

```
IDL> x = 15B
IDL> help, x
X              BYTE      =    15
```

TABLE 5.1   Examples of binary representation of some integers.

Binary	Decimal
0	0
1	1
10	2
11	3
1000	8
1001	9
1111	15
11111111	255

---

1   For technical reasons, on most computers integers are not represented internally exactly as given in Table 5.2, but the differences are not important for our purposes.

TABLE 5.2   Binary representation of integers using 1 byte (8 bits). The values of all 8 bits are shown for each number, including leading zeros.

Binary	Decimal
00000000	0
00000001	1
00000010	2
00000011	3
00000100	4
00000101	5
00000110	6
00000111	7
00001000	8
00001001	9
.	
.	
.	
11111110	254
11111111	255

When you type x = 15B, IDL will translate the decimal number 15 into a 1-byte internal binary representation (00001111). The value represented by the characters 15B is a *constant*. It is, obviously, always equal to 15. Because its value can be changed, the quantity indicated by the name x is a *variable*. It can be changed simply by assigning it a new value:

```
IDL> x = 19B
IDL> help, x
X               BYTE      =    19
```

If you omit the B, by default IDL will create a 32-bit (4-byte) integer called a LONG:[2]

```
IDL> y = 15
IDL> help, y
Y               LONG      =             15
```

More on LONG-type integers in Section 5.5.

Whatever the number of bits used, there are two main things to watch out for when using integer data types. The first is that there is a limited range of numbers that can be represented. If you do an arithmetic operation that results in a value that is outside the range for that type, the result is likely to be something that you don't expect. For example,

```
IDL> x = 240B
```

---

2   Make sure you have COMPILE_OPT IDL2 in your startup.pro file.

```
IDL> y = 32B
IDL> print, x + y
   16
```

Both 240 and 32 can be represented as BYTE-type variables, but their sum, 272, is too large to be represented with 8 bits. The result overflows or "wraps around" to give 16 $(240 + 32 - 256 = 16)$.[3]

Here is another example:

```
IDL> print, y - x
   48
```

If a BYTE variable could represent a negative integer, the result would be -208, but BYTE variables must lie between 0 and 255, so once again the result "wraps around." Notice that in each case *IDL did not issue an error message. Each of these results is completely correct insofar as BYTE arithmetic is defined.*

It is easy to get similar results when multiplying:

```
IDL> print, 16B * 16B
    0
```

Once again, the result wraps around $((16 \times 16) \bmod 256 = 0)$.

Division presents another type of problem, because the result of dividing two integers may not be an integer. BYTE type variables, however, can only represent integers:

```
IDL> x = 32B
IDL> y = 24B
IDL> print, x/y
    1
IDL> print, y/x
    0
```

When dividing two integer variables, *the fractional part is thrown away*. The result of 32/24 is 1. Similarly, the result of 24/32 is 0. In each case the fractional part cannot be represented by a BYTE variable, or by any other integer type, for that matter.

A numerical type that only allows storing integer values between 0 and 255 is of limited use for general numerical calculations. Imagine a scientific calculator with only three digits, no negative numbers, and so on. So what good are BYTE variables? One occasional use is when you *really* need to save space, *and* you only need to count things in a very limited range. Rather than using a 4-byte integer variable to store numbers, if you are *certain* that the values will be between 0 and 255, you can use a BYTE variable and save a factor

---

3   More generally, the result is $(240 + 32) \bmod 256 = 16$.

of 4 in memory or disk storage. The main use for BYTE variables, though, is to store *images*. A black-and-white (grayscale) photographic image can be stored digitally with fairly good fidelity using only 256 shades of gray for each small picture element, or pixel. Here's an example of a grayscale image:

```
IDL> window, xsize=400, ysize=400
IDL> image = bytscl(dist(400))
IDL> help, image
IMAGE           BYTE      = Array[400, 400]
IDL> print, min(image), max(image)
   0 255
IDL> tv, image
```

The resulting graphic is shown in Figure 5.1. First we create a new window that is 400 × 400 pixels. The DIST function creates a 400 × 400 array of floating-point values. (In this example, DIST is just a convenient way to create an array filled with numbers.) BYTSCL scales the values generated by the DIST function into the range 0 to 255. We check these things with HELP and PRINT. The TV command sends the array image to the screen as shades of gray. Color images can be stored using 3 bytes per pixel—one byte for red, one for green, and one for blue. Professional-quality digital imaging systems nowadays usually use more than 8 bits for each color (or *channel*), but 8-bit grayscale and 24-bit color images work very well for most computer applications.

See the DIST, BYTSCL, and TV functions in *IDL Reference Guide*.

FIGURE 5.1   A grayscale image created by using a BYTE array. (GRAYSCALE)

5.4 `INT` **Constants and Variables**

Fortunately, IDL has other integer types with more than 8 bits. In fact, the
standard default type for an integer variable is a *2-byte* integer type called an
INT (sometimes called a "short"). With 16 bits it would seem to be possible
to store values between 0 and $2^{16} - 1$, but this is not quite the case. The INT
type sets aside one bit as a *sign bit* to indicate whether the number is positive
or negative. Therefore, the INT type can represent integers between -2^{15} and
$+2^{15} - 1$ ($-32,768$ to $32,767$). (Note the small asymmetry between positive
and negative numbers.)

See *Integer Constants*
in *Building IDL
Applications.*

Unless you tell IDL otherwise (with the COMPILE_OPT statement, for example), when you use an integer constant, it will generally be taken as an INT
(2-byte) number. Beginning IDL programmers often unknowingly create
INT variables and then run into one of the problems seen above with BYTE
variables: trying to use numbers larger than the capacity of the type. To explicitly create an INT variable, the letter S (for *short* integer) is appended to the
numerals

```
IDL> x = 20000S
IDL> help, x
X               INT       =       20000
IDL> print, 2S * x
  -25536
```

The expected result in this case, 40,000, is too large to be represented by an
INT variable, and the arithmetic "wraps around." In this case, because negative
numbers *are* possible, it wraps around to a negative value. Once again, there
is no error message. One common way to make this mistake is to use an INT
as a loop counter and then attempt to count past 32,767.

There are two ways to avoid this problem. The first is to always explicitly
specify that an integer constant is a *4-byte* value, known as a LONG, by adding
an L to the number:

```
IDL> i = 15L
IDL> help, i
I               LONG      =               15
```

A lowercase l will work, but you should always use an uppercase L because
the lowercase l looks very much like the numeral 1 (one). In some computer
typefaces, the two are identical!

Writing all integer constants with an L at the end is a bit ugly; and until
it becomes a habit, it is easy to forget. A better way to avoid this problem of
inadvertently creating INTs is to change the default behavior of IDL by using
the COMPILE_OPT statement. The startup.pro file provided with this book
contains the following statement:

See the COMPILE_OPT
statement in *IDL
Reference Guide.*

```
COMPILE_OPT IDL2
```

This tells IDL that the default integer type should be LONG. (It also specifies that array subscripts must use square brackets.) Thus:

```
IDL> i = 15
IDL> help, i
I               LONG      =              15
```

You should include COMPILE_OPT IDL2 in every procedure and function that your write. (Unless you have a *very* good reason not to!)

There is one case where integer arithmetic *does* generate an error message: division by zero.

```
IDL> i = 3/0
% Program caused arithmetic error: Integer divide by 0
IDL> help, i
I               LONG      =               3
```

Note that the value 3 is assigned to i, but that is not the result of the operation specified. (The result is actually not a number.)

At one time there were advantages to using SHORT integers, notably faster execution speed and use of less memory. On current workstations and personal computers, however, those advantages have largely disappeared, so you should use 4-byte integers (LONGs) except for images. This does not completely eliminate the possibility of overflow, but does make it much less likely. The LONG type is discussed further in the following section.

5.5 LONG **Constants and Variables**

The LONG data type is a 32-bit (4-byte) signed integer. As you might expect, it allows values between -2^{31} and $+2^{31} - 1$ ($-2,147,483,648$ to $2,147,483,647$), or about ± 2 billion.

See *Integer Constants* in *Building IDL Applications.*

As with any integer type, it is possible to get unexpected results when you try to calculate something that is outside the range of values that the type can represent (see the exercises at the end of the chapter). And, of course, when dividing integers the fractional part is thrown away:

```
IDL> print, 5/2
      2
```

Note that by throwing away the fractional part, integer division "rounds toward zero." It does not round to the smaller number (that is, "to the left" on the number line):

```
IDL> print, -5/2
     -2
```

5.6   Other Integer Types

IDL does have other integer types, including unsigned versions of most types (in the same way that BYTEs are unsigned). There is also a 64-bit (8-byte) integer type, the LONG64. The range of LONG64 variables is -2^{63} to $+2^{63} - 1$ ($-9,223,372,036,854,775,808$ to $9,223,372,036,854,775,807$), which can be handy for those occasions when you need to count *really* high (that's 9 *quintillion*, by the way). LONG64 constants are written by appending an LL to the end of the numerals:

See *Integer Constants* in *Building IDL Applications.*

```
IDL> help, 2LL^63-1
<Expression>    LONG64    =    9223372036854775807
```

How long would it take to count from 0 to 2^{63}? If your computer could count once per clock cycle, and it had a clock frequency of 1 GHz, it would take approximately

```
IDL> print, ((2LL^63-1)/(10LL^9))/(365LL * 86400LL), 'years'
              292 years
```

(There are approximately $365 \times 86,400$ seconds in a year.)

5.7   Converting One Integer Type to Another

In some cases IDL will automatically convert one type to another. For example,

```
IDL> x = 20000S
IDL> help, x
X               INT       =    20000
IDL> print, 2*x
      40000
IDL> help, 2*x
<Expression>    LONG      =         40000
```

Because we used the COMPILE_OPT IDL2 statement in our startup file, the default integer type is LONG. Therefore, the constant 2 is treated as a LONG. Before the multiplication with x is carried out, x is converted to a LONG. IDL automatically *promotes* a variable to the "higher" type before carrying out an operation between two different types. The promotion prevented the operation from exceeding the limits of an INT variable.

You can also explicitly tell IDL to convert the type of a variable:

See *Type Conversion Functions* in *Building IDL Applications.*

```
IDL> help, 200B
<Expression>    BYTE      =    200
IDL> help, LONG(200B)
```

```
<Expression>    LONG    =           200
```

Be careful, though! If you convert to a "lower" type, strange things can happen:

```
IDL> help, BYTE(300L)
<Expression>    BYTE    =   44
```

5.8 Summary

The commonly used integer types are summarized in Table 5.3. The other integer types available in IDL are described in the IDL documentation (*Building IDL Applications*).

The two most commonly used integer types are BYTEs (for images) and LONGs (for most kinds of counting). On rare occasions it may be worthwhile to use BYTEs or INTs instead of LONGs to save some space in memory or in a file. If you need to use integers greater than about ±2 billion, you can use 64-bit integers (LONG64s).

There are three potential problems that you should always be aware of when using integers: arithmetic operations that result in values outside the range of the integer type used; division, which discards any fractional part of a result; and division by zero.

With all of these limitations, why use integer variable types at all? Why not just use floating-point numbers? One answer is that floating-point types have their own limitations, as will be discussed in Chapter 6.

5.9 Exercises

Unless otherwise indicated, do the following problems first without using IDL. Then, use IDL to check your answer.

1. What is the binary representation of 17? (No need to use IDL.)

2. What is the (decimal) result of the following numerical operations? (Assume that the default integer type is LONG.)

    7B + 5B

    128B + 128B

TABLE 5.3   Commonly used integer types. Other integer types that are available in IDL are described in the IDL documentation.

Type	Bits	Bytes	Range (powers of 2)		Range (powers of 10)	
			Minimum	Maximum	Minimum	Maximum
BYTE	8	1	0	$2^8 - 1$	0	255
INT	16	2	-2^{15}	$2^{15} - 1$	$-32{,}768$	$32{,}767$
LONG	32	4	-2^{31}	$2^{31} - 1$	$\sim -2 \cdot 10^9$	$\sim 2 \cdot 10^9$
LONG64	64	8	-2^{63}	$2^{63} - 1$	$\sim -9 \cdot 10^{18}$	$\sim 9 \cdot 10^{18}$

32/33

33/33

33/32

−33/32

3. Assume that you want to keep track of time using units of seconds. How many years can you count before a LONG variable is unable to represent the elapsed time?

4. Use IDL to print the values of the following constants.

300B

40000S

4000000000L

Floating-Point Constants and Variables

This chapter explains the basic principles of using floating-point numbers.

6.1 IDL Commands and Notation

- Floating and double-precision notation: `0.0`, `1.0E3`, `2.0D4`, `Inf`, `NaN`

- `FLOAT` function

- `DOUBLE` function

- `LONG` function

- `FINDGEN` function

- `!VALUES` system variable

- `TOTAL` function and `NAN` keyword

6.2 Development of Floating-Point Methods

As we saw in Chapter 5, the various integer types are useful for things that can be counted, but not for general-purpose scientific calculations, where types that can directly represent *real* numbers would be more appropriate. For this purpose, computers have several *floating-point* variable types that provide an approximate representation of the real number system.

Throughout the history of electronic computing, a number of different schemes have been devised for doing floating-point arithmetic. Each typically gave (slightly) different answers to any particular calculation. Each typically had its own incompatible binary representation for floating-point numbers; that is, the bits used to represent a number on one computer were different from the bits used on a different brand of computer. This made it very difficult to move data files from one computer to another. That was not a problem as long as you never bought a computer from a different company or worked with anyone who did.

Fortunately, order was brought to this situation by the development of a standard scheme for representing floating-point numbers and doing floating-point arithmetic. The standard was developed by the Institute of Electrical and Electronics Engineers (IEEE, pronounced I-triple-E) and is referred to as IEEE 754. Fortunately, the IEEE 754 standard has been adopted by all of the major computer manufacturers. Modern central processing units (CPUs) can usually do at least one floating-point operation (flop) per clock cycle. With current clock rates well above 1 GHz, most modern workstations and personal computers can perform more than 1 billion floating-point calculations per second (referred to as 1 gigaflop).

This chapter covers the most important aspects of floating-point arithmetic for beginning programmers.

6.3   Limitations of Floating-Point Arithmetic

To illustrate some of the problems that can occur when making calculations with floating-point numbers, we'll start with some examples using decimal notation.

As with integers, the fundamental problem with floating-point numbers on computers is that in practice we can use only a finite number of digits. There are, however, infinitely many real numbers. In fact, between any two (different) real numbers there are infinitely many other real numbers. With a finite number of digits, however, it is possible to exactly represent only a finite subset of those real numbers.

For simplicity, let's assume that we have a computer that stores floating-point numbers with three decimal digits in the *fraction* (also called the *mantissa* or the *significand*) and two digits in the *exponent*, along with the signs of both parts of the number. Some examples are shown in Table 6.1. We have chosen not to allow leading zeros to the right of the decimal point; that is, the smallest number that can be written is $+0.100 \times 10^{-99}$. These are referred to as *normalized* numbers. With some loss of precision, we could have written $+0.001 \times 10^{-99}$, which would be a *denormalized* form. Generally, IEEE floating-point numbers are stored in normalized form.

Note that the rational number 1/3 cannot be stored exactly because it is an infinitely repeating decimal number. The floating-point representation of 1/3 must be rounded to three significant digits. This can lead to odd results such as $3 \times (1/3) = 0.999 \times 10^0$, not 1. In this case, doing the inverse of

TABLE 6.1   Some floating-point numbers in decimal notation with three-digit precision.

Largest positive number	$+0.999 \times 10^{+99}$
Smallest positive number	$+0.100 \times 10^{-99}$
Smallest negative number	-0.100×10^{-99}
Largest negative number	$-0.999 \times 10^{+99}$
1/3 (approximate)	$+0.333 \times 10^0$

an operation does *not* return the original value. This is one of the possible problems that can occur with floating-point numbers due to round-off.

Here is another example of a problem that results from having only a finite number of digits. Let's say that you want to find the sum of 1 and 1×10^{-3}. These numbers are stored as 0.100×10^{01} and 0.100×10^{-02}. The first step in the addition is to align the decimal points. This would give $0.100 \times 10^{01} + 0.0001 \times 10^{01}$. The second number requires four digits, but only three are available. Therefore, the second number is rounded to 0, and the operation becomes $0.100 \times 10^{01} + 0.000 \times 10^{01}$, which gives a value of 0.100×10^{01}. In this case, adding a non-zero quantity to a number does not change its value!

The IEEE floating-point standard attempts to minimize these kinds of problems by rounding arithmetic results as carefully as possible and by providing extra digits of precision for intermediate results. The designers of the IEEE standard also tried to ensure that the same calculation carried out on two different computers (that both follow the standard) would give the same results. Some limitations are unavoidable, however, so you should plan carefully when doing floating-point arithmetic. Some additional examples are given below.

6.4 Single-Precision Constants and Variables

IDL distinguishes floating-point constants from integer constants by the presence of a decimal point:

See *Floating Point and Double Precision Constants* in *Building IDL Applications*.

```
IDL> a = 1.0
IDL> i = 1
IDL> help, a, i
A               FLOAT     =         1.00000
I               LONG      =               1
```

For readability, it is a good idea to always include at least one digit on each side of the decimal point when writing floating-point constants. That is, write 0.1, not .1 and 1.0, not 1.

The basic IEEE floating-point type uses 32 bits (4 bytes). This is referred to as a *single-precision floating-point number* (FLOAT). In a single-precision floating-point number, 1 bit is used to indicate the sign of the number, 8 bits for the exponent (positive and negative), and 23 bits for the fraction. In practice this allows for a precision of about seven to eight decimal digits, and a range from $\sim -3.4 \times 10^{38}$ to $\sim 3.4 \times 10^{38}$. The smallest numbers that can be written[1] have an absolute value of $\sim 1.2 \times 10^{-38}$.

Many numbers that can be written exactly with only a few decimal digits cannot be written in binary notation with a finite number of bits.

---

1   *Denormalized* numbers can be as small as $\sim 1.4 \times 10^{-45}$. The technical details are not of importance here.

For example, in decimal notation it is possible to write the number 1/10 exactly as 0.100×10^0. In binary notation 0.1 is a repeating binary number $1.1001100110011001100\ldots \times 2^{-4}$. In order to store the real number 0.1 as a floating-point number on a computer, it must be rounded to a binary number that *can* be stored exactly. Try this example in IDL:

```
IDL> x = 0.1
IDL> print, x
      0.100000
```

Everything looks precisely correct, but when you print more digits, the result may not be quite what you expect:

```
IDL> print, x, format = \dqt(F20.15)\dqt
      0.100000001490116
```

The decimal number 0.1 is stored as a binary number that is nearly, but not exactly, equal to 0.1.

Here are a few other examples of potential problems with decimal numbers:

```
IDL> a = 1.0
IDL> b = 1.0E-10
IDL> print, a, b, a + b, format ="(F20.15)"
      1.000000000000000
      0.000000000100000
      1.000000000000000
```

The notation 1.0E-10 is used to represent 1.0×10^{-10}. In this case the individual numbers can both be written with good precision, but the sum is incorrect. This is the same problem we saw in Section 6.3 when adding two numbers with very different magnitudes. If you do this repeatedly, you can get very inaccurate answers. The following example adds 1.0×10^{-6} together 1 million times. The result should be exactly 1:

```
IDL> a = 1.0E-6
IDL> b = 0.0
IDL> for i = 1, 1000000 DO b = b + a
IDL> print, b, format ="(F20.15)"
      1.009038925170898
```

Initially the values in the sum have similar magnitude ($a \approx b$), but as b gets larger, the errors that occur with each addition increase and accumulate. Even though single-precision floating-point numbers provide seven to eight digits of decimal precision, in this case the result of many accumulated errors is only accurate to about two significant figures. The result is ~ 1.01, rather than the correct answer, 1.

Another instance in which you can have serious loss of precision is when subtracting variables of similar magnitude:

```
IDL> x = 1.234567
IDL> y = 1.234566
IDL> print, x - y
   1.07288e-06
```

The correct answer would be 1.000000E-06. This result, however, is correct only to about two significant figures.

Think carefully about the order in which you do floating-point operations. You may be able to get better precision by doing the operations in the optimum order. For example, when summing the terms in a power series expansion, it is usually best to sum from smallest to largest. This helps to ensure that each addition is between two values with similar magnitudes.

6.5 Double-Precision Constants and Variables

With integers, we saw that storing larger numbers requires more bits. Similarly, with floating-point numbers, storing larger numbers *or* achieving higher precision requires more bits. All modern computers include a 64-bit (8-byte) floating-point type referred to as *double precision* (DOUBLE). Table 6.2 at the end of this chapter shows the range of values possible with double-precision floating-point types. To write a double-precision constant in IDL you must use both a decimal point *and* an exponent that begins with D (for double):

See *Floating Point and Double Precision Constants* in *Building IDL Applications.*

```
IDL> d = 1.0D0
IDL> help, d
D               DOUBLE    =        1.0000000
```

Double precision can reduce some floating-point errors. If we repeat the calculations from the previous section using double-precision arithmetic, we get the following:

```
IDL> a = 1.0D0
IDL> b = 1.0E-10
IDL> print, a, b, a + b, format ="(F20.15)"
   1.000000000000000
   0.000000000100000
   1.000000000100000
```

With double precision we have enough precision to add *these* two numbers together accurately, despite their widely different magnitudes. Similarly, for the following loop:

```
IDL> a = 1.0D-06
IDL> b = 0.0D0
```

```
IDL> for i = 1, 1000000 DO b = b + a
IDL> print, b, format ="(F20.15)"
   1.000000000007918
```

the final result is much more accurate than the single-precision calculation.

Using double precision does not solve all floating-point problems; it just expands the range of problems that can be done with good precision. On some computers double-precision operations are slower than single-precision, so you probably do not want to automatically do everything in double precision. (On other computers double-precision operations are just as fast as single-precision operations.) Also, double-precision numbers require twice as much computer memory as single-precision numbers. If you are using large arrays of numbers, the difference can be significant. Finally, if you write double-precision values to a file, the file will be twice as large as the equivalent file with single-precision values. One possible solution to this problem is to do the calculation in double precision, but convert the numbers to single precision before writing them to files. If speed and memory are not limitations, or your computer has full 64-bit arithmetic hardware, then you may want to routinely do all calculations in double precision.

6.6 Type Conversion

IDL has built-in functions to convert between different numerical types:

See *Type Conversion Functions* in *Building IDL Applications.*

```
IDL> a = 5.5
IDL> print, long(a)
         5
IDL> i = 5
IDL> print, float(i)
      5.00000
IDL> print, double(i)
      5.0000000
```

When a FLOAT or DOUBLE is converted to a LONG, the fractional part is thrown away (like integer division).

When doing *mixed* arithmetic (arithmetic between different types), IDL automatically *promotes* (converts) variables to the *higher* type:

```
IDL> help, i*a
<Expression>    FLOAT    =       27.5000
IDL> b=5.5d0
IDL> help, i*b
<Expression>    DOUBLE   =       27.500000
```

That is, the LONG variable i is converted to a FLOAT or a DOUBLE before the multiplication is carried out. If you must do mixed-type arithmetic, it is a good idea to *explicitly* convert the types to be sure that the calculation is carried out the way you want.

6.7 Rounding

IDL has built-in functions to control rounding of floating-point variables:

```
IDL> a = 5.6
IDL> b = -5.6
IDL> print, round(a), round(b)
          6          -6
IDL> print, floor(a), floor(b)
          5          -6
IDL> print, ceil(a), ceil(b)
          6          -5
```

The ROUND function rounds to the nearest integer, CEIL returns the closest integer greater than or equal to the argument, and FLOOR returns the closest integer less than or equal to the argument.

See the ROUND, CEIL, and FLOOR functions in *IDL Reference Guide*.

6.8 Infinities and Not-a-Numbers

The IEEE 754 floating-point standard has several additional features that are very useful when doing floating-point calculations. Two important features deal with calculations that produce results that cannot be represented as floating-point numbers. One example is the result of division by zero:

```
IDL> x = 3.0/0.0
% Program caused arithmetic error: Floating divide by 0
IDL> help, x
X               FLOAT     =             Inf
```

Note that trying to divide by zero produces two important effects. First, IDL issues an error message to inform you that something went wrong. Second, the value assigned to x is a special IEEE value (bit pattern) used to represent *infinity* (∞). The IEEE standard even distinguishes between $\pm\infty$:

See *Special Floating Point Values* in *Building IDL Applications*.

```
IDL> y = -3.0/0.0
% Program caused arithmetic error: Floating divide by 0
IDL> help, y
Y               FLOAT     =             -Inf
```

If you try to calculate 0.0/0.0, the result is another special value called a Not-a-Number (NaN):

```
IDL> z = 0.0/0.0
% Program caused arithmetic error: Floating illegal operand
```

```
IDL> help, z
Z               FLOAT      =             NaN
```

One very important feature of Infs and NaNs is that they propagate through a calculation. That is, if intermediate calculations generate an Inf or a NaN, the final result will be an Inf or a NaN. This is important so that intermediate errors are not hidden by later calculations.

You should design your programs so that you only get floating-point errors when something has really gone wrong. Don't write programs that generate floating-point errors while producing "correct" results. Because you normally only get one floating-point exception message when your program terminates, if your program generates a floating-point exception in normal operation, it can hide a real floating-point error that occurred elsewhere in the program. Whenever IDL reports a floating-point error, you need to figure out where something went wrong.[2]

NaNs can be very useful for representing missing data. That way, if you inadvertently do a calculation with a missing value (NaN), the result will be an NaN. Before IEEE arithmetic, programmers often tried to use special values like −999.0 to represent missing values in a data set. If you inadvertently use the "missing" value in a calculation, however, you may never know it, because −999.0 is a valid floating-point number. With the IEEE NaN, the special value propagates through the calculation, and the final result will reveal an obvious problem.

Many built-in IDL functions automatically exclude all NaNs if you use the proper keyword. Here is an example. First we create a short array and use the TOTAL function to find the sum of the value in the array:

See the TOTAL function in *IDL Reference Guide.*

```
IDL> x = findgen(5)
IDL> print, x
      0.00000      1.00000      2.00000      3.00000      4.00000
IDL> print, total(x)
      10.0000
```

Next, we replace one of the values in the array by a NaN to represent a missing observation. Conveniently, IDL has built-in constants containing the special IEEE values. They are stored in the *system variable* !VALUES. (Recall that the names of all system variables begin with an exclamation point; that is, the exclamation point is part of the variable name.) The system variable !VALUES is actually a *structure* that contains four separate values: NaNs and Infs for both single- and double-precision types. You can see the contents of the !VALUES structure by using the HELP command. (For more on structures, see Chapter 9.)

See *System Variables* in *Building IDL Applications.*

---

2   A good start is to set !EXCEPT = 2 and rerun your calculation. That will cause IDL to report errors, if any, immediately after they occur.

```
IDL> help, !values, /structure
** Structure !VALUES, 4 tags, length=24, data length=24:
   F_INFINITY       FLOAT           Inf
   F_NAN            FLOAT           NaN
   D_INFINITY       DOUBLE          Infinity
   D_NAN            DOUBLE          NaN
```

To reference a value within a structure, a period is used to separate the *variable name* (!VALUES) from the *tag name* (F_NAN):

```
IDL> x[2] = !values.f_nan
IDL> print, x
      0.00000      1.00000          NaN      3.00000      4.00000
```

If we sum all of the values in x, the result is NaN (because *one* of the values in the sum is a NaN):

```
IDL> print, total(x)
         NaN
```

To treat the NaN as *missing* data, and omit it from the sum, use the NaN keyword:

```
IDL> print, total(x, /nan)
      8.00000
```

Be careful, however, if your array is completely filled with NaNs:

```
IDL> x = replicate(!values.f_nan, 5)
IDL> print, x
          NaN          NaN          NaN          NaN          NaN
IDL> print, total(x)
         NaN
IDL> print, total(x, /nan)
      0.00000
```

RSI erred in the implementation of the NAN keyword in the TOTAL function (and several other functions). It would be more convenient for the programmer if the result in this case were also a NaN, but as you can see, it is not. Therefore, if you want to use the NAN keyword to treat NaNs as missing values, you must still check your arrays for the possibility that *all* values might be NaNs. This greatly reduces the utility of the NAN keyword.

6.9 Summary

The commonly used floating-point types are summarized in Table 6.2. The other floating-point types available in IDL are described in the IDL documentation (*Building IDL Applications*).

TABLE 6.2   Commonly used floating-point types.

Type	Bits	Decimal Digits	Range	Minimum Magnitude
Single precision	32	7 to 8	$\pm 3.4 \times 10^{38}$	$\pm 1.2 \times 10^{-38}$
Double precision	64	15 to 16	$\pm 1.8 \times 10^{308}$	$\pm 2.2 \times 10^{-308}$

Some general guidelines for floating-point calculations:

1. Do not use floating-point numbers when integers are more natural (for example, for counting things, especially loop counters).

2. Try to avoid adding numbers that have different magnitudes.

3. Try to avoid subtracting numbers that have similar magnitudes.

4. Double precision can expand the range of calculations that you can do with good precision.

5. Use explicit type conversions.

6. Use NaNs for missing data.

7. Write your programs so they do not generate floating-point errors unless something has gone wrong.

6.10   Exercises

1. Try some interactive experiments to find the largest values of x for which you can compute e^x and e^{-x} without floating-point underflow or overflow errors. Try the calculations using both single- and double-precision numbers.

2. Try some interactive experiments to find the smallest value of x for which you can compute $sin(x)$ without floating-point underflow errors. Try the calculations using both single- and double-precision numbers.

7

Using Arrays

This chapter describes how to create arrays and use them efficiently to do some common arithmetic operations using IDL's built-in *array syntax*.

7.1   IDL Procedures and Functions

The following IDL procedures are discussed:

- Array-creation functions (BYTARR, INTARR, LONARR, LON64ARR, FLTARR, DBLARR, COMPLEXARR, STRARR, MAKE_ARRAY, REPLICATE)

- Index-generation functions (BINDGEN, INDGEN, LINDGEN, L64INDGEN, FINDGEN, DINDGEN, CINDGEN, SINDGEN, MAKE_ARRAY)

- N_ELEMENTS function

- SIZE function

- REFORM function and the OVERWRITE keyword

- REBIN function and the SAMPLE keyword

- REVERSE function

- ROTATE function

- SHIFT function

7.2   Creating Arrays

An array is a multidimensional, rectangular grid or lattice of variables. The variables in an array can be any IDL variable type, including integers, floats, strings, and even structures (see Chapter 9 for information about structures). All of the elements of an array must be the same type. IDL arrays can have up to eight dimensions. The elements of an array are referenced by *subscripts*. If the size of a dimension is n, the subscripts for that dimension range from 0 to $n - 1$.

Here are some simple examples that use built-in IDL array-creation functions to create new array variables:

```
IDL> i = lonarr(4)
IDL> help, i
I               LONG      = Array[4]
IDL> print, i
        0           0           0           0

IDL> x = fltarr(4, 2)
IDL> help, x
X               FLOAT     = Array[4, 2]
IDL> print, x
    0.00000     0.00000     0.00000     0.00000
    0.00000     0.00000     0.00000     0.00000
```

In the examples, the arguments specify the sizes of each dimension of the arrays to be created. The array i is a one-dimensional LONG array with four elements. The array x is a two-dimensional FLOAT array with dimensions 4 and 2 (8 elements total). By default, arrays created with the basic array-creation functions are filled with zeroes. To create an array that is filled with a non-zero value, use the REPLICATE or MAKE_ARRAY function. Alternatively, you can create a new array and then use an array assignment statement to assign the same value to all elements, as illustrated here:

```
IDL> x = fltarr(3, 2)
IDL> print, x
    0.00000     0.00000     0.00000
    0.00000     0.00000     0.00000
IDL> x[*] = 3.2
IDL> print, x
    3.20000     3.20000     3.20000
    3.20000     3.20000     3.20000
```

Notice that you can use the [*] notation to refer to all of the elements in an array, even if it has multiple dimensions. More on *array syntax* follows.

Some of the available array creation functions are given in Table 7.1. Other type-specific functions are available for the unsigned integer types. The MAKE_ARRAY and REPLICATE functions can be used to create arrays of any of the available types.

7.3 Arithmetic with Arrays

From its initial conception, IDL was designed as an *array-oriented* language. It owes some of its design features to the interactive array-oriented language

TABLE 7.1   Array creation functions.

Type	Function
BYTE	BYTARR
INT	INTARR
LONG	LONARR
LONG64	LON64ARR
FLOAT	FLTARR
DOUBLE	DBLARR
COMPLEX	COMPLEXARR
STRING	STRARR
specified by keyword	MAKE_ARRAY
specified by variable	REPLICATE

APL. Using IDL's array features has several major benefits. Programs written using array syntax are easier to write, easier to read, and less likely to have errors. Additionally, operations that use array syntax are much faster than those that use explicit loops.

We begin with a look at two different ways to carry out a basic operation: adding together two one-dimensional floating-point arrays of size n, element by element, to create a new array, also of size n. If you know Fortran 77, you would probably write this operation in IDL in the following way. (We assume that the arrays x and y already exist and have the same number of elements.)

```
n = N_ELEMENTS(x)
z = FLTARR(n)
FOR i = 0, n-1 DO z[i] = x[i] + y[i]
```

The N_ELEMENTS function determines the number of elements in the array x. The FLTARR function creates a new floating-point array z with n elements. Recall that when an array is created, the elements of the array are set equal to zero. The FOR loop then counts from 0 to $n - 1$ and adds the i-th elements of x and y together to get the i'th element of z. (Remember that IDL array indices start at 0.) Subscripts are indicated by using *square* brackets. If you use a FOR loop, the output array z must be created ahead of time with the FLTARR statement.

See the N_ELEMENTS and FLTARR functions and the FOR statement in *IDL Reference Guide*.

Although this Fortran-like approach gives the correct result, it is definitely not the best way to do this operation in IDL. In IDL, there is a much simpler way using array syntax:

```
z = x + y
```

With array syntax, the FLTARR statement is not needed. IDL automatically creates a new array of the correct type and size to store the result of the operation x + y.

If the two arrays have a different number of elements, IDL will produce a result with as many elements as there are in the smaller array:

```
IDL> x = findgen(5)
IDL> print, x
      0.00000      1.00000      2.00000      3.00000      4.00000
IDL> y = findgen(3)
IDL> print, y
      0.00000      1.00000      2.00000
IDL> print, x + y
      0.00000      2.00000      4.00000
```

As mentioned above, there are two important differences between the Fortran approach (with the IDL equivalent of a Fortran DO loop) and the IDL array-oriented approach. First, although the FOR loop does not appear that complicated, it is remarkably easy to make a blunder or typographical error when writing loops. All of the detail (indices, brackets, loop limits, etc.) adds greatly to the complexity of that one line of IDL. The array-oriented approach is much easier to read, understand, and program correctly. Second, the first version is much slower than the second. We can show this with the following IDL script, named add_arrays:

```
;  Compare times for different methods of adding two arrays

n = 10^6
x = FINDGEN(n)
y = FINDGEN(n)
z = FLTARR(n)

time0 = SYSTIME(/SECONDS)
FOR i = 0, n-1 DO z[i] = x[i] + y[i]
time_for = SYSTIME(/SECONDS) - time0


time0 = SYSTIME(/SECONDS)
z = x + y
time_array = SYSTIME(/SECONDS) - time0

PRINT, 'Time using FOR loop      = ', time_for
PRINT, 'Time using array syntax = ', time_array
PRINT, 'Array syntax is           ', time_for/time_array, 'times faster.'
```

In this script, the input and output arrays x, y, and z are created. Then the time is compared for the FOR loop and the array syntax by calculating the elapsed time with the SYSTIME function. (This includes only the time to do

See the SYSTIME function in *IDL Reference Guide*.

the arithmetic operation, omitting the time required to allocate the arrays in memory.) After running the script several times, the results are:

```
IDL> @add_arrays
Time using FOR loop     =        2.8655750 s
Time using array syntax =        0.075492978 s
Array syntax is                  37.958165 times faster.
```

If you run the script again, the answers will vary slightly depending on what else the computer is doing. On this computer the array syntax is almost 40 times faster than the FOR loop. If you are doing multiple array operations, the differences can really add up.

So, one very important guideline for writing IDL programs is to *use array syntax and avoid* FOR *loops whenever possible*.

7.4 Index Arrays

It is often possible to avoid using FOR loops in IDL by creating *index arrays*. An index array is simply an array that contains, in order, n values from 0 to $n - 1$. IDL has built-in functions to create index arrays of any type of variable. Here are some examples:

```
IDL> i = lindgen(5)
IDL> help, i
I               LONG      = Array[5]
IDL> print, i
         0           1           2           3           4

IDL> x = findgen(3, 2)
IDL> help, x
X               FLOAT     = Array[3, 2]
IDL> print, x
      0.00000      1.00000      2.00000
      3.00000      4.00000      5.00000
IDL> print, x[1,0]
      1.00000
IDL> print, x[1,1]
      4.00000
```

In the examples, the arguments of the LINDGEN and FINDGEN functions specify the size of the array to be created. The last two PRINT commands are examples of array subscripting. The order in which x is stored in the computer's memory is x[0,0], x[1,0], x[2,0], x[0,1], x[1,1], x[2,1]; that is, the first subscript varies fastest.

Some of the available index generation functions are given in Table 7.2. Other type-specific functions are available for the unsigned integer types.

TABLE 7.2   Index-generation functions.

Type	Function
BYTE	BINDGEN
INT	INDGEN
LONG	LINDGEN
LONG64	L64INDGEN
FLOAT	FINDGEN
DOUBLE	DINDGEN
COMPLEX	CINDGEN
STRING	SINDGEN
specified by keyword	MAKE_ARRAY with /INDEX keyword

When used with the INDEX keyword, MAKE_ARRAY can be used to generate index arrays.

7.5   Generating a Coordinate Array

One very common array operation is generating a "coordinate" variable. For example, you might wish to compute

$$y = \sin(2\pi x) \tag{7.1}$$

for a set of n evenly spaced values of x between 0 and 1. That is, you want to calculate

$$y_i = \sin(2\pi x_i), \quad \text{where} \quad x_i = i \cdot \delta x, \, \delta x = 1/(n-1), \quad \text{and}$$

$$\langle i = 0, 1, 2, \dots, n-1. \rangle \tag{7.2}$$

In order to compute y_i, it is first necessary to compute the values of the independent coordinate x_i. The Fortran approach to this problem using FOR loops is:

```
IDL> n = 10
IDL> x = fltarr(n)
IDL> for i = 0, n-1 do x[i] = float(i)/(n-1)
IDL> print, x
      0.00000      0.111111      0.222222      0.333333      0.444444
      0.555556      0.666667      0.777778      0.888889      1.00000
```

Remember that array subscripts use square brackets, whereas function references (such as the FLOAT function) use parentheses. Because i is explicitly converted to a FLOAT, the expression n-1 is automatically promoted to a FLOAT. You can write it this way

```
IDL> for i = 0, n-1 do x[i] = float(i)/float(n-1)
```

to be certain that the operation is carried out using the correct variable types.

The IDL approach using array syntax is:

```
IDL> x = findgen(n)/(n-1)
IDL> print, x
      0.00000      0.111111      0.222222      0.333333      0.444444
      0.555556      0.666667      0.777778      0.888889      1.00000
```

Again, because the result of the FINDGEN function is a floating-point array, the result of the expression (n-1) is automatically promoted to a FLOAT. The array-syntax method works because the FINDGEN function creates an array of n elements filled with the values [0.0, 1.0, 2.0,..., n-1]. Each element of this array is multiplied by δx, that is, by 1.0/(n-1). IDL *automatically creates* the floating-point output array x to store the result.

Note that if you want 10 equal-sized *intervals*, rather than 10 *points*, then you need 11 points:

```
IDL> n = 11
IDL> x = findgen(n)/(n-1)
IDL> print, x
      0.00000      0.100000      0.200000      0.300000      0.400000
      0.500000      0.600000      0.700000      0.800000      0.900000
      1.00000
```

Now that we have x, it is easy to calculate y using IDL array syntax:

```
IDL> y = sin(2.0 * !pi * x)
IDL> print, y
      0.00000      0.587785      0.951057      0.951056      0.587785
    -8.74228e-08  -0.587786    -0.951056    -0.951056    -0.587785
      1.74846e-07
```

The *system variable* !PI contains the numerical value of π:

```
IDL> print, !pi
      3.14159
```

Due to round-off error, the values are not exactly zero at $x = 0.5$ and $x = 1.0$. They are, however, zero to within the expected precision of a single-precision floating-point number.

Check your result with the PLOT command:

```
IDL> plot, x, y
```

7.6   Changing the Shape of an Array

Every IDL array variable carries with it information about the type, size, and shape of the array. For example:

```
IDL> x = findgen(4, 4)
IDL> print, x
      0.00000       1.00000       2.00000       3.00000
      4.00000       5.00000       6.00000       7.00000
      8.00000       9.00000       10.0000       11.0000
      12.0000       13.0000       14.0000       15.0000
IDL> help, x
X                 FLOAT     = Array[4, 4]
```

Within a program you can access this information using the SIZE function:

```
IDL> print, size(x)
        2             4             4             4            16
```

See the SIZE function in
IDL Reference Guide.

The array returned by the SIZE function includes the number of dimensions (2), the size of each dimension (4 and 4), the type of the variable (4 means FLOAT), and the total number of elements (16). This is very different from C and Fortran, where a variable is nothing but an address in memory that contains the first element of the array.

To access a single element of an array, you supply subscripts for each dimension:

```
IDL> print, x[2,1]
      6.00000
```

This is column index 2 and row index 1. Remember that IDL indices start at 0, so in this example we get the third column and second row. You can access an entire row or column by using the * notation. This example prints the second row:

```
IDL> print, x[*,1]
      4.00000       5.00000       6.00000       7.00000
```

IDL has the very nice property that you can treat an array as though it were one-dimensional, even if it has multiple dimensions. Here are two examples:

```
IDL> print, x[6]
      6.00000
IDL> print, x[*]
      0.00000       1.00000       2.00000       3.00000       4.00000
      5.00000       6.00000       7.00000       8.00000       9.00000
      10.0000       11.0000       12.0000       13.0000       14.0000
      15.0000
```

The * notation returns *all* index values (0 through 15). You can even do arithmetic with arrays of different shape, as this example demonstrates:

```
IDL> y = findgen(16)
IDL> help, x, y
X                 FLOAT     = Array[4, 4]
Y                 FLOAT     = Array[16]
IDL> print, x + y
      0.00000       2.00000       4.00000       6.00000
      8.00000       10.0000       12.0000       14.0000
      16.0000       18.0000       20.0000       22.0000
      24.0000       26.0000       28.0000       30.0000
```

It is sometimes convenient to change the shape of an array without changing its values. This is done with the REFORM command:

See the REFORM function in *IDL Reference Guide*.

```
IDL> x = findgen(4, 4)
IDL> print, x
      0.00000       1.00000       2.00000       3.00000
      4.00000       5.00000       6.00000       7.00000
      8.00000       9.00000       10.0000       11.0000
      12.0000       13.0000       14.0000       15.0000
IDL> y = reform(x, 2, 8)
IDL> print, y
      0.00000       1.00000
      2.00000       3.00000
      4.00000       5.00000
      6.00000       7.00000
      8.00000       9.00000
      10.0000       11.0000
      12.0000       13.0000
      14.0000       15.0000
```

In this example a new array y is created with the same values as x but a different shape (2×8 instead of 4×4).

You can also change the shape of an array without making a new array:

```
IDL> x = reform(x, 8, 2, /overwrite)
IDL> print, x
      0.00000       1.00000       2.00000       3.00000       4.00000
      5.00000       6.00000       7.00000
      8.00000       9.00000       10.0000       11.0000       12.0000
      13.0000       14.0000       15.0000
```

The /OVERWRITE keyword tells REFORM to change the shape of the data but not to copy the data itself. With the /OVERWRITE keyword, re-forming an array is a very fast operation.

Note that the total number of elements in the new array must match the
number in the original array:

```
IDL> x = reform(x, 1, 8)
% REFORM: New subscripts must not change the number elements in X.
% Execution halted at: $MAIN$
```

You can even change the *number of dimensions*, as long as the total number
of *elements* does not change:

```
IDL> x = reform(x, 2, 2, 2, 2, /overwrite)
IDL> print, x
      0.00000       1.00000
      2.00000       3.00000

      4.00000       5.00000
      6.00000       7.00000

      8.00000       9.00000
      10.0000       11.0000

      12.0000       13.0000
      14.0000       15.0000
```

Sometimes it is useful to think of an array as a row vector:

```
IDL> y = findgen(4)
IDL> print, y
      0.00000       1.00000       2.00000       3.00000
IDL> help, y
Y                 FLOAT     = Array[4]
```

and sometimes as a column vector:

```
IDL> y = reform(y, 1, 4, /overwrite)
IDL> print, y
      0.00000
      1.00000
      2.00000
      3.00000
IDL> help, y
Y                 FLOAT     = Array[1, 4]
```

IDL arrays can have dimensions of size 1, although in some situations
IDL automatically removes *trailing* dimensions of size 1. If you want
to get *rid* of any dimensions of size 1, use REFORM without specifying any

dimensions:

```
IDL> y = reform(y, /overwrite)
IDL> help, y
Y               FLOAT     = Array[4]
```

7.7 Using Part of an Array

IDL has several shortcuts for working with only part of an array. These are referred to as *subarrays*. Subarrays are conveniently specified by using *subscript ranges*. Below are some examples of using subscript ranges on a 4×4 floating-point array:

See *Subscript Ranges* in *Building IDL Applications.*

```
IDL> x = findgen(4, 4)
IDL> print, x
      0.00000      1.00000      2.00000      3.00000
      4.00000      5.00000      6.00000      7.00000
      8.00000      9.00000      10.0000      11.0000
      12.0000      13.0000      14.0000      15.0000
IDL> print, x[*]              ;Example 1
      0.00000      1.00000      2.00000      3.00000      4.00000
      5.00000      6.00000      7.00000      8.00000      9.00000
      10.0000      11.0000      12.0000      13.0000      14.0000
      15.0000
IDL> print, x[*,1]            ;Example 2
      4.00000      5.00000      6.00000      7.00000
IDL> print, x[1,*]            ;Example 3
      1.00000
      5.00000
      9.00000
      13.0000
IDL> print, x[1:2,0:3]        ;Example 4
      1.00000      2.00000
      5.00000      6.00000
      9.00000      10.0000
      13.0000      14.0000
IDL> print, x[2:*,0:1]        ;Example 5
      2.00000      3.00000
      6.00000      7.00000
IDL> print, x[0:*:2,*]        ;Example 6
      0.00000      2.00000
      4.00000      6.00000
      8.00000      10.0000
      12.0000      14.0000
```

A single asterisk * by itself means all elements of the array, even if it has multiple dimensions (Example 1). Using an asterisk to subscript a particular dimension will return all possible subscripts of that dimension (Examples 2 and 3 above). Note the difference between row and column subscripts. You can select a limited range from a given dimension using the : notation (Example 4). You can think of this as indexing from:to. An asterisk after the colon means "to the largest subscript for that dimension" (Example 5). Finally, recent versions of IDL allow a from:to:by notation. In Example 6, the first subscript goes from 0 to the last element of that dimension, by 2. The by value is referred to as the *stride*. As the examples show, you can use different types of subscript ranges for each dimension.

The different types of array subscript ranges are listed in Table 7.3.

7.8 Expanding or Shrinking (Rebinning) an Array

Using subscript ranges with a stride, it is possible to extract a regular subgrid of elements from an array (like selecting only the black squares on a checkerboard). This operation can also be done with the REBIN function, but only when the dimensions of the new array are an integral divisor of the input array. For example, to extract every other element of an array, use REBIN in the following way:

See the REBIN function in IDL Reference Guide.

```
IDL> x = findgen(4, 4)
IDL> print, x
      0.00000       1.00000       2.00000       3.00000
      4.00000       5.00000       6.00000       7.00000
      8.00000       9.00000       10.0000       11.0000
      12.0000       13.0000       14.0000       15.0000
IDL> print, rebin(x, 2, 2, /sample)
      0.00000       2.00000
      8.00000       10.0000
```

REBIN in this form is not as versatile as subscript ranges with strides, but REBIN has other useful abilities.

If the /SAMPLE keyword is omitted, for example, REBIN *averages* the values within blocks of adjacent array elements:

```
IDL> print, rebin(x, 2, 2)
      2.50000       4.50000
      10.5000       12.5000
```

TABLE 7.3   Forms of subscript ranges.

Form	Meaning	Example
i	A simple subscript expression	x[3]
$i_0:i_1$	Subscript range from i_0 to i_1	x[3:5]
$i_0:i_1:i_2$	Subscript range from i_0 to i_1 with a stride of i_2	x[3:9:2]
$i_0:*$	All points from element i_0 to end	x[3:*]
$i_0:*:i_2$	All points from element i_0 to end with a stride of i_2	x[3:*:3]
*	All points in the dimension	x[*]

REBIN can also be used to *expand* an array. The following is an example that illustrates some of the power of REBIN. Section 7.5 of this chapter shows how to compute a one-dimensional coordinate variable with array syntax by using the FINDGEN function. It is convenient (and fast) to use the same approach with multidimensional arrays. For example, you might wish to compute

$$z(x, y) = \sin(2\pi x) \; \sin(2\pi y) \qquad (7.3)$$

for a set of $N_x \times N_y$ grid points that are evenly spaced between 0 and 1 in both x and y, that is

$$z_{i,j} = \sin(2\pi x_i) \sin(2\pi y_j) \qquad (7.4)$$

where $x_i = i \cdot \delta x$, $\delta x = 1/(N_x - 1)$, and $i = 0, 1, 2, \ldots, N_x - 1$ $\quad(7.5)$

and $y_j = j \cdot \delta y$, $\delta y = 1/(N_y - 1)$, and $j = 0, 1, 2, \ldots, N_y - 1$ $\quad(7.6)$

To compute $z_{i,j}$, it is first necessary to compute the values of the independent coordinates x_i and y_j. In order to use IDL array syntax, x and y must be 2-D arrays.

The trick to doing this in IDL is to create one-dimensional coordinate arrays and then *expand* them into two-dimensional arrays by using the REBIN function. Here is a simple example that expands x in the y direction by duplicating rows:

```
IDL> x = findgen(4)
IDL> print, x
      0.00000      1.00000      2.00000      3.00000
IDL> print, rebin(x, 4, 3, /sample)
      0.00000      1.00000      2.00000      3.00000
      0.00000      1.00000      2.00000      3.00000
      0.00000      1.00000      2.00000      3.00000
```

To do the same with y, it is necessary to first transform a 1-D row vector into a 2-D column vector (with a leading dimension of 1) by using REFORM:

```
IDL> y = findgen(3)
IDL> print, y
      0.00000      1.00000      2.00000
IDL> y = reform(y, 1, 3, /overwrite)
IDL> print, y
      0.00000
      1.00000
      2.00000
IDL> y = rebin(y, 4, 3, /sample)
IDL> print, y
```

```
   0.00000        0.00000        0.00000       0.00000
   1.00000        1.00000        1.00000       1.00000
   2.00000        2.00000        2.00000       2.00000
```

Here is a complete script that will create 2-D *x* and *y* coordinates, compute
z from the formula above, and plot a contour graph of the result:

```
;  Generate 2-D coordinates and plot a sample function

nx = 21                                  ;Number of x-grid points
ny = 26                                  ;Number of y-grid points

dx = 1.0/(nx-1)                          ;x-grid point spacing
dy = 1.0/(ny-1)                          ;y-grid point spacing

x  = dx*FINDGEN(nx)                      ;Compute 1-D x-coordinates
y  = dy*FINDGEN(ny)                      ;Compute 1-D y-coordinates

xx = REBIN(x, nx, ny, /SAMPLE)           ;Expand x-coordinates to 2-D
yy = REBIN(REFORM(y, 1, ny), nx, ny, /SAMPLE) ;Expand y-coordinates to 2-D

z  = SIN(2.0*!PI*xx) * SIN(2.0*!PI*yy)   ;Compute z
HELP, xx, yy, z

CONTOUR, z, x, y, /FOLLOW, $             ;Plot contour graph
   LEVELS = -1.0+0.2*FINDGEN(11), $
   TITLE  = 'Plot of sin(2 pi x) * sin(2 pi y)', $
   XTITLE = 'x', $
   YTITLE = 'y'
```

For clarity, the coordinate arrays are created in three separate steps: first,
compute dx and dy; next, compute the 1-D coordinates x and y; and finally,
expand x and y into 2-D coordinates xx and yy. These steps could be combined
into one line for each coordinate, but the resulting IDL statements would be
harder to read. Executing the script gives:

```
IDL> @two_d_coords
X                FLOAT     = Array[21, 26]
Y                FLOAT     = Array[21, 26]
Z                FLOAT     = Array[21, 26]
```

The graph produced by the script is shown in Figure 7.1.

7.9 Reversing an Array

IDL has a built-in function to reverse the order of the elements in an array.
This *does* require that values be moved around in memory. As with most array
operation, it is much faster to use REVERSE than a FOR loop. Here is an

See the REVERSE function
in *IDL Reference Guide.*

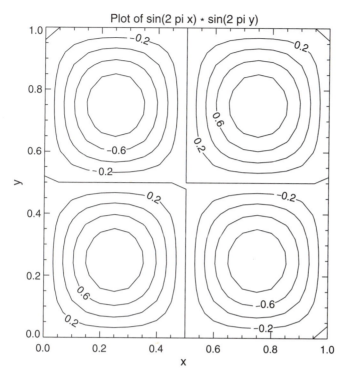

FIGURE 7.1   A simple contour graph. (TWO_D_COORDS_PS)

example:

```
IDL> a = findgen(5)
IDL> print, a
      0.00000      1.00000      2.00000      3.00000      4.00000
Idl> b = reverse(a)
% Compiled module: REVERSE.
IDL> print, b
      4.00000      3.00000      2.00000      1.00000      0.00000
```

You can also use REVERSE to reverse the elements of any dimension of a multidimensional array. The second argument indicates which dimension of i should be reversed:

```
IDL> i = lindgen(3, 3)
IDL> print, i
           0           1           2
           3           4           5
           6           7           8
IDL> print, reverse(i, 1)
           2           1           0
           5           4           3
           8           7           6
```

```
IDL> print, reverse(i, 2)
          6            7            8
          3            4            5
          0            1            2
```

7.10   Rotating or Transposing an Array

The built-in IDL function to rotate or transpose an array is ROTATE.[1] ROTATE only works on 1- and 2-D arrays and only rotates in 90° increments. The first argument to ROTATE is the array to be rotated; the second is the type of rotation or transposition. There are eight possible rotation/transposition options. The table in the *IDL Reference Guide* entry for ROTATE describes the effects of each option on the elements of a 2-D array. Here are some examples:

See the ROTATE function in *IDL Reference Guide.*

```
IDL> print, i
          0            1            2
          3            4            5
          6            7            8
IDL> print, rotate(i, 0)          ;No rotation or transposition
          0            1            2
          3            4            5
          6            7            8
IDL> print, rotate(i, 1)          ;Rotate 90, no transposition
          6            3            0
          7            4            1
          8            5            2
IDL> print, rotate(i, 4)          ;No rotation, transpose
          0            3            6
          1            4            7
          2            5            8
IDL> print, rotate(i, 5)          ;Transpose, then rotate 90
          2            1            0
          5            4            3
          8            7            6
```

7.11   Shifting an Array

The built-in IDL function to shift an array is SHIFT. SHIFT works on arrays with any number of dimensions. For multidimensional arrays, you must specify the shift to be applied to each dimension. All shifts are circular.

See the SHIFT function in *IDL Reference Guide.*

---

1   There is also a TRANSPOSE function that allows dimension permutation of multidimensional arrays.

Elements shifted off the end of a dimension are shifted onto the other end. Positive shifts are to the right, negative shifts to the left. Here are some examples:

```
IDL> x = lindgen(4, 4)
IDL> print, x
           0           1           2           3
           4           5           6           7
           8           9          10          11
          12          13          14          15
IDL> print, shift(x, 1, 0)
           3           0           1           2
           7           4           5           6
          11           8           9          10
          15          12          13          14
IDL> print, shift(x, -1, 0)
           1           2           3           0
           5           6           7           4
           9          10          11           8
          13          14          15          12
IDL> print, shift(x, 0, 3)
           4           5           6           7
           8           9          10          11
          12          13          14          15
           0           1           2           3
```

7.12 Summary

IDL programs are generally faster and easier to read if you use array operations rather than loops. In addition to standard arithmetic operations with arrays, IDL has a number of built-in functions that can rotate, reverse, reform, rebin, and shift arrays. These functions can be used to carry out most array operations that require loops in Fortran or C.

7.13 Exercises

1. Make a small two-dimensional string index array using the SINDGEN function and print the results.

2. Create a 2 × 2 FLOAT index array and rebin it to a 6 × 6 array with and without the /SAMPLE keyword. Print the results. Try the same operations with a LONG array.

3. Create a coordinate array with n values equally spaced between -1.0 and 1.0. Compare the results when n is even and when n is odd.

4. Generate a two-dimensional array containing the values of the function

$$z(x, y) = xy^2 \qquad\qquad (7.7)$$

Plot the array using contour or surface. Examine the effects of using ROTATE, REVERSE, or SHIFT on the array.

Searching and Sorting

This chapter covers how to *search* for specific values within IDL arrays and *sort* the values of IDL arrays into increasing or decreasing order.

8.1 IDL Procedures and Functions

The following IDL procedures are discussed:

- WHERE function and the COUNT, COMPLEMENT, and NCOMPLEMENT keywords
- SORT function
- VALUE_LOCATE function

8.2 Finding Values in an Array That Satisfy a Logical Condition

A common programming task is to find the elements of an array that satisfy a particular condition. For example, if you have an array filled with floating-point numbers, you might want to know which elements of the array are less than some threshold value. Here is a six-element array filled with pseudorandom numbers[1] between 0 and 1:

```
IDL> seed = 11
IDL> x = randomu(seed, 6)
IDL> print, x
      0.0187254      0.717428      0.0846801      0.320515      0.713097
      0.949264
```

To find the values less than 0.5, use the WHERE function:

```
IDL> i = where(x LT 0.5, count)
IDL> print, i
           0          2          3
```

See the WHERE function in *IDL Reference Guide*.

---

1 Setting seed to 11 ensures that you will see the same sequence of pseudorandom numbers as in the example. If you want to try these operations with a different set of numbers, omit the statement seed = 11.

```
IDL> print, count
           3
IDL> print, x[i]
    0.0187254     0.0846801       0.320515
```

The array i contains the *subscripts* of all of the elements in x that satisfy the logical expression x LT 0.5. Note that i contains the subscripts of the elements, not the elements themselves. If you print i, you see that in this example elements 0, 2, and 3 are less than 0.5. The optional scalar variable count is also returned by the WHERE function. It contains the number of elements for which the logical expression is true (3 in this case).

The last line in the example above shows the real power of the WHERE function. You can use the array i to subscript the array x, which picks out all of the elements that satisfy the logical expression. This is referred to as an *array subscript*. If you like, you can copy the selected values to a new array:

```
IDL> y = x[i]
IDL> help, y
Y                    FLOAT      = Array[3]
IDL> print, y
    0.0187254     0.0846801       0.320515
```

The first argument of the WHERE function is always a logical expression. IDL includes the standard relational operators for arithmetic comparisons, which are listed in Table 8.1. Note that you do not use the mathematical symbols $<$, $>$, and so forth for relational expressions. Those symbols have a different function in IDL. The IDL relational symbols are similar to those in Fortran. IDL also includes the logical or Boolean operators listed in Table 8.2.

See *Relational Operators* in *Building IDL Applications.*

The second argument of the WHERE function, count, is optional, *but you should include* count *every time you use the* WHERE *function.* The example below shows why. (As this example shows, the name of the count variable does not have to be count.)

See *Boolean Operators* in *Building IDL Applications.*

```
IDL> j = where(x GT 2.0, jcount)
IDL> print, j
          -1
```

TABLE 8.1   Relational operators.

Operator	Description
EQ	Equal to
NE	Not equal to
GE	Greater than or equal to
GT	Greater than
LE	Less than or equal to
LT	Less than

TABLE 8.2   Boolean operators.

Operator	Description
AND	Logical and
OR	Logical or
NOT	Logical not (opposite)
XOR	Logical exclusive or

```
IDL> print, x[j]
% Attempt to subscript X with J is out of range.
% Execution halted at: $MAIN$
IDL> if (jcount GT 0) then print, x[j]
IDL>
```

In this example, *no elements satisfy the logical condition.* The value returned for j is −1. If you try to subscript x with j, an error results. The lesson here is that you should *always test the value of* count *before using the subscript array returned by the* WHERE *function.* In the example above, the logical expression (jcount GT 0) is false, so the PRINT statement is not executed and does not generate an error.

As with other array operations in IDL, WHERE is generally much faster than the equivalent Fortran-style program that uses a FOR loop. Avoid programming like this:

```
FOR i = 0, n-1 DO BEGIN
   IF (x[i] LT x0) THEN
      ... do one thing
   ENDIF ELSE BEGIN
      ... do something else
   ENDELSE
ENDFOR
```

Instead use this form:

```
i = WHERE(x LT x0, icount, COMPLEMENT = j, NCOMPLEMENT = jcount)
IF (icount GT 0) THEN x[i] = ... do one thing
IF (jcount GT 0) THEN x[j] = ... do something else
```

The COMPLEMENT keyword returns an array (in this case called j) that contains the indices of the elements that *do not* satisfy the logical condition. The NCOMPLEMENT keyword contains the number of elements that do not satisfy the logical condition.

8.3   Sorting an Array

The built-in IDL function to sort the elements of an array is SORT. In a manner similar to WHERE, SORT returns a list of the *indices* of the array sorted

See the SORT function in *IDL Reference Guide.*

in the proper order, not the elements themselves. This example sorts the pseudorandom numbers contained in x:

```
IDL> k = sort(x)
IDL> print, k
           0            2            3            4            1
           5
IDL> print, x[k]
    0.0187254    0.0846801    0.320515    0.713097    0.717428
    0.949264
```

To get the values in descending order, reverse the subscript array:

```
IDL> print, x[reverse(k)]
% Compiled module: REVERSE.
    0.949264    0.717428    0.713097    0.320515    0.0846801
    0.0187254
```

To sort the actual values of x into ascending order, use the array subscript:

```
IDL> x = x[SORT(x)]
IDL> print, x
    0.0187254    0.0846801    0.320515    0.713097    0.717428
    0.949264
```

8.4   Finding a Value in a Sorted Array

The WHERE function can be used to find a single value within an array:

```
IDL> print, x
    0.0187254    0.0846801    0.320515    0.713097    0.717428
    0.949264
IDL> x0 = x[3]
IDL> print, x0
    0.713097
IDL> i = where(x EQ x0, count)
IDL> print, i, count
           3
           1
```

It is important to remember, however, that the WHERE function applies the logical test to *every element of an array*. If you are repeatedly searching for a single value within an array using WHERE, each time you call WHERE, it will search the entire array. If there are n elements in the array, then WHERE will do n comparisons. For repeated searches of large arrays, this can be very slow.

If you sort the elements of the array first, however, you can use much faster searching techniques, such as a binary search. A binary search requires at most only $\log_2(n)$ comparisons. For an array with 10^6 elements, that is only $\sim$20 comparisons, which is an improvement by a factor of 50,000 over the *linear* search used by WHERE. The IDL function to carry out a binary search is called VALUE_LOCATE. VALUE_LOCATE also finds the element in the array with the value closest to the value you are searching for. This makes it very useful, for example, when interpolating irregularly spaced data.

See the VALUE_LOCATE function in *IDL Reference Guide.*

The procedure SEARCH_COMPARE compares the search times for WHERE and VALUE_LOCATE when carrying out 1000 searches on an array of 10^6 pseudo-random numbers. The results are shown below:

```
IDL> .r search_compare
% Compiled module: SEARCH_COMPARE.
IDL> SEARCH_COMPARE
Time required for        1000 searches in a      1000000-element array.
Time using WHERE         =        70.726247 s
Time using VALUE_LOCATE  =        3.5786340 s
VALUE_LOCATE is                   19.763476 times faster.
```

The difference in this example is about a factor of 20. (Remember that using VALUE_LOCATE does require sorting the array first, which takes some time.)

As you can see, if you have to search an array only once, a single WHERE statement is faster and easier than sorting the array and then using VALUE_LOCATE. If you are searching an array many times, however, it may well prove faster to use SORT and then VALUE_LOCATE.

As the number of searches increases, the overhead of sorting the values first becomes less important, and the difference between the two methods becomes much larger. Here is a comparison for 10,000 searches:

```
IDL> SEARCH_COMPARE
Time required for        10000 searches in a      1000000-element array.
Time using WHERE         =        684.59085 s
Time using VALUE_LOCATE  =        3.5752939 s
VALUE_LOCATE is                   191.47820 times faster.
```

In this case, the time used by the VALUE_LOCATE method is almost entirely for the initial sort (about 3 seconds); the time required to do the searches is almost negligible. The times for the two methods in this case are $\sim$11 minutes using WHERE and $\sim$4 seconds using SORT and VALUE_LOCATE!

8.5 Summary

The WHERE function is the essential tool for doing fast conditional array operations in IDL. Most operations that could be done in a Fortran-like style using FOR loops and IF statements can be done faster and more elegantly in IDL using WHERE.

WHERE applies the logical test to *every* element of the array. SORT and VALUE_LOCATE sort arrays and search ordered arrays, respectively.

8.6 Exercises

1. Create an array of integers from 100 to 199 by 1. Use WHERE to find the indices of all of the even and odd values in the array. Hint: i MOD 2 is 0 if i is even and 1 if i is odd. Print the resulting lists of even and odd numbers.

2. Create a coordinate variable x that goes from 1 to 10 by 0.1 and use it to compute a table of logarithms $y = \log_{10} x$. Generate a pseudorandom number x_0 between 1 and 10 using RANDOMU and use VALUE_LOCATE to estimate the logarithm of x_0 by finding the index of the closest x. Print the actual logarithm of x_0, the value estimated from the table, and the error (difference). For extra credit, linearly interpolate the table of logarithms to the point x_0.

Structures

In IDL, *structures* are collections of variables that can be referenced with a single name. Their primary purpose is to allow you to keep logically or functionally related variables together. Structures can help you to organize your variables (data) like procedures and functions help you to organize your program (algorithms). This chapter describes IDL structures and how to use them.

9.1   IDL Commands and Keywords

The following IDL commands can be used to create structures or get information about existing structures:

- CREATE_STRUCT procedure

- N_TAGS function

- TAG_NAMES function

9.2   Named Structures

IDL provides two types of structures: *named structures* and *anonymous structures*. This section describes named structures.

Like other IDL data types (scalars, arrays, etc.), structures can be created dynamically at any point in a program. Here is a script that creates a named structure:

```
;  named_structure.pro

data = COORDINATE, $
        values : FINDGEN(4), $
        n      : 4

PRINT, 'Structure contents :'
PRINT, data.values
PRINT, data.n
```

Executing the script produces the following:

```
IDL> @named_structure
Structure contents :
      0.00000      1.00000      2.00000      3.00000
           4
```

The structure variable named data is created by providing a list with the structure name at the beginning (COORDINATE in this case), followed by pairs of *tag names* and *tag definitions*. Each pair consists of a tag name (which must satisfy the IDL rules for variable names), a colon, and the tag definition (a variable or expression). Each pair of items identified by a tag name is referred to as a *field*. The structure itself (that is, the name plus the list of fields) is delimited by braces { and }. The structure name does not have a tag definition associated with it.

In this example, the tag names are values and n. Structure definitions are much easier to read and debug if they are written as above, one tag_name : tag_definition pair per line, with the colons lined up to create a two-column table.

As the last two lines in the script illustrate, a variable stored within a structure is referenced by using the syntax variable_name.tag_name. You can use the same tag name within multiple structures because the field can only be referenced if the variable name is also included. If you try to access a variable inside a structure, n, for example, without providing the structure variable name, an error occurs:

```
IDL> print, n
% PRINT: Variable is undefined: N.
% Execution· halted at: $MAIN$
IDL> print, data.n
           4
```

You can also use HELP to inquire about the variables contained in a structure:

```
IDL> help, data, /structure
** Structure COORDINATE, 2 tags, length=20, data length=18:
   VALUES          FLOAT      Array[4]
   N               INT             4
```

There is an important difference between structure fields and regular IDL variables. The size and type of regular IDL variables can be changed at any time simply by assigning a new expression to the old variable name. With variables *inside a structure* (structure *fields*), this is not possible. The size and

type of each field is fixed when the structure is defined. Attempting to change
`data.values` to a larger array, for example, causes an error:

```
IDL> data.values = findgen(10)
% Conflicting data structures: structure tag,<FLOAT    Array[10]>.
% Execution halted at: $MAIN$
```

You can change the value of a variable inside a structure, but not its size
or type:

```
IDL> data.values = SQRT(data.values)
IDL> print, data.values
      0.00000      1.00000      1.41421      1.73205

IDL> data.values[2] = 13.0
IDL> print, data.values
      0.00000      1.00000      13.0000      1.73205
```

Although you cannot change the internal definition of structure fields, you
can change a structure *variable* just like any other IDL variable. A structure
variable can be dynamically replaced by another variable of any type:

```
IDL> data = fltarr(2, 2)
IDL> help, data
DATA            FLOAT     = Array[2, 2]
```

Once a named structure is defined, its definition is stored within your IDL
session. To create a new structure variable with the same type, just reference
the structure name:

```
IDL> newdata = {coordinate}
IDL> help, newdata, /str
** Structure COORDINATE, 2 tags, length=20, data length=20:
   VALUES          FLOAT     Array[4]
   N               LONG             4
IDL> print, newdata.values
      0.00000      0.00000      0.00000      0.00000
```

Note that when a new structure is created using a previously defined structure,
the fields are *zeroed*. String fields are set to the null string.

9.2.1 Automatic Structure Definition

Named structures can be defined automatically by putting the structure definition for a named structure into a special kind of procedure. The first time the
named structure is referenced, the procedure is automatically compiled and
executed. The procedure below, WX_OB__DEFINE, shows how to use automatic
structure definition:

```
PRO WX_OB__DEFINE

;  Structure definition for named structure WX_OB

data = WX_OB, $
        station_name : '', $
        T            : 0.0, $
        T_units      : '', $
        p            : 0.0, $
        p_units      : ''

END
```

Note that the name of the procedure must match the structure name,
with __DEFINE added at the end. (That's *two* underscores before DEFINE!)
Attempting to create a WX_OB structure variable, ob, causes IDL to search for
a procedure named WX_OB__DEFINE. If it exists, it is automatically compiled
and executed. The structure variable that is created is zeroed, as expected:

```
IDL> ob = wx_ob
% Compiled module: WX_OB__DEFINE.
IDL> help, ob, /str
** Structure WX_OB, 5 tags, length=44, data length=44:
   STATION_NAME    STRING    ''
   T               FLOAT          0.00000
   T_UNITS         STRING    ''
   P               FLOAT          0.00000
   P_UNITS         STRING    ''
```

Values can be stored in ob using standard assignment statements:

```
IDL> ob.station_name = 'CLL'
IDL> ob.T = 83.0
IDL> ob.T_units = 'degrees F'
IDL> ob.p = 1012.5
IDL> ob.p_units = 'hPa'
IDL> help, ob, /str
** Structure WX_OB, 5 tags, length=44, data length=44:
```

```
STATION_NAME    STRING    'CLL'
T               FLOAT            83.0000
T_UNITS         STRING    'degrees F'
P               FLOAT          1012.50
P_UNITS         STRING    'hPa'
```

The end result is a single variable (ob) that carries around a collection of related information. One important feature of structures is that all of the variables inside a structure can be passed between procedures and functions by using only the structure variable name, ob.

9.3 Anonymous Structures

As the name suggests, the primary way that anonymous structures differ from named structures is by *not* having an explicit name associated with the structure.

Here is a short script that creates two variables, a STRING variable called name and a floating-point array called x. Those variables are copied into a structure variable named data, along with the size of the array x:

```
;  anonymous_structure.pro

name = 'Example anonymous structure'
x    = FINDGEN(5)

data = name    : name, $
       values : x, $
       n       : N_ELEMENTS(x)

PRINT, 'Variable info :'
PRINT, name
PRINT, x

PRINT, 'Structure info :'
PRINT, data.name
PRINT, data.values
PRINT, data.n
```

In this example, the tag names are name, values, and n. Note that name is a *field name*, not the structure name. Executing the script produces this output:

```
IDL> @anonymous_structure
Variable info :
Example anonymous structure
      0.00000      1.00000      2.00000      3.00000      4.00000
```

```
Structure info :
Example anonymous structure
      0.00000      1.00000      2.00000      3.00000      4.00000
          5
```

Note that the ordinary variables name and x are *copied* into the structure. The original variables, name and x, are not affected by the creation of the structure.

To store values into a structure field, use the "dot" syntax to identify the field:

```
IDL> data.values[2] = -2.0
IDL> print, data.values
      0.00000      1.00000     -2.00000      3.00000      4.00000
```

As with named structures, you can inquire about an anonymous structure variable by using the HELP procedure. By itself, HELP merely tells you that data is a structure:

```
IDL> help, data
DATA               STRUCT     = -> <Anonymous> Array[1]
```

Adding the /STRUCTURE keyword to HELP (abbreviated /STR) produces a list of the structure's tag names and definitions:

```
IDL> help, data, /str
** Structure <11d4020>, 3 tags, length=36, data length=36, refs=1:
   NAME              STRING     'Example structure'
   VALUES            FLOAT      Array[5]
   N                 LONG                 5
```

You also can get information about a structure using the N_TAGS and TAG_NAMES functions:

See the N_TAGS and TAG_NAMES functions in *IDL Reference Guide.*

```
IDL> help, n_tags(data)
<Expression>    LONG      =            3
IDL> help, tag_names(data)
<Expression>    STRING    = Array[3]
IDL> print, tag_names(data)
NAME VALUES N
```

Structures can also be created dynamically using the CREATE_STRUCT function.

9.4 Hierarchical Structures

Structure variables can be placed inside other structures to create *hierarchical structures*. Here is a script that creates a hierarchical structure:

See the CREATE_STRUCT function in *IDL Reference Guide*.

```
;  hierarchical_structure.pro

nx   = 20
x    = name    : 'Longitude', $
       values : FLTARR(nx)

ny   = 25
y    = name    : 'Latitude', $
       values : FLTARR(ny)

data = name    : 'Temperature', $
       values : FLTARR(nx, ny), $
       x       : x, $
       y       : y

HELP, data,   /str
HELP, data.x, /str
HELP, data.y, /str

PRINT, data.name
PRINT, data.x.name
PRINT, data.y.name
```

Running the script gives the following results:

```
IDL> @hierarchical_structure
** Structure <165730>, 4 tags, length=2216, data length=2216, refs=1:
   NAME              STRING      'Temperature'
   VALUES            FLOAT       Array[20, 25]
   X                 STRUCT      -> <Anonymous> Array[1]
   Y                 STRUCT      -> <Anonymous> Array[1]
** Structure <e1e00>, 2 tags, length=92, data length=92, refs=3:
   NAME              STRING      'Longitude'
   VALUES            FLOAT       Array[20]
** Structure <e18a0>, 2 tags, length=112, data length=112, refs=3:
   NAME              STRING      'Latitude'
   VALUES            FLOAT       Array[25]
Temperature
Longitude
Latitude
```

The last three lines of the script show how to access variables within the structure hierarchy. The `values` field within the field x is accessed with, for example,

```
IDL> print, data.x.values[0:4]
      0.00000      0.00000      0.00000      0.00000      0.00000
```

9.5 Additional Topics

Structures can be organized into arrays of structures; that is, each element of the array is a structure. In an array of structures, all of the structures must be identical. For information on structure arrays, see *Building IDL Applications*.

9.6 Summary

This chapter has covered the basics of creating and using named and anonymous structures. Anonymous structures are suitable for most instances in which you need to use structures, particularly when you do not know the specifics of the structure content ahead of time.

Named structures are convenient for those structures where you know the exact types and sizes of the variables in the structure ahead of time. With named structures you should use automatic structure definition. It is much easier to find the structure definition if it is stored in a `__DEFINE` procedure rather than buried within some function or procedure. This also helps prevent inadvertently using two structures with the same name.

9.7 Exercises

1. Create a named structure to contain the date and time to the nearest second. If you wished to have higher precision, what would you do?

2. Create an anonymous structure to hold a coordinate variable. It should contain the following fields: coordinate values (an array), name, units, and the number of points in the coordinate. You could also include fields to indicate whether the coordinate grid is regular or irregular, and whether it is stored in increasing or decreasing order. Including that information in the structure can make it easier to use the coordinate information in your programs.

Part II

INPUT AND OUTPUT

Printing Text

This chapter covers how to send text output to the terminal screen or to a file; that is, how to prepare output for *humans* to read. This is referred to as *text* or *formatted* or *ASCII* output. ASCII (pronounced as-key) is an acronym for American Standard Code for Information Interchange. The ASCII code is simply a table that assigns upper- and lowercase letters in the Latin alphabet, numerals, punctuation marks, and other items to different byte values between 0 and 127. For example, the uppercase letter A is assigned the value 65 in the ASCII table. ASCII provides a simple way to store text in a file composed of bytes, one byte per character.[1]

Generally, when you need to transfer *numerical* data between programs or between computers, you should use *binary* formats, which are covered in Chapters 12, 13, and 14.

10.1 IDL Commands and Keywords

The following IDL commands and keywords are used for printing text to the terminal screen and to files:

- PRINT procedure and FORMAT keyword

- OPENW procedure and GET_LUN keyword

- PRINTF procedure and FORMAT keyword

- FREE_LUN procedure

10.2 Free-Format Output

We have already used the PRINT command many times to print the values of IDL constants, expressions, and variables. Like most IDL commands, PRINT has a *default* behavior. If you PRINT the BYTE variable x in the example below,

See *Using Free Format Input/Output* in *Building IDL Applications.*

---

1 ASCII is being replaced gradually by a new standard called UNICODE. UNICODE tables can contain thousands of characters and symbols, which allows them to support a much wider set of languages.

the internal binary representation (8 bits) of the BYTE variable are converted
to the characters 1 and 5 (that is, a string) and displayed on the screen:

See the PRINT
procedure in *IDL
Reference Guide.*

```
IDL> x = 15B
IDL> y = 250B
IDL> print, x, y
  15 250
```

As you can see, you can supply more than one expression or variable to be
printed in a list of items separated by commas. Because BYTE variables cannot
have more than three decimal digits, and negative values are not allowed, the
output for a BYTE is allotted four characters by default. This allows for a space
between successive output values.

You can print various kinds of variables or expressions in a single
statement:

```
IDL> i = 34567
IDL> a = 15.0
IDL> b = 123456.7
IDL> c = 9.876E23
IDL> d = 7.654D-21
IDL> text = 'This is a string.'
IDL> print, i, a, b, c, d, text
       34567       15.0000       123457.   9.87600e+23
       7.6540000e-21 This is a string.
```

Note that the string variable text, unlike the other variables, did not get any
extra blanks. You must provide those yourself:

See *String Constants*
in *Building IDL
Applications.*

```
IDL> print, i, a, b, c, d, " , text
       34567       15.0000       123457.   9.87600e+23
       7.65400e-21 This is a string.
```

IDL has built-in rules for writing each type of variable. This default behavior is called *free-format* output because the format of the output is not specified
explicitly. Free-format output is usually adequate for interactive calculations.
If free-form output is not satisfactory, you can specify the output format using
the FORMAT keyword (see the next section).

Be careful! If you try to print a large array, IDL will happily print millions
of numbers to the screen. (Don't try this example unless you are very patient!)

```
IDL> x = findgen(100000)
IDL> print, x
       0.00000       1.00000       2.00000       3.00000       4.00000
       5.00000       6.00000       7.00000       8.00000       9.00000
       10.0000       11.0000       12.0000       13.0000       14.0000
```

15.0000	16.0000	17.0000	18.0000	19.0000
20.0000	21.0000	22.0000	23.0000	24.0000
25.0000	26.0000	27.0000	28.0000	29.0000
30.0000	31.0000	32.0000	33.0000	34.0000
35.0000	36.0000	37.0000	38.0000	39.0000

.
.
.

You can use control-c to interrupt output, but it may take some time for the interrupt to work.

10.3 Formatted Output

10.3.1 Printing Integers

The PRINT command accepts optional arguments called *keywords* to control the output. The only keyword that we are concerned with here is the FORMAT keyword. Here is a simple example of how to use the FORMAT keyword:

See *Using Explicitly Formatted Input/Output* in *Building IDL Applications.*

```
IDL> print, x, y, format = "(I2, I10)"
15        250
```

The expression inside the double quotes is a string that contains a standard Fortran *format specification.*[2] The complete rules for format specification are complex, but this simple case is fairly easy to understand. In the example there are two format specifications, separated by a comma. The first number is output as an integer using 2 columns (I2), the second is also output as an integer, in this case using 10 columns (I10). Be careful when you specify explicit formats like this. If you reverse the order of the output arguments, you get this:

```
IDL> print, y, x, format = "(I2, I10)"
**        15
```

The number 250 cannot be printed with only two digits. This error is indicated by the ** printed in the first two columns.

At times it is useful to be able to print integers with leading zeros. For example, if you need to print a sequence of file names: file001, file002, etc. you could use the following format[3].

---

2   IDL PRINT statements can also use C printf-style format codes. For information about using C-style codes, see **Format Codes** in *Building IDL Applications.*
3   Creating standardized file names like this can make other tasks easier.

```
IDL> i = lindgen(4)
IDL> print, i, FORMAT = "('file',I3.3)"
file000
file001
file002
file003
```

This format definition has two parts. First, it writes the string `file`. Because it is contained *within* the larger string that makes up the complete format specification, `file` must be enclosed in *single* quotes. Next, a three-column integer is written with enough leading zeros to fill all three columns (indicated by the I3.3 format code). Because the output uses a format specification, it does not automatically insert any blanks. The PRINT command prints all four values contained in the array i, even though the format specification only provides for printing a single value. When the end of the format is reached, if there are still items to be output, a new output line is started and processing starts over from the beginning of the format specification. This "automatic repeat" function is convenient for printing lists or arrays.

10.3.2 Printing Floating-Point Numbers

Floating-point numbers have slightly more complicated format codes than integers:

```
IDL> a = 15.0
IDL> b = 123456.7
IDL> c = 9.876E23
IDL> d = 7.654D-21
IDL> print, a, b, c, d
      15.0000      123457.   9.87600e+23    7.6540000e-21
```

By default, IDL prints FLOATs with about six-digit precision and provides blanks so that successive numbers do not run together. As we have seen, six-digit precision is about all that can be expected from a 32-bit floating-point number. Because d is double precision, it is printed with eight digits by default. When writing floating-point variables, IDL automatically rounds the output to the precision specified (the default precision, in this case). Note that the printed value of b is rounded up to 123457. *The value of* b *stored in computer memory is not changed.* The rounding by PRINT affects only the way the FLOAT is translated into decimal characters in the printed output. If the number is large or small enough to need it, exponential notation is used.

You can force IDL to provide more precision:

```
IDL> print, b, format = "(F15.6)"
  123456.703125
```

This format specifies that the result should occupy 15 columns, with 6 digits to the right of the decimal place. *Note that the output value is not the same as the constant specified above.* This happens because many decimal numbers cannot be represented exactly in binary notation using only 32 bits (see Chapter 6).

10.4 Printing a Table

In this section we use free-form and formatted output to print a short table of base-10 logarithms:

```
IDL> x = findgen(10)
IDL> y = alog10(x)
% Program caused arithmetic error: Floating divide by 0
```

Oops! We forgot that we cannot take the logarithm of zero:

```
IDL> x = 1.0 + findgen(10)
IDL> y = alog10(x)
IDL> print, x
      1.00000      2.00000      3.00000      4.00000      5.00000
      6.00000      7.00000      8.00000      9.00000      10.0000
IDL> print, y
      0.00000      0.301030     0.477121     0.602060     0.698970
      0.778151     0.845098     0.903090     0.954243     1.00000
```

We do a quick PRINT to make sure our values look correct. Next we will format these values into a more easily readable table. Remember that the formatting is entirely to make the data easier to read.

```
IDL> x = 1.0 + findgen(10)
IDL> y = alog10(x)
IDL> FOR i = 0, 9 DO PRINT, x[i], y[i], FORMAT = "(2F12.5)"
      1.00000     0.00000
      2.00000     0.30103
      3.00000     0.47712
      4.00000     0.60206
      5.00000     0.69897
      6.00000     0.77815
      7.00000     0.84510
      8.00000     0.90309
      9.00000     0.95424
     10.00000     1.00000
```

The statement FOR i = 0, 9 DO... is another example of a *loop*. In this case, the variable i counts from 0 to 9 by 1. Each time i is incremented by one, IDL executes the PRINT statement, which prints the values of the *i*'th elements of x and y using the format provided.

You can ensure that there is space between each of the items that are printed either by making the format code wide enough to leave space at the beginning of each number or by explicitly inserting spaces, either with the X format specifier:

```
IDL> FOR i = 0, 3 DO PRINT, x[i], y[i], FORMAT = "(F12.5, 5X, F12.5)"
      1.00000         0.00000
      2.00000         0.30103
      3.00000         0.47712
      4.00000         0.60206
```

or by inserting an explicit string containing spaces:

```
IDL> FOR i = 0, 3 DO PRINT, x[i], y[i], FORMAT = "(F12.5, '        ', F12.5)"
      1.00000         0.00000
      2.00000         0.30103
      3.00000         0.47712
      4.00000         0.60206
```

10.5   Output to Files

IDL can send printed output to a file as well as to the terminal screen. Before printing to a file, IDL has to know to which file you want to send the output. This information is provided through the OPEN command. There are actually three different versions of the OPEN command: OPENW, OPENR, and OPENU. OPENW opens a new file for writing. If the file already exists, it is overwritten, and any previous content is lost (unless writing is prohibited by the operating system). OPENR opens a file for reading only. If you only want to read from a file, but not write to it, you should use OPENR to reduce the possibility of a programming blunder that might destroy the file. OPENU opens an existing file for both input and output. This is called *update* mode. Generally it is better to avoid reading from and writing to the same file. It is very easy to make a programming error that damages or destroys the contents of an existing file.

See the OPEN procedure in IDL Reference Guide.

Here is an example of how to write the table in the previous section to a file by using OPENW:

```
IDL> openw, ounit, 'table.txt', /GET_LUN
IDL> print, ounit
         100
IDL> FOR i = 0, 9 DO PRINTF, ounit, x[i], y[i], FORMAT = "(2F12.5)"
IDL> free_lun, ounit
```

The OPENW command tells IDL to open a connection to a file called table.txt. Because we have not provided a complete path to the file (that is, including all parent directories), IDL creates a file inside the current directory, which is usually your home directory. Within IDL the file is referred to by a tag called a *logical unit number* or LUN. The LUN, which is simply an integer, is stored in the variable named ounit, which is a short name for "output unit number." The /GET_LUN keyword tells IDL to find the first available unused LUN between 100 and 128. After entering the OPENW command, we print the value of ounit and see that it is set to 100.

To print the table to the file, we use the PRINTF command rather than the PRINT command (PRINT sends output to the terminal). The first argument of the PRINTF command must be the unit number.

See the PRINTF procedure in *IDL Reference Guide*.

When the output is complete, the LUN is freed and the file is closed with the FREE_LUN command. You should always close a file when you are finished reading from it or writing to it. This frees the LUN for use with another file. Among other things, there is a limit to the number of files that can be open simultaneously. Closing files when finished with them will help you avoid running out of LUNs.

See the FREE_LUN procedure in *IDL Reference Guide*.

You can also specify an LUN explicitly,

```
IIDL> openw, 21, 'table.txt', /GET_LUN
IDL> FOR i = 0, 9 DO PRINTF, 21, x[i], y[i], FORMAT = "(2F12.5)"
IDL> close, ounit
```

but why do that when IDL can find an available LUN for you?

Using a text editor or the IDL Development Environment, open the file table.txt and compare its contents to the terminal output in the previous section:

```
 1.00000     0.00000
 2.00000     0.30103
 3.00000     0.47712
 4.00000     0.60206
 5.00000     0.69897
 6.00000     0.77815
 7.00000     0.84510
 8.00000     0.90309
 9.00000     0.95424
10.00000     1.00000
```

10.6 Summary

This chapter has covered the basics of sending printed output to the terminal or to a file. Here are some points to remember:

- PRINT sends output to the terminal, PRINTF to a file.

- You must open a file before writing to it.

- Close files when you are finished writing to them.

- Avoid reading from and writing to the same file.

- Use the /GET_LUN keyword with the OPENW command and the FREE_LUN command to avoid having to provide a logical unit number.

- ASCII output (either free-form or formatted) is for humans to read. It is, however, a bad way to transfer data between computer programs. When writing data for computers to read, use a binary format (see Chapters 12, 13, and 14).

- Format codes are hard to get right the first time. Plan on some trial and error when preparing a format specification.

10.7 Exercises

1. Write a script to print a table of $\sin(\theta)$ and $\cos(\theta)$ for θ between 0 and 2π. Check some sample values with a hand calculator. Hint: Like most computer languages, IDL expects the arguments of trigonometric functions to be in radians.

2. Write a script to print a table of $\ln(x)$, e^x, and e^{-x} for x between 1 and 10.

3. Using the Planck function, write a script to print a table of the radiance emitted by a blackbody at 300 K for wavelengths between 1 nm and 30 nm.

4. Using the Clausis-Clapeyron equation, write a script to print a table of the saturation vapor pressure from water between 0 and 50 °C.

5. Print a table of the major constituent gases of the Earth's atmosphere, their chemical symbol, molecular weight, and mass or mole fraction. Hint: You can explicitly specify an array of strings like this:

```
gas = ['Nitrogen', 'Oxygen', 'Argon']
```

Reading Text

This chapter shows how to read text data (*formatted* or *ASCII* data) from the terminal or a file.

11.1 IDL Commands and Keywords

The following IDL commands and keywords are used for reading text from the terminal prompt and from files:

■ READ procedure

■ READF and FORMAT keywords

■ OPENR procedure and GET_LUN keyword

■ FREE_LUN procedure

11.2 Reading Text from the Terminal

You may need to write IDL programs that get input from the user. Here is a simple example:

```
PRO PLOT_POWER

;  Demonstrate reading from the terminal.

COMPILE_OPT IDL2                          ;Set compile options

n = 0                                     ;Make sure n is an integer

READ, n, PROMPT = 'Enter exponent and <cr>: '  ;Read the exponent

x = FINDGEN(10)                           ;Create x-array
y = x^n                                    ;Compute y-array
```

```
PLOT, x, y, $                                    ;Plot y(x)
   TITLE  = 'Plot of x^' + STRTRIM(STRING(n), 2), $
   XTITLE = 'x', $
   YTITLE = 'y'

END
```

The program is run as follows:

```
IDL> plot_power
% Compiled module: PLOT_POWER.
Enter exponent : 3
IDL>
```

Following the colon, the user enters an integer and then a carriage return. The program stores the value 3 in n and then computes and plots x^n.

When you use READ to input the value of a variable that does not already exist, by default IDL creates a FLOAT (regardless of the *name* of the variable). In this case we would like to input an integer, not a float. To accomplish this, a LONG variable called n is created *before* the READ statement. Then the value of n is read from the terminal with the READ statement. This is an example of one of the few instances in IDL in which it is necessary to explicitly declare the type of a variable before using it.

See the READ procedure in *IDL Reference Guide*.

Whenever a program expects input from the keyboard, it is a good idea to print a prompt so the user knows what the program expects. In this example the prompt "Enter exponent and <cr>: " is generated by the line

```
READ, n, PROMPT = 'Enter exponent and <cr>: '
```

The PROMPT keyword provides a string to be printed with the READ statement (<cr> is standard shorthand for carriage return).

11.3 Reading Text from Files

As we saw in Chapter 10, text (ASCII) files have advantages and disadvantages as a means of storing data. The primary advantage of text files is that they are human readable (with a text editor). Additionally, you can use a text editor to create a text file to be read by your computer program. Finally, text files are relatively portable, and can be moved from one computer to another with little difficulty.

The major disadvantages of text files are that input and output are slow relative to binary files (this is important for large files) and the transformation from internal binary numbers to formatted text characters and back to binary numbers is not exact.

IDL usually handles simple cases with sensible default behavior. Here is an example. We can use the logarithm table that we created in Chapter 10, table.txt, as a test case.

The following short IDL procedure demonstrates how to read values from a file into IDL variables:

```
PRO READ_LOG_TABLE, x, logx

;  Demonstrate reading from a file

infile = !Bowman + 'data/table.txt'      ;Input file name

n    = FILE_LINES(infile)                ;Get number of lines in the file
x    = FLTARR(n)                         ;Create array for x values
logx = FLTARR(n)                         ;Create array for log(x) values
x0   = 0.0                               ;FLOAT input variable
logx0 = 0.0                              ;FLOAT input variable

OPENR, iunit, infile, /GET_LUN           ;Open input file

FOR i = 0, n-1 DO BEGIN
   READF, iunit, x0, logx0               ;Read one line from the file
   x[i]    = x0                          ;Store x value
   logx[i] = logx0                       ;Store log(x) value
ENDFOR

FREE_LUN, iunit                          ;Close input file

FOR i = 0, n-1 DO PRINT, x[i], logx[i], $ ;Print values to terminal
   FORMAT = "(2F12.5)"

END
```

The built-in procedure to read from files is called READF. There are several important details in this example that you should note. First, it is easier to read data into a program if you know the size of the arrays to be read ahead of time. The FILE_LINES function is an easy way to get that information. IDL has a number of other functions (the function names begin with FILE_) to get information about files or change their attributes. It is possible to read arrays of unknown size, but as you might expect, programs that do so are more complex. (Another way to deal with this problem is to include the size of the arrays within the file itself.) Second, when reading elements of an array, as opposed to entire arrays, you must use scalar variables in the READ statement itself (x0 and logx0 in READ_LOG_TABLE). You cannot use the Fortran method of reading directly into an array element like this:

See the READF procedure in IDL Reference Guide.

See the FILE_LINES function in IDL Reference Guide.

```
READF, iunit, x[i], y[i]
```

For reasons having to do with how arguments are passed to procedures and functions, *this does not work in IDL.*

Running the program gives the following:

```
IDL> .r read_log_table
% Compiled module: READ_LOG_TABLE.
IDL> READ_LOG_TABLE, a, loga
      1.00000      0.00000
      2.00000      0.30103
      3.00000      0.47712
      4.00000      0.60206
      5.00000      0.69897
      6.00000      0.77815
      7.00000      0.84510
      8.00000      0.90309
      9.00000      0.95424
     10.00000      1.00000
IDL> print, a
      1.00000      2.00000      3.00000      4.00000      5.00000
      6.00000      7.00000      8.00000      9.00000      10.0000
IDL> print, loga
      0.00000      0.301030      0.477120      0.602060      0.698970
      0.778150      0.845100      0.903090      0.954240      1.00000
```

The READF command also accepts the FORMAT keyword, which can be used to specify an exact format with which to read the data. You should use the FORMAT keyword only for reading files for which the contents of the file are known exactly.

See *Using Explicitly Formatted Input/Output* in *Building IDL Applications.*

11.4 Summary

This chapter has covered the basics of reading text (ASCII) output from the terminal or a file. Here are some points to remember:

- READ reads input from the terminal, READF reads from a file.

- You must open a file before reading from it.

- Close files when you are finished reading from them.

- Avoid reading from and writing to the same file.

- Use the /GET_LUN keyword with the OPENR command and the FREE_LUN command to avoid having to provide logical unit numbers.

- Free-form and formatted (ASCII) output are for humans to read. They are a bad way to transfer data between programs. When writing data for computers to read, use binary formats (see Chapters 12, 13, and 14).

11.5 Exercises

1. Write an IDL program to read and plot some of the data from the following text files:

   - `wc151_1804_new.txt`
   - `wc151_18010_new.txt`
   - `wc151_18016_new.txt`
   - `wc151_18112_new.txt`

   in the directory `data/flux/`. In these files the variables are organized into columns. A README file in that directory describes the contents of the files.

2. Write an IDL program to read and plot some of the data from the text files:

   - `wc151_1804.txt`
   - `wc151_18010.txt`
   - `wc151_18016.txt`
   - `wc151_18112.txt`

   in the directory `data/flux/`. These files are a little harder to read than the files from Exercise 1. A README file in that directory describes the contents of the files.

Writing and Reading Binary Files

This chapter describes how to write data to and read data from *binary* files. As we saw in Chapters 10 and 11, it is possible to write IDL variables to text (ASCII) files. When writing text files, the internal binary representation of each variable is translated to text characters. You can choose to use the default formatting rules (free-format) or specify exactly how to translate them by using a format specification. Data can be read from text files and the information converted back into internal IDL variables (integers, floating-point variables, etc.).

Text files have the big advantage that they are human-readable, but they have several disadvantages. The conversion process from binary to text and back is relatively slow. Also, due to the translation from binary to ASCII characters, it is not easy to ensure that the process is exactly reversible; that is, that the numbers that you read are exactly the numbers you wrote.

Binary files make a different set of trade-offs. Reading and writing binary files is very fast, and you can read into one program exactly what was written by another program. On the other hand, you must know *exactly* how the file is written. You cannot look at a binary file with a text editor and expect to see anything intelligible. Remember, each byte of computer memory can store 255 different patterns of bits, but only about 75 of those patterns represent printable characters (letters, numbers, punctuation, etc.). Because the contents of the file are an exact copy of the variables in memory, a particular byte in a binary file might be a byte from a floating-point number, an integer, or a character string. Without knowing the variable type, it is impossible to know what a given byte represents. In practical terms, this means that in order to read a binary file you need to have either the program that wrote the file or an exact description of how the file was written.

12.1 IDL Commands and Keywords

The following IDL commands and keywords are used for writing and reading binary files:

- OPENW procedure and GET_LUN and F77_UNFORMATTED keywords

- OPENR procedure and GET_LUN and F77_UNFORMATTED keywords

- WRITEU procedure

- READU procedure
- FREE_LUN procedure

12.2 Writing Binary Files

Here is a short example of a program to write a binary file:

```
PRO WRITE_MY_BINARY

;+
; Name:
;      WRITE_MY_BINARY
; Purpose:
;      Write a binary file containing different data types.
; Calling sequence:
;      WRITE_MY_BINARY
; Inputs:
;      None.
; Output:
;      Binary file binary.dat containing different data types.
; Keywords:
;      None.
; Author and history:
;      Kenneth P. Bowman, 2004.
;-

COMPILE_OPT IDL2                      ;Set compile options

outfile = !Bowman + 'data/binary.dat' ;Binary output file name

n =  20                              ;Array i dimension size
m = 400                              ;Array z dimension size
i = LINDGEN(n, n, n)                 ;Create array i
z = DIST(m)                          ;Create array z
b = BYTSCL(z)                        ;Create array b

HELP, n, m, i, z, b                  ;Print info on variables
PRINT, z[0:3,0:3]                    ;Print part of z
PRINT, 'File size = ', $             ;Print file size in bytes
    4*(1+1+n*n*n+m*m) + m*m

OPENW,  ounit, outfile, /GET_LUN     ;Open output file

WRITEU, ounit, n, m                  ;Write array dimensions
WRITEU, ounit, i, z, b               ;Write arrays
```

```
FREE_LUN, ounit                         ;Close binary output file

END
```

The output file is named `binary.dat`. Because we have not specified a full file path, the file is created in the current directory.

The first part of this example program creates several different kinds of IDL variables: n, m, and i are LONG variables (two scalars and an array), z is a two-dimensional floating-point array, and b is a 2-D BYTE array. To confirm that the variables are what we expect, we use the HELP command to print their properties. We also print a small part of the array z. For an extra check, before writing all of these variables to the output file, we calculate and print the size of the file by adding up the number of bytes in each variable. The first four variables are all 4 bytes per element, the array b is 1 byte per element.

The next step is to open `binary.dat` for writing. The GET_LUN keyword tells OPENW to get the next available logical unit number (LUN) and assign it to the variable ounit. The next two lines use the WRITEU procedure to write the two scalar variables n and m, followed by the three arrays, i, z, and b. (The reason for using two separate calls to WRITEU is discussed below.) Each call to WRITEU transfers all of the bytes that make up the variables in the argument list from computer memory to the output device (usually a file on a disk drive). Thus, WRITEU, ounit, n, m writes 8 bytes in the output file (4 bytes each for the integers n and m). The total size of the arrays i, z, and b is 832,000 bytes, so the second WRITEU statement transfers 832,000 bytes to the file. Finally, the program frees the logical unit number ounit and closes the output file using FREE_LUN.

The output from this program looks like this:

See the OPENW procedure in *IDL Reference Guide*.

See the WRITEU procedure in *IDL Reference Guide*.

See the FREELUN procedure in *IDL Reference Guide*.

```
IDL> WRITE_MY_BINARY
% Compiled module: WRITE_BINARY.
% Compiled module: DIST.
N               LONG      =              20
M               LONG      =             400
I               LONG      = Array[20, 20, 20]
Z               FLOAT     = Array[400, 400]
B               BYTE      = Array[400, 400]
       0.00000      1.00000       2.00000       3.00000
       1.00000      1.41421       2.23607       3.16228
       2.00000      2.23607       2.82843       3.60555
       3.00000      3.16228       3.60555       4.24264
File size =        832008
```

We use the command line to check the file size,

```
csrp3> ls -l binary.dat
-rw-r--r--  1 bowman   unknown   832008 Aug 23 14:14 binary.dat
```

which is what we expect: 832,008 bytes.

If you try to open binary.dat with a text editor, you'll see gibberish. Most of the bytes in the file do not translate into printable characters. Text editors typically display blanks or boxes for unprintable characters. Go ahead and try it; you won't break anything. Just don't try to print the file!

12.3 Reading Binary Files

A program to read binary.dat is very similar to the program that wrote it:

```
PRO READ_MY_BINARY

;+
; Name:
;       READ_MY_BINARY
; Purpose:
;       Read a binary file containing different data types.
; Calling sequence:
;       READ_MY_BINARY
; Inputs:
;       Binary file containing different data types.
; Output:
;       None.
; Keywords:
;       None.
; Author and history:
;       Kenneth P. Bowman, 2004.
;-

COMPILE_OPT IDL2                    ;Set compile options

infile = !Bowman + 'data/binary.dat' ;Input file name

OPENR, iunit, infile, /GET_LUN     ;Open input file

n = 0                              ;Make n a LONG
m = 0                              ;Make m a LONG
READU, iunit, n, m                 ;Read n and m

i = LONARR(n, n, n)                ;Create i array
z = FLTARR(m, m)                   ;Create z array
b = BYTARR(m, m)                   ;Create b array
READU, iunit, i, z, b              ;Read i, z, and b

FREE_LUN, iunit                    ;Close input file
```

```
HELP, n, m, i, z, b                    ;Print variable info
PRINT, z[0:3,0:3]                      ;Print part of z

END
```

Notice that in this program we use OPENR (for open-read) rather than OPENU or OPENW (for open-update or open-write). This prevents accidentally writing to the file and destroying its contents due to a programming error. Before reading the two integers n and m, we ensure that the program knows that they are integers. We do this by creating two integer variables m and n, both equal to 0. Only then can we read the integers with the READU command. (If you do not explicitly create integers, IDL automatically creates FLOATs.)

> See the OPENR procedure in *IDL Reference Guide*.

At this point it should be clearer why we used two separate WRITEU statements in the first program. Doing so allows us to read the values of n and m, and then use those values to create the array variables i, z, and b. (It is not strictly necessary to use two separate WRITEUs, but it helps make the logic of the program easier to understand.) After reading those variables, we use HELP to display the variable information, close the file, and print the same small section of the array z:

> See the READU procedure in *IDL Reference Guide*.

```
IDL> READ_MY_BINARY
N               LONG      =              20
M               LONG      =             400
I               LONG      = Array[20, 20, 20]
Z               FLOAT     = Array[400, 400]
B               BYTE      = Array[400, 400]
      0.00000       1.00000       2.00000       3.00000
      1.00000       1.41421       2.23607       3.16228
      2.00000       2.23607       2.82843       3.60555
      3.00000       3.16228       3.60555       4.24264
```

As we expected, the values in z are *exactly* what was written by the previous program.

What if we had made a mistake about the variable type, thinking z was an integer? Our program would look almost identical, except for the line that creates the array z, where we replace FLTARR with LONARR:

```
PRO READ_MY_BINARY2

;+
; Name:
;       READ_MY_BINARY2
; Purpose:
;       Read a binary file containing different data types.
```

```
; Calling sequence:
;       READ_MY_BINARY2
; Inputs:
;       Binary file containing different data types.
; Output:
;       None.
; Keywords:
;       None.
; Author and history:
;       Kenneth P. Bowman, 2004.
;-

COMPILE_OPT IDL2                      ;Set compile options

infile = !Bowman + 'data/binary.dat' ;Input file name

OPENR, iunit, infile, /GET_LUN        ;Open input file

n = 0                                 ;Make n a LONG
m = 0                                 ;Make m a LONG
READU, iunit, n, m                    ;Read n and m

i = LONARR(n, n, n)                   ;Create i array
z = LONARR(m, m)                      ;Create z array
b = BYTARR(m, m)                      ;Create b array
READU, iunit, i, z, b                 ;Read i, z, and b

FREE_LUN, iunit                       ;Close input file

HELP, n, m, i, z, b                   ;Print variable info
PRINT, z[0:3,0:3]                     ;Print part of z

END
```

Now the program output looks like this:

```
N               LONG     =            20
M               LONG     =           400
I               LONG     = Array[20, 20, 20]
Z               LONG     = Array[400, 400]
B               BYTE     = Array[400, 400]
            0   1065353216  1073741824  1077936128
   1065353216   1068827891  1074731965  1078616770
   1073741824   1074731965  1077216499  1080475994
   1077936128   1078616770  1080475994  1082639286
```

As it happens, the bytes in the file that represent floating-point numbers between 0.0 and 5.0 also represent integers in the range of 1,000,000,000! READU and WRITEU simply transfer bytes between memory and file. They don't know or care what the variable type is. This example emphasizes the point that it is necessary to know *exactly* what is in a binary file in order to be able to read it.

12.4 Exchanging Files with Fortran Programs

Many scientific data files are written and read using Fortran programs. In Fortran, each binary (unformatted) WRITE statement writes the bytes that make up the variables in the argument list to the file. Each Fortran WRITE also writes an integer that contains the number of bytes of data transferred (twice, once before and once after the data itself). That is, each Fortran WRITE statement also writes the size of the data written. This size is used by Fortran when *reading* the data. IDL includes these additional length bytes when writing files, and uses them properly when reading, if the file is opened with the F77_UNFORMATTED keyword set. Use this keyword when you need to write a file to be read by a Fortran program, or read a file that was written by a Fortran program.

12.5 Summary

This chapter has covered the basics of writing and reading binary files. Binary input and output has the advantage of speed and simplicity. It has the disadvantage of obscurity and limited portability. The files are obscure because a binary file tells you nothing about its contents, and a text editor generally won't help. Binary files have limited portability because different computer systems use different binary representations for integers or floating-point numbers (IEEE arithmetic notwithstanding). One common problem is that different computers store the bits within each byte in different orders. (In homage to Jonathan Swift's *Gulliver's Travels*, these are referred to as "little-endian" and "big-endian" computers.)

IDL has keywords to swap "endian-ness," but any scientific programmer who has worked with binary data files can tell you what a hassle it is to try to read a binary file from another system. There are several alternatives for writing and reading binary files that avoid many of these problems. These are discussed in Chapters 13 and 14.

I find nowadays that I *very* rarely write a plain binary file. Although it is useful to know how to read and write binary files, think long and hard, and know what you are getting into, before resorting to the quick fix of plain binary input and output.

12.6 Exercises

1. Write an IDL program to generate an array containing 1 million pseudo-random numbers. (See Chapter 23 for a description of how to generate pseudorandom numbers.) Write the array to a binary file. Close the file. Reopen it and read the numbers back into the program. Compare the numbers to see if they are exactly what was written.

2. Do the same exercise as above, but write the random numbers to a text file. When you read the array, do the values exactly match what was written?

3. Using the programs above, compare the time required to write and read the binary file and the text file.

13

Reading NetCDF Files

Several file formats and software libraries have been developed to overcome some of the limitations of plain binary files. NetCDF is one. The HDF and CDF formats, which are not covered in this book, are two others. All three file types can be read and written with IDL.

NetCDF (for Networked Common Data Form) is a file format that is designed for efficient reading and writing of many types of scientific data, particularly array data. NetCDF files are *self-documenting*; that is, each netCDF file contains the basic information needed to read the file. With a little extra work, programs that create netCDF files can go beyond basic information to include a full and detailed description of the file contents.

The netCDF format and software to read and write netCDF files were developed by the University Data Program (Unidata) at the University Corporation for Atmospheric Research (UCAR). Through the use of special libraries, netCDF files are highly portable between different computers and can be written or read quickly using Fortran, C, IDL, and a number of other languages. The netCDF interface also provides *random access* to any part of the file. Because reading netCDF files is somewhat simpler than writing them, this chapter describes how to read netCDF files. Writing netCDF files is discussed in Chapter 14.

13.1 IDL Procedures and Functions

The IDL commands used to read and write netCDF files are described in a separate manual, *Scientific Data Formats*, which also contains the documentation for HDF and CDF commands.

The following IDL procedures are used to read netCDF files:

- NCDF_OPEN function

- NCDF_VARGET procedure

- NCDF_ATTGET procedure

- NCDF_CLOSE procedure

The chapter also discusses the ncdump command-line procedure.

13.2 NetCDF Basics

NetCDF files can contain a variety of types of data, including BYTE, CHAR, SHORT, LONG, FLOAT, and DOUBLE. NetCDF files are primarily intended to store rectangular arrays of data (like IDL arrays). NetCDF files are *not* the best choice for storing irregular data structures, such as lists of items with different lengths or large amounts of text.

One of the biggest advantages of netCDF files is that they contain not only data, but also a *description* of the data. The descriptive part of the file is referred to as the *metadata*, that is, data about data. Storing the metadata within the file itself means that you can find out what is in a netCDF file without having external documentation or the program that created the file.[1] It is possible to create netCDF files with minimal metadata, but don't be lazy! When you create a netCDF file, you should always make the extra effort to include enough metadata so that you can understand the file when you go back to it long after you originally wrote it. That will happen more often than you expect!

It is possible to write IDL programs that use the IDL netCDF *inquire* functions to find out what is in a netCDF file. In many cases it is simpler to use a command-line utility called ncdump to print a description of the file contents. The ncdump utility is not part of IDL, but is included with the general distribution of the netCDF software libraries from Unidata.[2] Source code is available, and binary distributions are available for most operating systems. If you plan to use netCDF files, you should install the netCDF libraries on your system or ask your system administrator to do so.

A listing of the metadata for a netCDF file named random.ncd, as produced by ncdump, is shown below:

```
csrp3> ncdump -h random.ncd

netcdf random {
dimensions:
    Time = UNLIMITED ; // (1000 currently)
variables:
    int Time(Time) ;
        Time:longname = "Time since 2003-08-19 18:00:00Z" ;
        Time:units = "s" ;
    float w(Time) ;
        w:longname = "Vertical velocity" ;
        w:units = "m s^-1" ;
    float T(Time) ;
        T:longname = "Temperature" ;
        T:units = "K" ;
```

---

1 Given an unfamiliar ASCII file, it is sometimes possible to decipher its contents. With plain binary files, it is generally impossible.

2 The web address for Unidata is http://www.unidata.ucar.edu.

```
// global attributes:
        :Description = "Near surface measurements of vertical
velocity and temperature" ;
}
```

The -h flag tells ncdump to print only the *header* information (the metadata), not the entire file. If you use the -c flag instead, ncdump will also print the *coordinate variables* (more on coordinate variables in the following paragraph). If you omit both flags, ncdump will print the entire contents of the file, data and all![3] The file random.ncd has one *dimension* called Time, and three *variables*: Time, T, and w. Time is a LONG array, whereas the other two are FLOATs. All three of the variables are dimensioned by Time. The size of the Time dimension is 1000, so each variable is a one-dimensional array containing 1000 elements.

It may seem confusing to have two different things within the file both named Time, but in fact, this does make sense. There is a *dimension* named Time, and there is also a *variable* named Time that contains the actual values for that dimension, in this case time in seconds. A variable that has the same name as a dimension is referred to as a *coordinate variable*. Coordinate variables generally contain the values associated with a particular physical dimension, such as longitude or time, and can be thought of as the *independent variables* of a data set. Coordinate variables are not mandatory, but it usually makes sense to include them. The other two variables, w and T (which represent Vertical velocity and Temperature), both depend on time and can be thought of as *dependent variables*.

Three notes on ncdump and netCDF files: First, the ncdump utility uses the C-language convention for displaying array dimensions. That means that when a variable has more than one dimension, the dimensions are listed in the *reverse order* of the way the array would be used in IDL. Second, also following the C convention, an int in an ncdump listing is a 4-byte integer (a LONG in IDL), not a 2-byte integer (an INT in IDL). Third, unlike IDL, *netCDF dimension and variable names are case sensitive*. That means that it is possible to have one variable named T and another named t in the same file. That does not mean it is a good idea, though!

After using the ncdump command to display the file metadata, it is a simple matter to write an IDL program to read the file. Here is a short IDL program called READ_NETCDF1 that reads the contents of the file random.ncd and plots a scatterplot of T vs. w.

---

3   A useful Unix trick to browse through the actual data in a netCDF file is to send the output of the ncdump command to more, which will display text one page at a time. For a file named random.ncd, this is done with the Unix command ncdump random.ncd | more.

```
PRO READ_NETCDF1, infile

;+
; Name:
;       READ_NETCDF1
; Purpose:
;       This program reads a simple netCDF file and
;       plots a scatterplot.
; Calling sequence:
;       READ_NETCDF1
; Inputs:
;       infile : name of input file
; Output:
;       Scatterplot of data from the netCDF file.
; Keywords:
;       None.
; Author and history:
;       Kenneth P. Bowman, 2004.
;-


COMPILE_OPT IDL2                       ;Set compile options

IF (N_ELEMENTS(infile) EQ 0) THEN $   ;Default input file
    infile = !Bowman + 'data/random.ncd'


iid = NCDF_OPEN(infile)                ;Open input file
NCDF_VARGET, iid, 'Time', time         ;Read time
NCDF_VARGET, iid, 'T',    T            ;Read temperature
NCDF_VARGET, iid, 'w',    w            ;Read vertical velocity
NCDF_CLOSE,  iid                       ;Close input file

HELP, time, T, w                       ;Print info about variables

PLOT, w, T, PSYM = 1, /YNOZERO, $      ;Plot data
    XTITLE = 'w', $
    YTITLE = 'T'

END
```

Running the program READ_NETCDF1 gives the following results:

```
IDL> read_netcdf1
% Compiled module: READ_NETCDF1.
% Loaded DLM: NCDF.
TIME            LONG     = Array[1000]
T               FLOAT    = Array[1000]
W               FLOAT    = Array[1000]
```

As you can see in *Scientific Data Formats*, about 25 different functions and procedures are used with netCDF files. Fortunately, to read netCDF files we only need to use three of those procedures. The first step is to open the netCDF file for reading. This is done with the NCDF_OPEN function. This function returns a file ID, which is a LONG variable that we save with the name iid (for "input ID"). We use this variable in other NCDF_ commands to refer to this particular file. If you need to have a second netCDF file open at the same time (when reading from one file and writing to another, for example), you save its ID with a different name, such as oid. (NCDF_OPEN is the equivalent of OPENR, and iid is equivalent to the LUN for text and binary files.)

See the NCDF_OPEN function in *Scientific Data Formats*.

The next three lines of the program use the NCDF_VARGET procedure to read the variables Time, T, and w. The three arguments to the NCDF_VARGET procedure tell it which file to read from, which variable in the file to read, and the name of the local IDL variable in which the data will be stored in memory. Because the netCDF file contains all of the metadata needed to describe its own contents, IDL is able to get the type and size of the data in the file from the file itself and then create the necessary IDL variables. The NCDF_VARGET procedure transfers data from the file to the IDL program. The result is three array variables named time, T, and w. The names of the variables in the file and the names of the local IDL variables do not have to match, but it usually makes the program easier to understand. We use the HELP command to check that we are getting what we expect, three floating-point arrays of size 1000.

See the NCDF_VARGET procedure in *Scientific Data Formats*.

It is possible to read a subsection of an array by using the OFFSET, COUNT, and STRIDE keywords with the NCDF_VARGET procedure. If the keywords are omitted, as we have done here, the default behavior is to read the entire variable. This is a good example of IDL's ability to create variables on the fly. In this case, the NCDF_functions are smart enough to automatically create arrays of the proper size and type. Unlike Fortran, in IDL it is not necessary to define the variables' sizes and types first.

The next line closes the file with the NCDF_CLOSE procedure. IDL can have only a limited number of netCDF files open at one time, so it is important to close a file when you are finished with it. If your program crashes before reaching NCDF_CLOSE, the file is left open. Therefore, it is a good idea to close a file as soon as you are finished reading from it or writing to it. Exiting IDL closes any open files.

See the NCDF_CLOSE procedure in *Scientific Data Formats*.

Lastly, the program plots a scatterplot of T vs. w. The results are shown in Figure 13.1.

13.3 Reading Attributes

You may have noticed that the ncdump utility showed some additional information in the netCDF file that we have not made use of. The variables Time, T, and w all have *units* and *long names* associated with them. These metadata are known as *attributes*. Attributes can be attached to variables or to the file itself (*global* attributes). An attribute is nothing but extra information that can be referenced by using the *attribute name*. Attributes are often strings (character

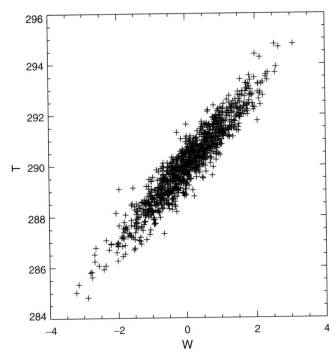

FIGURE 13.1   A scatterplot of T vs. w from the values in the file random.ncd.
(READ_NETCDF1_PS)

variables), but they can be numbers or even arrays. Note that multiple variables can have attributes with the same name.

Attributes are read with the NCDF_ATTGET procedure. We can use the attribute information from the file to improve the plots. Here is an example of a program that reads the attribute data from the file and uses it to provide more informative labels for the plots. Note that STRING variables are read as BYTE arrays, which can be converted to IDL strings by using the STRING function.

```
PRO READ_NETCDF2, infile

;+
; Name:
;       READ_NETCDF2
; Purpose:
;       This program reads a simple netCDF file
;       and plots several graphs.
; Calling sequence:
;       READ_NETCDF2
; Inputs:
;     infile    : name of input file
; Output:
;       Plots of data from netCDF file.
```

```
; Keywords:
;       None.
; Author and history:
;       Kenneth P. Bowman, 2004.
;-

COMPILE_OPT IDL2                         ;Set compile options

IF (N_ELEMENTS(infile) EQ 0) THEN $      ;Default input file
   infile = !Bowman + 'data/random.ncd'

iid = NCDF_OPEN(infile)                  ;Open input file

NCDF_VARGET, iid, 'Time', time           ;Read time
NCDF_VARGET, iid, 'T',    T              ;Read temperature
NCDF_VARGET, iid, 'w',    w              ;Read vertical velocity

NCDF_ATTGET, iid, 'Time', 'longname', $  ;Get long name of time
   time_name
NCDF_ATTGET, iid, 'Time', 'units',    $  ;Get units of time
   time_units
NCDF_ATTGET, iid, 'T',    'longname', $  ;Get long name of T
   T_name
NCDF_ATTGET, iid, 'T',    'units',    $  ;Get units of T
   T_units
NCDF_ATTGET, iid, 'w',    'longname', $  ;Get long name of w
   w_name
NCDF_ATTGET, iid, 'w',    'units',    $  ;Get units of w
   w_units

NCDF_CLOSE, iid                          ;Close input file

time_name  = STRING(Time_name)           ;Convert to string
time_units = STRING(Time_units)          ;Convert to string
T_name     = STRING(T_name)              ;Convert to string
T_units    = STRING(T_units)             ;Convert to string
w_name     = STRING(w_name)              ;Convert to string
w_units    = STRING(w_units)             ;Convert to string

b = REGRESS(w, t, YFIT = T_fit, $        ;Linear regression
   CONST = a, /DOUBLE)

!P.MULTI = [0, 2, 2, 0, 0]               ;Set plots per page

PLOT, time, w, /YNOZERO, $               ;Plot w(time)
   XTITLE = time_name + ' (' + time_units + ')', $
   YTITLE = w_name + ' (' + w_units + ')'
```

```
PLOT, time, T, /YNOZERO, $              ;Plot T(time)
   XTITLE = time_name + ' (' + time_units + ')', $
   YTITLE = T_name + ' (' + T_units + ')'

PLOT, w, T, PSYM = 3, /YNOZERO, $        ;Plot T vs. w
   XTITLE = w_name + ' (' + w_units + ')', $
   YTITLE = T_name + ' (' + T_units + ')'
OPLOT, [!X.CRANGE[0], !X.CRANGE[1]], $    ;Plot linear fit
   [a + b[0]*!X.CRANGE[0], a + b[0]*!X.CRANGE[1]]

!P.MULTI = 0                             ;Reset !P.MULTI

END
```

The resulting graphs are shown in Figure 13.2. These graphs also illustrate the importance of looking at your data in different ways. It is difficult to see any relationship between T and w when comparing the noisy time series plots. The scatterplot, however, shows a very clear correlation between the two variables. We have used the IDL REGRESS procedure to compute the linear least-squares fit between the data and plotted the results on the lower graph using the OPLOT command.

See the REGRESS and OPLOT procedures in *IDL Reference Guide.*

13.4   A Real Data File

A sample netCDF file containing real surface-flux data from a field experiment is included with the example programs and data files.[4] The file is named wc151_18010.ncd. It contains one hour of velocity, temperature, humidity, and carbon dioxide measurements made near the Earth's surface. In order to measure the effects of turbulence close to the surface, the data were collected at a rate of 20 Hz (20 times per second). Therefore, the file contains 72,000 observations. The original text file used to create the netCDF file, wc151_18010.txt, is also included.

Here is the metadata (header information) from the files:

```
netcdf wc151_18010 {
dimensions:
   Time = 72000 ;
variables:
   int Year(Time) ;
   int Month(Time) ;
   int Day(Time) ;
   int Hour(Time) ;
   int Minute(Time) ;
```

4   Many thanks to Prof. Tony Cahill of the Civil Engineering Department at Texas A&M for providing these data.

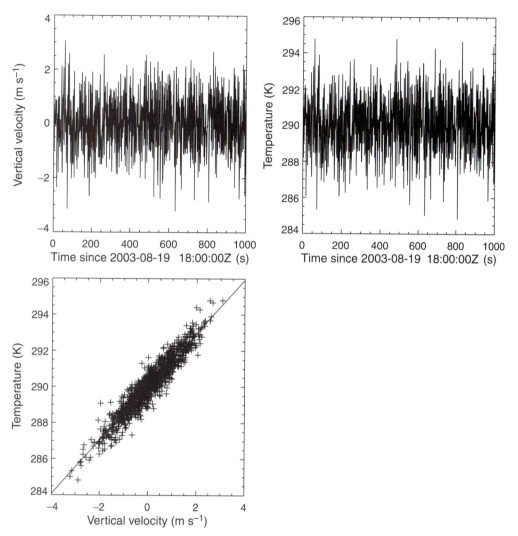

FIGURE 13.2   Multiple plots of the variables in the file random.ncd that make use of the variable attributes. (READ_NETCDF2_PS)

```
int Second(Time) ;
int Millisecond(Time) ;
float u(Time) ;
   u:longname = "U-velocity" ;
   u:units = "m s^-1" ;
float v(Time) ;
   v:longname = "V-velocity" ;
   v:units = "m s^-1" ;
float w(Time) ;
   w:longname = "W-velocity" ;
   w:units = "m s^-1" ;
float T(Time) ;
   T:longname = "Temperature" ;
   T:units = "degrees C" ;
```

```
    int flag(Time) ;
    float CO2(Time) ;
        CO2:longname = "CO2 density" ;
        CO2:units = "mg m^-3" ;
    float H2O(Time) ;
        H2O:longname = "H2O density" ;
        H2O:units = "g m^-3" ;
    float p(Time) ;
        p:longname = "Pressure" ;
        p:units = "kPa" ;

// global attributes:
        :Site name = "Walnut Creek, Iowa, USA" ;
        :Site number = 151 ;
        :Longitude = 263.7f ;
        :Latitude = 42.f ;
        :Instrument height = "3.1 m" ;
        :Description = "Flat cornfield" ;
}
```

One of the exercises for this chapter is to write a program to read this file and plot some of the data. Some sample output is shown in Figure 13.3.

13.5 Summary

This chapter has covered the basics of reading data from netCDF files:

- Use ncdump to show the contents of a netCDF file (the metadata).

- First open the file with NCDF_OPEN.

- Read data with NCDF_VARGET.

- Read attributes with NCDF_ATTGET.

- Don't forget to close files with NCDF_CLOSE when you are finished reading from them.

13.6 Exercises

1. Write an IDL program to read the data in the text file wc151_18010.txt. Write the data to a new netCDF file similar to wc151_18010.ncd. A description of the text file is contained in the README file in the flux/ directory.

2. Write an IDL program to read wc151_18010.ncd and plot the graphs shown in Figure 13.3. The file wc151_18010_ncdump.txt contains an ncdump of the file's header information.

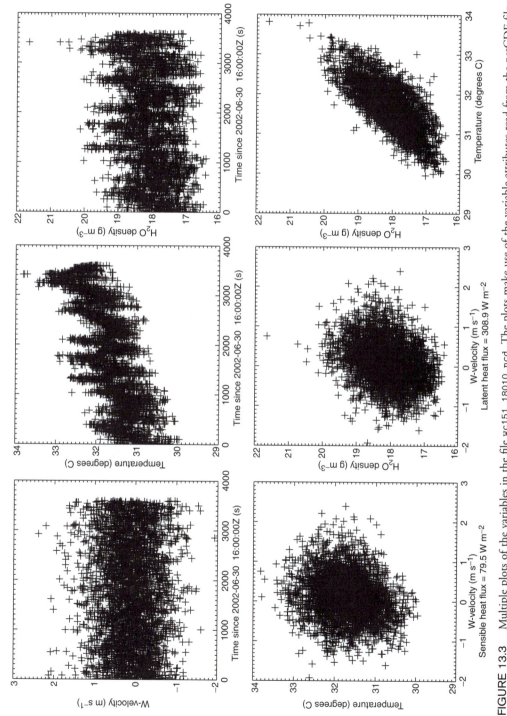

FIGURE 13.3 Multiple plots of the variables in the file wc151_18010.ncd. The plots make use of the variable attributes read from the netCDF file. Because the large number of data points tends to make the plots difficult to read, only every 20th point is plotted.

Writing NetCDF Files

Chapter 13 covers the basics of reading netCDF files. NetCDF files are particularly easy to read with IDL because each netCDF file contains *metadata* that describes the file's contents. The IDL functions that read netCDF files can automatically read the metadata and create IDL variables with the appropriate types and array sizes to store the data read from the files.

In order for this magical process to work, the metadata (description of the file contents) must be written into the file at the time it is created. For this reason, writing netCDF files is slightly more complicated than reading them. This chapter describes the steps required to write simple netCDF files.

14.1 IDL Procedures and Functions

The IDL commands used to read and write netCDF files are described in a separate manual, *Scientific Data Formats*, along with the documentation for HDF and CDF commands.

The following IDL procedures are used to write netCDF files:

- `NCDF_CREATE` function and `CLOBBER` keyword

- `NCDF_DIMDEF` function

- `NCDF_VARDEF` function

- `NCDF_ATTPUT` procedure

- `NCDF_CONTROL` procedure and `ENDEF` keyword

- `NCDF_VARPUT` procedure

- `NCDF_CLOSE` procedure

14.2 Writing a NetCDF File

Although it is possible to write to an existing netCDF file (or other kinds of files, for that matter), you should generally avoid doing so. One minor bug in a program can easily destroy a file, obliterating its contents. For simplicity and safety, the programs in this chapter create new files from scratch.

When you create a new netCDF file (with the NCDF_CREATE function),
you need to decide what to do if a file already exists with the same name.
The default behavior is to stop, issue an error message, and *not* destroy
the old file. If you wish to wipe out the existing file and replace it with
a new file with the same name, either use the operating system to delete
the file before running your IDL program or add the CLOBBER keyword
to NCDF_CREATE. (NCDF_CREATE is equivalent to OPENW for text and binary
files.)

See the NCDF_CREATE
function in *Scientific
Data Formats*.

The quickest way to learn how to write a netCDF file is with an example program. The following program creates the file random.ncd used in
Chapter 13:

```
PRO WRITE_RANDOM_NETCDF, outfile, n, seed, a, b, eps


;+
; Name:
;     WRITE_RANDOM_NETCDF
; Purpose:
;     This program creates a simple netCDF file containing
;     random, correlated data.
; Calling sequence:
;     WRITE_RANDOM_NETCDF, outfile, n, seed, a, b, eps
; Input:
;     outfile : name of output file
;     n       : number of pairs of random numbers to generate
;     seed    : seed for random number generator
;     a       : intercept
;     b       : slope
;     eps     : magnitude of random component
; Output:
;     NetCDF file containing random output
; Keywords:
;     None.
; Author and history:
;     Kenneth P. Bowman, 2004.
;-


COMPILE_OPT IDL2

IF (N_PARAMS() EQ 0) THEN BEGIN
   outfile = !Bowman + 'data/random.ncd' ;Default output file name
   n       = 1000                         ;Default number of points
   seed    =    117                       ;Random number seed
   a       = 290.0                        ;Intercept
   b       =   1.5                        ;Slope
   eps     =   0.5                        ;Default scaling factor
ENDIF
```

```
description = 'Near surface measurements of ' + $
    'vertical velocity and temperature'

time        = LINDGEN(n)                 ;Generate time
time_name   = $                          ;Variable name
    'Time since 2003-08-19 18:00:00Z'
time_units  = 's'                        ;Variable units

w           = RANDOMN(seed, n)           ;Generate random vertical velocity
w_name      = 'Vertical velocity'        ;Variable name
w_units     = 'm s^-1'                    ;Variable units

T           = a+b*w+eps*RANDOMN(seed, n) ;Compute correlated temperature
t_name      = 'Temperature'              ;Variable name
t_units     = 'K'                        ;Variable units

oid = NCDF_CREATE(outfile, /CLOBBER)     ;Create output file

NCDF_ATTPUT, oid, 'Description', $       ;Write time units
    description, /GLOBAL

tid = NCDF_DIMDEF(oid, 'Time', $         ;Define time dimension
    /UNLIMITED)

vid = NCDF_VARDEF(oid, 'Time', [tid], $  ;Define time variable
    /LONG)
vid = NCDF_VARDEF(oid, 'w',    [tid], $  ;Define vertical velocity variable
    /FLOAT)
vid = NCDF_VARDEF(oid, 'T',    [tid], $  ;Define temperature variable
    /FLOAT)

NCDF_ATTPUT, oid, 'Time', 'longname', $  ;Write time long name
    time_name
NCDF_ATTPUT, oid, 'Time', 'units',   $   ;Write time units
    time_units
NCDF_ATTPUT, oid, 'w',    'longname', $  ;Write vertical velocity long name
    w_name
NCDF_ATTPUT, oid, 'w',    'units',   $   ;Write vertical velocity units
    w_units
NCDF_ATTPUT, oid, 'T',    'longname', $  ;Write temperature long name
    t_name
NCDF_ATTPUT, oid, 'T',    'units',   $   ;Write temperature units
    t_units

NCDF_CONTROL, oid, /ENDEF                ;Exit define mode

NCDF_VARPUT, oid, 'Time', time           ;Write the time
```

```
NCDF_VARPUT, oid, 'T',    T              ;Write the temperature
NCDF_VARPUT, oid, 'w',    w              ;Write the vertical velocity

NCDF_CLOSE, oid                          ;Close the netCDF file

b = REGRESS(w, t, YFIT = T_fit, $        ;Compute linear regression
   /CONST = a, DOUBLE)

PLOT, w, T, PSYM = 3, /YNOZERO, $        ;Plot data
   XTITLE = w_name + ' (' + w_units + ')', $
   YTITLE = T_name + ' (' + T_units + ')'
OPLOT, [!X.CRANGE[0], !X.CRANGE[1]], $   ;Plot linear fit
   [a + b[0]*!X.CRANGE[0], a + b[0]*!X.CRANGE[1]]


END
```

The first part of this program creates the data arrays that will be written to the netCDF file: time, w, and T. The variable time is created with the LINDGEN function, while w and T are created by using the built-in IDL pseudorandom number generator, RANDOMN. Some additional STRING variables, such as w_name and w_units, are created with descriptive information about each of the data variables. These will be used to add variable attributes to the netCDF file. The middle part of the program defines the contents of the netCDF file, and the last part (after the NCDF_CONTROL statement) actually writes the data to the file.

See the RANDOMN function in IDL Reference Guide.

The first step in writing a netCDF file is to create the file with the NCDF_CREATE statement. In this case, if the output file already exists, we have chosen to CLOBBER (overwrite) it. The NCDF_CREATE function returns a LONG variable (named oid, for "output ID") containing the file ID. The netCDF file ID is similar to the logical unit numbers (LUNs) used to identify text and plain binary files. You need the ID to do any other operation with the file (writing to it, closing it, etc.)

Next, a *global attribute* is written to the file with NCDF_ATTPUT. Global attributes can contain any descriptive information about the file that you want to include in the file itself. We choose to name this attribute Description. You can write multiple global attributes to a file.

Next, dimensions are defined with the NCDF_DIMDEF function. Each call to the NCDF_DIMDEF function returns a LONG variable that is used to refer to that particular dimension. This file has only one dimension, called Time. The dimension ID is saved in the variable tid (for 'time ID'). Remember that names of netCDF attributes, dimensions, and variables are *case sensitive*.

See the NCDF_DIMDEF function in Scientific Data Formats.

The netCDF standard allows two types of dimensions, *fixed* and *unlimited*. Unlimited dimensions grow as needed when data are written to the file. NetCDF files can contain more than one dimension, but *only one unlimited dimension is allowed per netCDF file*.

The next three lines use NCDF_VARDEF to define the three variables in the file. In this example, each variable is dimensioned by Time, which is indicated by the array containing the dimension ID, [tid]. A three-dimensional array would have a list of three dimension IDs, such as [xid, yid, tid]. If there is an unlimited dimension, it must be the last one in the list of IDs. NetCDF files can contain BYTE, CHAR, SHORT, LONG, FLOAT, and DOUBLE data types. In this case, Time is a LONG array, whereas w and T are FLOATs. Because variables can be referred to by name (as well as by ID number), it is not necessary to save the variable IDs for each variable. (This is why we can reuse the same variable ID name (vid) for each variable.) Using variable names instead of ID numbers makes the program easier to read.

See the NCDF_VARDEF function in Scientific Data Formats.

The next six lines of the program use NCDF_ATTPUT to write the variable attributes to the file. In this case the attributes are strings containing the long name and units for each of the variables. The names of the attributes are longname and units. The values of the attributes are things such as "Vertical velocity".

See the NCDF_ATTPUT procedure in Scientific Data Formats.

At this point, all of the metadata for the file have been defined (dimension names and sizes, variable names and dimensions, and attributes). The NCDF_CONTROL, id, /ENDEF statement takes the file out of *define mode* (that is, defining the file contents) and puts it into *data mode* (ready to read or write data). It is a minor limitation of the netCDF software that it has these two modes. The practical effect is that a program can be either defining the file contents or writing to the file, but the two cannot be intermingled. It is possible to switch back to define mode and add more dimensions, variables, or attributes, but it should be avoided. Among other things, it requires that a new copy be made of the entire file.

See the NCDF_CONTROL procedure in Scientific Data Formats.

Toward the bottom of the program the arrays time, w, and T are written to the output file by using NCDF_VARPUT commands.

See the NCDF_VARPUT procedure in Scientific Data Formats.

Finally, the output file is closed with NCDF_CLOSE.

The listing of the metadata for the file as given by ncdump is below (identical to Chapter 13). As you can see, writing a netCDF file is a little more involved than writing a plain binary file. The payoff is that the file is *very* portable, easy to access, and self-documenting. These features may not seem important until you have spent several days moving a plain binary file between two different computers or deciphering the contents of a binary file (yours or someone else's).

See the NCDF_CLOSE procedure in Scientific Data Formats.

14.3 Writing Parts of an Array

It is important to point out that netCDF files do not require you to read and write entire arrays at one time. Indeed, due to computer memory limitations it is often necessary to work on only part of a data file at one time. The netCDF interface makes it very easy to read or write arbitrary portions of a data array.

If you use the code snippet below to replace the three NCDF_VARPUT statements in the earlier program, the resulting output file is the same in both cases,
although the use of the FOR loop and multiple writes will make the program
somewhat slower:

```
FOR s = 0, n-1 DO BEGIN
    NCDF_VARPUT, oid, 'Time', time[s], $ ;Write the time
        OFFSET = [s], COUNT = [1]
    NCDF_VARPUT, oid, 'T',    T[s],   $ ;Write the temperature
        OFFSET = [s], COUNT = [1]
    NCDF_VARPUT, oid, 'w',    w[s],   $ ;Write the vertical velocity
        OFFSET = [s], COUNT = [1]
ENDFOR
```

In this version the values in the three arrays are written one element at a time
to the output file. The index s counts through all of the possible subscripts
for the arrays time, w, and T. For each s, one value from each array is written
to the output file. The OFFSET keyword contains the index of the array in the
file where writing should begin. The COUNT keyword tells how many values
should be written (just 1 in this case). These two keywords make it possible to
easily write any "rectangular" chunk of a multidimensional array. The COUNT
and OFFSET keywords can also be used with NCDF_VARGET to *read* parts of
an array.

*See the OFFSET and
COUNT keywords for
NCDF_VARGET and
NCDF_VARPUT in Scientific
Data Formats.*

14.4   Summary

NetCDF files are a great way to store array-oriented scientific data in an
eminently portable, self-documenting format. NetCDF is usually not a good
format for more irregular data structures.

The hardest part of writing a netCDF file is not understanding the technical
details of the various NCDF_functions and procedures. That will come with a
little practice. The next hardest part is having the patience and discipline to
write all of the metadata to the file. Try to think ahead!

The basic steps for creating a netCDF file are:

1. Create a new netCDF file with NCDF_OPEN.

2. Write global attributes to the file with NCDF_ATTPUT.

3. Define the dimensions with NCDF_DIMDEF.

4. Define the variables with NCDF_VARDEF.

5. Write variable attributes to the file with NCDF_ATTPUT.

6. Exit define mode with NCDF_CONTROL.

7. Write data with NCDF_VARPUT.

8. Close the file with NCDF_CLOSE when finished writing.

14.5 Exercises

1. Write an IDL program to create a netCDF file containing a synthetic two- or three-dimensional data array.

2. Write an IDL program to read a surface-flux data file from Chapter 13 and rewrite that data to a new netCDF file.

Part III

PROGRAM STRUCTURE AND CONTROL

Procedures and Functions

Procedures and functions are the building blocks of all but the simplest programs. Deciding how to break the different parts of a complex program into components is one of the most difficult aspects of software development. This chapter covers the basic mechanics of how to use procedures and functions. It touches only briefly on the more difficult problem of how to organize the procedures and functions into a working program.

Procedures and functions are much easier to write, debug, and use if they are written in a clear, consistent style. You should develop the habits of including comments and using a consistent programming style in all of your programs. Good style will save you much time and frustration down the line. The example programs included in this book follow the style guidelines discussed in A.

15.1   IDL Commands and Keywords

The following IDL commands and keywords are used for printing text to the terminal screen and to files:

- PRO statement

- FUNCTION statement

- RETURN statement

- END statement

15.2   Built-in Procedures and Functions

IDL comes with hundreds of built-in procedures and functions. We have used some already, such as the PLOT procedure, which plots line graphs, and the ALOG10 function, which computes base-10 logarithms. Each of the procedures and functions supplied by RSI are described in *IDL Reference Guide*.

Although IDL is an interactive language, user procedures and functions, and some built-in functions, must be *compiled* before they are used. Because the IDL compiler does not spend much effort on optimization, it compiles very quickly. Most of the RSI-supplied procedures and functions are *precompiled*, so when you use them, they are immediately available. This statement uses the PRINT procedure to print the results of the FINDGEN function:

```
IDL> print, findgen(5)
      0.00000      1.00000      2.00000      3.00000      4.00000
```

The actual programs (source code) that carry out the PRINT and FINDGEN operations are not available to users.

Other procedures and functions provided by RSI are written in the IDL language. An example is the REGRESS function, which performs linear regression. You can examine the actual REGRESS program in the file regress.pro, which is in the lib directory of the IDL installation. You can also copy the REGRESS function to your own directory, change both file and function names (I would name it REGRESS_KPB), and modify it for your special purposes.

See the REGRESS function in *IDL Reference Guide.*

When you use the REGRESS function, IDL first locates the file regress.pro (the lib directory is included in the IDL search path by default). IDL then automatically *compiles* the REGRESS function and executes it:

```
IDL> a = regress(findgen(10), findgen(10))
% Compiled module: REGRESS.
IDL> print, a
      1.00000
```

Note the message indicating that the REGRESS procedure was compiled.

IDL automatically compiles your procedures and functions if:

- Each procedure or function is in a separate file.

- The file name matches the procedure or function name *exactly* and ends in .pro.

- The file name is all lowercase.

- The file is in your IDL search path.

If these conditions are not true, IDL *may* find the file and compile it, depending on how your computer system matches file names.

IDL does not automatically keep track of whether you have changed a procedure or function. If you make changes to a program unit that has already been compiled in your current IDL session, you must recompile it before using it. Otherwise you will actually be executing the previously compiled version. You can manually compile (or recompile) a procedure or function using the .compile or .run commands.

The .compile command can be shortened to .com, and the .run command can be shortened to .r. I have gotten into the habit of using .r to compile procedures and functions:

See *Running IDL Program Files* in *Using IDL.*

```
IDL> .com regress
% Compiled module: REGRESS.
```

```
IDL> .r regress
% Compiled module: REGRESS.
```

Each time you compile an IDL program unit, the new version replaces the previous version in your current session.

15.3 Writing Procedures

IDL provides for two kinds of programming modules: *procedures* and *functions*. The difference between procedures and functions is actually relatively minor. With a few minor changes, any procedure could potentially be turned into a function, and any function could be turned into a procedure. Which to choose is largely a matter of convenience and should become clear after studying a few examples of each.

See *Procedures and Functions* in *Building IDL Applications*.

This section covers the basics of procedures, but almost everything applies equally to functions.

A procedure is a sequence of IDL statements that carries out a specific operation. As you can see, this is a very general definition. An IDL program, even a very complex program, *could* be written as a single, very long procedure. Programmers have learned by experience, however, that it is much better to organize programs into modules or program units. Modules are typically of short to medium length, that is, from a few IDL commands to at most a few hundred. Well-designed modules usually do one thing and do it well. For example, if you have a program that reads data from a file, performs some calculations with the data, and then plots a graph, it would be logical to organize the program into four modules, one to read the data, one to do the calculations, and one to plot the graph. The fourth module would be a procedure that is usually called the *main program*. Executing it would execute the other three modules. Depending on their complexity, the subtasks (reading, calculating, and plotting) might be part of the main program.

Writing four procedures to carry out one "program" might seem needlessly complex, but in fact, long, single programs are more difficult to write, debug, and modify than well-designed modular programs. Another advantage of modular programming: You may be able to reuse the individual modules in future programs, saving much time and effort.

An IDL procedure always begins with a PRO statement and ends with an END statement. Any statements after the END statement are ignored. You can put comments before the PRO statement, but I recommend against doing that. It can make it hard to find the PRO statement when you look at a procedure file. For readability, the PRO statement should be the first line in the file. (You will find many IDL library files in which this is not true, however.)

See the PRO statement in *IDL Reference Guide*.

A procedure looks like this:

```
PRO PROCEDURE_TEMPLATE, arg1, arg2, KEY1 = key1

;+
```

```
; Name:
;       PROCEDURE_TEMPLATE
; Purpose:
;       This is a template for creating IDL procedure files.
; Calling sequence:
;       PROCEDURE_TEMPLATE, arg1, arg2
; Input:
;       arg1 : positional parameter 1
; Output:
;       arg2 : positional parameter 2
; Keywords:
;       key1 : keyword parameter 1
; Author and history:
;       Kenneth P. Bowman.
;-


COMPILE_OPT IDL2                            ;Set compile options



END
```

This is the template that I use for creating new procedures. A similar template for functions is available in the file FUNCTION_TEMPLATE. The name of the procedure, which is how it is referred to in an IDL program, immediately follows the word PRO. If you use this template, replace "PROCEDURE_TEMPLATE" with the name of the procedure that you are writing. Don't forget to save the file with a new name (lowercase) that matches the procedure name.

After the procedure name is a list of the *arguments* or *parameters* of the procedure. (The two terms are used interchangeably.) The template contains three parameters: two *positional parameters* (arg1 and arg2), and one *keyword parameter* (KEY1 = key1).

The template contains a standard block of comments near the top of the procedure that is used to describe what the procedure does, how it does it, and how to use it. The two lines at the beginning and end of the comment block, one starting with ;+ and one starting with ;- are not mandatory. The IDL procedure MK_HTML_HELP uses those tags to create Hypertext Markup Language (HTML) help files. Here is a one-line procedure to make an HTML file containing the comment blocks from all of the example programs.

```
PRO MAKE_HTML_HELP

MK_HTML_HELP, !Bowman, !Bowman + 'examples.html', $
TITLE = 'IDL Example Programs', /VERBOSE

END
```

The HTML output file is called `examples.html`. It is included with the example programs. You should be able to open it with any Web browser.

After the comment block is the IDL statement

```
COMPILE_OPT IDL2                    ;Set compile options
```

I include this statement in *every* IDL procedure or function that I write. The `COMPILE_OPT IDL2` statement ensures that integers defined within the procedure, such as i = 3, are created as 4-byte LONGs, rather than 2-byte INTs. It also requires that array subscripts be written using square brackets [and], not parentheses (and). Parentheses can be used only for function calls. The reasons for doing this are slightly obscure. Suffice it to say that it will help to avoid occasional problems distinguishing between arrays and functions.

See COMPILE_OPT in *IDL Reference Guide*.

The IDL statements to be executed follow the `COMPILE_OPT` statement, and the procedure ends with the `END` statement.

The key to writing and using procedures is understanding two concepts: (1) local variables and (2) argument passing. These are often among the most difficult concepts for new programmers to understand. Here are the basic principles of using procedure and function parameters in IDL:

- First, the variables and variable names in a procedure are *local* to the procedure. This means that a variable in one procedure cannot be accessed in another procedure unless it is passed through the argument list.[1] If variables were not local, you would have to ensure that your variable names did not inadvertently match variables in *any* of the other modules that you use.

- Second, variables in the argument list are matched between the *calling* procedure and the *called* procedure according to their *order* in the argument list. The *names* of the variables in the calling procedure and the called procedure do not have to be the same.

These principles are best illustrated with an example. (The comments are omitted for brevity.) Here are two simple procedures, a main procedure called MYPRO:

```
PRO MYPRO

COMPILE_OPT IDL2                    ;Set compile options

a = 2.0                             ;Set a to 2.0
d = 4.0                             ;Set d to 4.0

PRINT, 'Step 1:  Values in MYPRO before calling MYSUB.'
HELP, a, b, c, d, x, y, z, t
```

---

1   Or placed in a *common block* or a *system variable*.

```
MYSUB, a, b, c                              ;Call procedure MYSUB

PRINT
PRINT, 'Step 4:  Values in MYPRO after calling MYSUB.'
HELP, a, b, c, d, x, y, z, t

END
```

and a subprocedure called MYSUB:

```
PRO MYSUB, x, y, z

COMPILE_OPT IDL2                            ;Set compile options

PRINT
PRINT, 'Step 2:  Values when entering MYSUB.'
HELP, a, b, c, d, x, y, z, t

y = x^2                                     ;Compute square of x
z = 3.0                                     ;Set z to 3.0
t = 5                                       ;Set t to 5

PRINT
PRINT, 'Step 3:  Values when exiting MYSUB.'
HELP, a, b, c, d, x, y, z, t

END
```

MYPRO, which has no arguments, sets the values of the variables a and d and then *calls* (executes) the procedure MYSUB. In MYPRO, the argument list for MYSUB contains the three variables a, b, and c. (These are sometimes referred to as *actual arguments*.) Within MYSUB, these variables are referred to by the names x, y, and z. (These are sometimes called *dummy arguments*.) To illustrate that variables are *local*, the two procedures use the HELP function to show the values of all variables at several stages of the program evolution. If you execute MYPRO, you get the following output on the terminal screen:

```
IDL> mypro
% Compiled module: MYPRO.
Step 1:  Values in MYPRO before calling MYSUB.
A               FLOAT     =       2.00000
B               UNDEFINED = <Undefined>
C               UNDEFINED = <Undefined>
D               FLOAT     =       4.00000
X               UNDEFINED = <Undefined>
Y               UNDEFINED = <Undefined>
Z               UNDEFINED = <Undefined>
```

```
T               UNDEFINED = <Undefined>
% Compiled module: MYSUB.

Step 2:   Values when entering MYSUB.
A               UNDEFINED = <Undefined>
B               UNDEFINED = <Undefined>
C               UNDEFINED = <Undefined>
D               UNDEFINED = <Undefined>
X               FLOAT     =      2.00000
Y               UNDEFINED = <Undefined>
Z               UNDEFINED = <Undefined>
T               UNDEFINED = <Undefined>

Step 3:   Values when exiting MYSUB.
A               UNDEFINED = <Undefined>
B               UNDEFINED = <Undefined>
C               UNDEFINED = <Undefined>
D               UNDEFINED = <Undefined>
X               FLOAT     =      2.00000
Y               FLOAT     =      4.00000
Z               FLOAT     =      3.00000
T               LONG      =            5

Step 4:   Values in MYPRO after calling MYSUB.
A               FLOAT     =      2.00000
B               FLOAT     =      4.00000
C               FLOAT     =      3.00000
D               FLOAT     =      4.00000
X               UNDEFINED = <Undefined>
Y               UNDEFINED = <Undefined>
Z               UNDEFINED = <Undefined>
T               UNDEFINED = <Undefined>
```

First, IDL automatically finds the file `mypro.pro` and compiles it for execution.

At Step 1, within MYPRO, the values of a and d are known, but the other variables have not been defined. IDL then finds the file `mysub.pro` and compiles it for execution. Execution passes into MYSUB.

The variables in MYPRO and MYSUB are matched, as shown in Table 15.1, according to their order in the argument lists.

Step 2 shows the values of all variables at the beginning of MYSUB. As you can see, at this point MYSUB does not know anything about the variables a, b, c, and d. If you match the internal argument list of MYSUB (x, y, and z) with the arguments actually passed to MYSUB from MYPRO (a, b, and c), you can see that within MYSUB the variable a goes by the name x. Because b and c were undefined in MYPRO, y and z are undefined in MYSUB. MYSUB then computes a value for y using x and sets the values of z and t.

TABLE 15.1   Pairing of arguments in the calling and called procedures.

MYPRO		MYSUB
a	⇔	x
b	⇔	y
c	⇔	z
d		(none)
(none)		t

Step 3 shows that x, y, z, and t are now all defined. The execution now returns to MYPRO.

At Step 4, the variables a, b, c, and d are all known. The variables x, y, z, and t, which are local to MYSUB, are undefined.

You can use the same names for variables in a calling and called procedure. Often, that is the logical way to define the names in the calling procedure. Remember, though, a variable named x in the calling procedure and another variable named x in the called procedure are not the same thing unless they occur in the same position in the argument lists of the calling procedure and the called procedure.

You do not have to use variables in an argument list in the calling procedure; you can also use constants:

```
IDL> print, 0.5
      0.500000
```

15.4 Writing Functions

There are only two real differences between procedures and functions. The first is how they are used in the *calling* procedure. The PLOT procedure, for example, is used in the following way, in this case interactively at the command line:

```
IDL> x = findgen(11)
IDL> y = x^2
IDL> plot, x, y
```

In this example, the variables x and y are passed to the PLOT procedure. The values of x and y are used to plot a graph. In this case both x and y are *input* variables. This procedure does not return any variables in the argument list.

A function, on the other hand, *always returns a value*, so it can only be used in the calling program in a context where a returned value is needed. For example,

```
IDL> x = 1.0
IDL> y = sin(x)
```

```
IDL> print, x, y
      1.00000      0.841471
```

or

```
IDL> print, x, sin(x)
       1.00000      0.841471
```

You can think of the function as returning a value, in this case the floating-point number 0.841471, that *replaces* the expression sin(x) in the statement where it is used.

Just as it makes no sense to type

```
IDL> 0.841471
```

```
0.841471
 ^
% Syntax error.
```

it makes no sense to enter

```
IDL> sin(x)
```

```
sin(x)
 ^
% Syntax error.
```

You could convert the SIN function into a procedure like this:

```
PRO MYSIN, x, y
```

```
y = SIN(x)
```

```
END
```

You can use this procedure form of the SIN function as follows:

```
IDL> mysin, x, y
% Compiled module: MYSIN.
IDL> print, y
      0.841471
```

When you try to execute the procedure MYSIN, IDL automatically searches and finds the file mysin.pro (assuming it is in your IDL search path), compiles the procedure, and then executes it. Note that the MYSIN procedure does not have a RETURN statement. All values are returned through the positional parameter y.

A function can return more than a single value. For example:

```
IDL> x = findgen(4)
IDL> y = sin(x)
IDL> print, x
      0.00000      1.00000      2.00000      3.00000
IDL> print, y
      0.00000     0.841471     0.909297     0.141120
IDL> help, x, y
X               FLOAT    = Array[4]
Y               FLOAT    = Array[4]
```

In this case the input argument is an array of four elements. IDL automatically returns an output array that is the same size as the input array.

As stated above, a function *always returns a value*. The second difference between a function and a procedure is that a function *must* contain a RETURN statement that specifies the variable to be returned to the calling program. Procedures can also have RETURN statements (procedures and functions can, in fact, have more than one RETURN statement), but RETURN statements in a procedure must not provide a variable to be returned. When you write your own functions, you must include a RETURN statement that specifies the value to be returned.

See the RETURN statement in *IDL Reference Guide.*

Here is a simple function:

```
FUNCTION MYSQUARE, x

y = x^2

RETURN, y

END
```

Note that a function always begins with a FUNCTION statement instead of a PRO statement. You can use this function in the usual way:

See the FUNCTION statement in *IDL Reference Guide.*

```
IDL> y = mysquare(x)
% Compiled module: MYSQUARE.
IDL> print, y
      0.00000      1.00000      4.00000      9.00000
```

Once again, IDL searched the directories in the search path, found the file mysquare.pro, compiled the function, and executed it. (There is, of course, no reason to write a new function to compute the squares of the elements in an array; you can simply use the exponentiation operator ^.)

So, as you can see, functions are useful when you want to return a variable to use immediately in a mathematical operation, when used in a print statement, and so on. One very nice feature of IDL is that you can return any type of IDL variable: scalars, arrays, and even structures.

Like procedures, functions can have multiple arguments in the argument list, including keyword arguments.

15.5 Keyword Parameters

As we saw above, positional parameters are matched between calling and called procedures according to the order they are given in the argument list. IDL provides another way to match parameters between the calling and called procedure: *keyword parameters*. Instead of depending on position (order), keyword parameters have a tag (the *keyword*) that is used to match the variables between the calling and called routines. Because keyword parameters are matched by keyword name, they can be given in any order in the argument list. They can even be mixed in with the positional parameters. IDL does not count keyword parameters when determining position. Because of their flexibility, keywords are often used for *optional* parameters.

A good example of a procedure with keyword parameters is the PLOT procedure, as in this code snippet:

```
title   = 'Position vs. time'
abscissa = 'Time (s)'
ordinate = 'Distance (m)'
PLOT, x, y, $                          ;Plot y(x)
   TITLE = title, $
   XTITLE = abscissa, $
   YTITLE = ordinate
```

The variables title, abscissa, and ordinate are string variables that contain labels for the graph drawn by PLOT. These variables are passed into the PLOT procedure by associating them with the appropriate keywords. The PLOT program contains similar keyword definitions that connect the keyword tags to local variables within the PLOT procedure.

Within a procedure or function, it usually makes sense for the variable associated with a keyword to have the same name as the keyword, but it is not required.

Keywords are frequently used as *toggles* or *switches* to turn a particular option within a procedure or function on or off. For example, you might write a program whose default behavior is to display a graph on the screen. The program could include an optional keyword to allow the user to send the graph to a printer instead. IDL has special notation and functions to make this easy. Here is a program that works in the way described:

```
PRO PLOT_MY_GRAPH, PRINT = print, LANDSCAPE = landscape

IF KEYWORD_SET(print) THEN PRINTER_ON, LANDSCAPE = landscape

    ... program to create a plot

IF KEYWORD_SET(print) THEN PRINTER_OFF

END
```

This program has two keywords, PRINT and LANDSCAPE. In this example, the keyword names are the same as the local variables to which any keyword values are passed. Writing the keyword name in uppercase and the local variable name in lowercase helps to distinguish the two things conceptually. (Because IDL is not case sensitive, you could also write PRINT = PRINT or print = print and get the same result.) It usually makes sense for the names to match, but it is not required. You could do this instead:

```
PRO PLOT_MY_GRAPH, PRINT = send_to_printer, LANDSCAPE = print_wide

IF KEYWORD_SET(send_to_printer) THEN PRINTER_ON, LANDSCAPE = print_wide

    ... create a plot

IF KEYWORD_SET(send_to_printer) THEN PRINTER_OFF

END
```

Note that the KEYWORD_SET function checks the value of the *local variable* send_to_printer, not the keyword name PRINT.

The KEYWORD_SET function, not surprisingly, checks to see if a keyword is set. If it is, the PRINTER_ON procedure is called at the beginning of the program to switch the graphics device from the screen to a printer. At the end of the program the PRINTER_OFF procedure is called to send the graphics output to the printer and switch the output back to the screen.

See the KEYWORD_SET function in *IDL Reference Guide.*

If the PRINT keyword is omitted or equal to zero

```
IDL > plot_my_graph
```

or

```
IDL > plot_my_graph, PRINT = 0
```

then the variable print is either undefined or zero within PLOT_MY_GRAPH. In that case KEYWORD_SET(print) returns FALSE, and the PRINTER_ON and PRINTER_OFF procedures are not executed.

If the PRINT keyword is nonzero

```
IDL > plot_my_graph, /PRINT
```

or

```
IDL > plot_my_graph, PRINT = 1
```

then the variable print *is* set within PLOT_MY_GRAPH. In that case KEYWORD_SET(print) returns TRUE, and the PRINTER_ON and PRINTER_OFF procedures *are* executed.

The main program above, PLOT_MY_GRAPH, also includes the keyword LANDSCAPE. The value of this keyword, if it is defined, is passed through to the PRINTER_ON procedure.

The notation /PRINT is shorthand for PRINT = 1. Because of the somewhat peculiar way in which KEYWORD_SET evaluates its arguments, the KEYWORD_SET function should be used only with keywords like the one illustrated here, in which the keyword is used to indicate on or off.

If a keyword is not being used as an on-off switch, and you need to see whether the variable attached to the keyword is defined, do not use KEYWORD_SET. Use the function N_ELEMENTS instead. If the variable is undefined, N_ELEMENTS returns zero. If it is defined, it will return a number greater than zero.

15.6 Optional Parameters

IDL allows for programs to be written with optional parameters. The PLOT procedure is a good example. PLOT can be called either with two arguments

```
IDL > plot, x, y
```

or with one

```
IDL > plot, y
```

In the second case, PLOT automatically generates a default array for x using FINDGEN(n), where n is the number of elements in y.

Using optional arguments requires careful planning and is somewhat advanced for this book. If you want to learn more about writing procedures and functions with optional arguments, see *Practical IDL Programming* or *IDL Programming Techniques*.

15.7 Summary

This chapter has covered the basics of writing and using procedures and functions. Remember the following essential points about IDL programming modules:

- Variables are local to the procedure or function that contains them unless they are included in the argument list.

- Arguments in the argument list are matched according to the order in the list in the calling procedure and the called procedure.

- Keyword parameters can be given in any order and even mixed with positional parameters.

- Within a procedure or function, the keyword *name* should generally be the same as the local variable it is associated with (for example, PRINT = print). The capitalization simply emphasizes that there is a keyword tag PRINT.

15.8 Exercises

1. Convert the scripts from the exercises in Chapter 4 into procedures.

2. The intensity of the radiation emitted by a blackbody, $B_\lambda(T)$, as a function of temperature T and wavelength λ is given by the Planck function

$$B_\lambda(T) = \frac{2hc^2}{\pi \lambda^5 (e^{hc/k\lambda T} - 1)}.$$

In this equation, $h = 6.6262 \cdot 10^{-34}$ J s is Planck's constant, $c = 2.99793 \cdot 10^8$ m s^{-1} is the speed of light, and $k = 1.38062 \cdot 10^{-23}$ J K^{-1} is Boltzmann's constant. The temperature T is in Kelvin (K) and the wavelength λ in meters (m). The units of B_λ are W m^{-2} m^{-1}.

Write a function to compute the Planck (blackbody) function for a given temperature and wavelength.

3. Write a function to compute the solar declination δ as a function of time of year using the following Fourier series expansion:

$$\delta = \sum_{k=0}^{3} \left[a_k \cos(2\pi kt) + b_k \sin(2\pi kt) \right]$$

where t is the time in years, and the coefficients a_k and b_k are given in the following table:

k	a_k	b_k
0	0.006918	
1	−0.399912	0.070257
2	−0.006758	0.000907
3	−0.002697	0.001480

The series expansion is from Spencer (1971).

4. Write a function to compute the solar-distance parameter $(d^-/d)^2$ as a function of time of year using the following Fourier series expansion:

$$\left(\frac{d^-}{d}\right)^2 = \sum_{k=0}^{2} \left[a_k \cos\left(2\pi\,kt\right) + b_k \sin\left(2\pi\,kt\right)\right]$$

where t is the time in years, and the coefficients a_k and b_k are given in the following table:

k	a_k	b_k
0	1.000110	
1	0.034221	0.001280
2	0.000719	0.000077

The series expansion is from Spencer (1971).

5. Write a function to compute the hour of sunrise and sunset h_0 as a function of latitude ϕ and time of year t using the functions above. The hour of sunrise is given by

$$\cos(h_0) = -\tan(\phi)\,\tan(\delta)$$

Care must be taken in high latitudes during the polar night or day (times of year when the sun does not rise or does not set), particularly at the poles, as $\tan(\delta) \to \pm\infty$ as $\delta \to \pm\pi/2$.

6. Write a function to compute the solar zenith angle θ_s as a function of latitude ϕ, time of year t, and local time h using the functions above. The solar zenith angle is given by

$$\cos(\theta_s) = \sin(\phi)\sin(\delta) + \cos(\phi)\cos(\delta)\cos(h)$$

7. Write a function to compute the daily-mean insolation $\bar{Q}$ as a function of latitude ϕ and time of year t using the functions from Exercises 3, 4, and 5 above. The daily-mean insolation is given by

$$\bar{Q} = \frac{S_0}{\pi}\left(\frac{d^-}{d}\right)^2 \left[h_0 \sin(\phi)\sin(\delta) + \cos(\phi)\cos(\delta)\sin(h_0)\right]$$

8. Use the approximate form of the Clausius-Clapeyron equation below (Bohren and Albrecht, 1998) to write a function to compute the saturation vapor pressure of water e_s as a function of temperature T

$$e_s(T) = e_{s_0}e^{(a-b/T)}$$

where $e_{s_0} = 611$, Pa is e_s at $0°C$, $a = 19.83$, $b = 5417$ K, and T is in Kelvin (K).

Program Control

Normally IDL executes each statement in a program or script in sequence. Often it is useful to *conditionally* execute a statement or block of statements, or to repeatedly execute a statement or block of statements (that is, to execute a loop). IDL has a number of different program control options to do this kind of thing. This chapter covers the most frequently used control structures: IF...THEN statements, FOR loops, and WHILE loops.

16.1 IDL Commands and Keywords

The following IDL commands and keywords are used to control the execution of IDL statements and to repeatedly execute statements (loop):

- BEGIN...END statements
- IF...THEN...ENDIF...ELSE...ENDELSE statements
- FOR...DO...ENDFOR statements
- WHILE...DO...ENDWHILE statements
- REPEAT...UNTIL...ENDREP statements
- CASE...ENDCASE statements

16.2 BEGIN...END Statements

Most IDL control structures can be used either in "single-line" form, in which a single statement is executed conditionally or repeatedly, or in "block" form, in which a sequence of multiple statements is executed. The IDL reserved words BEGIN and END are used to identify the beginning and end of a block. Each type of IDL control structure has a matching form of the END statement: ENDIF, ENDELSE, ENDFOR, ENDWHILE, etc. You are not required to use the specific forms of the END statement; you can use a plain END statement. I strongly recommend, however, that you *always* use the specific forms because they make it much easier to find the beginning and end of blocks.

See the BEGIN...END statements in *IDL Reference Guide*.

In an IDL script or batch job (executed with the @ sign), statements are executed one at a time. As a result, scripts cannot use blocks. If you need to use blocks, write a procedure or function, not a script.

16.3 `IF...THEN...ELSE` **Statements**

16.3.1 **Single-Line Form**

The `IF...THEN...ELSE` statement evaluates a *logical expression* and executes a statement or block of statements if the expression evaluates to true. Here are some examples of the single-line form:

See the
`IF...THEN...ELSE`
statements in *IDL
Reference Guide.*

```
IF (i NE 0) THEN y = x^i
IF (N_ELEMENTS(z) GT 0) THEN z = z^2
IF ((a EQ 0) AND (b EQ 0)) THEN PLOT, x, y
```

In each of these examples, if the logical expression in parentheses is true, the statement following `THEN` is executed. If false, the statement following `THEN` is not executed, and execution continues with the next statement in the procedure or function.

    `IF...THEN` statements can have an optional `ELSE` part:

```
IF (i NE 0) THEN y = x^i ELSE y = 0.0
```

If the logical expression is true, the first statement is executed. If it is false, the statement following `ELSE` is executed. In either case, only one of the two statements is executed.

    If the statements to be executed are short, as above, the whole thing can be placed on a single line. Often, the structure of the statement is clearer if it is split over two or more lines using the continuation character $.

```
IF (i NE 0) THEN y = x^i $
            ELSE y = 0.0
```

16.3.2 **Block Form**

`IF...THEN` statements can be used to execute a block of statements by using the `BEGIN...END` construction described earlier:

```
IF (i NE 0) THEN BEGIN
   y = x^i
   z = 0.0
ENDIF
```

Blocks do not have to contain multiple statements. You can create blocks that contain only one statement:

```
IF (i NE 0) THEN BEGIN
   y = x^i
```

```
ENDIF ELSE BEGIN
   y = 0.0
ENDELSE
```

The indentation is not mandatory, but it makes the structure of the program much easier to identify.

An IF...THEN statement can have multiple sections:

```
IF (i GT 0) THEN BEGIN
   y = x^i
ENDIF ELSE IF (i EQ 0) THEN BEGIN
   y = 0.0
ENDIF ELSE BEGIN
   y = SQRT(x)
ENDELSE
```

If an IF...THEN statement has multiple sections, IDL tests each of the logical expressions in order. If it finds an expression that is true, the statement or block of statements following that expression is executed. None of the other blocks are executed. If an ELSE statement is included and none of the logical expressions is true, the ELSE block is executed. ELSE statements are not required, however. If an ELSE statement is *not* included and none of the expressions is true, none of the blocks are executed.

16.4 FOR **Loops**

16.4.1 **Single-Line Form**

FOR loops use a loop counter variable to repeatedly execute a statement or block of statements. A single-line FOR loop looks like this:

See the FOR...DO statement in *IDL Reference Guide.*

```
IDL> FOR i = 0, 4 DO PRINT, i^2
            0
            1
            4
            9
           16
IDL> PRINT, i
            5
```

This statement could be read as "For i equals 0 to 4 by 1, execute the statement PRINT, i^2." In detail, this is how the statement works. The variable i is initialized to 0. The statement following DO is executed repeatedly. Each time the statement is executed, i is incremented by 1 *after* the statement is executed. When i is greater than 4, execution jumps to the line following the FOR statement. Note that when the loop is finished, i = 5.

FOR loops can count backwards or by increments other than 1:

```
IDL> FOR i = 4, 0, -1 DO PRINT, i
       4
       3
       2
       1
       0
IDL> FOR i = 0, 7, 2 DO PRINT, i
       0
       2
       4
       6
```

You can also use variables other than integers as the loop counter:

```
IDL> FOR x = 0.0, 1.0, 0.2 DO PRINT, x
      0.00000
      0.200000
      0.400000
      0.600000
      0.800000
       1.00000
```

Be very careful when you do this. Roundoff errors in floating-point arithmetic may cause the loop to execute more or fewer times than you expect. Whenever you can, use integers as loop counters.

16.4.2 Block Form

A FOR loop with a block of statments looks like this:

```
FOR i = 0, n-1 DO BEGIN
   y[i] = x[i]^2
   z[i] = SQRT(y[i])
ENDFOR
```

IDL FOR loops work essentially exactly like Fortran DO loops.

Most operations with arrays can be done in a faster and clearer way using array syntax rather than FOR loops (see Chapter 7). Fortran programmers, in particular, should always think twice (or ask an IDL expert) before writing a FOR loop to do an array operation.

16.5 WHILE Loops

WHILE loops can be thought of as general-purpose FOR loops in which the programmer is responsible for managing the "loop" variable. Here is an example:

See the WHILE...DO statement in *IDL Reference Guide*.

```
i = 1
WHILE (i NE 0) DO BEGIN
    PRINT, 'Enter an integer other than 0 (enter 0 to exit): '
    READ, i
    PRINT, 'The square of ', i, ' is ', i^2
ENDWHILE
```

The statements between the BEGIN and END are executed repeatedly until the logical expression in parentheses is false. In this case, the loop control variable i is initialized to 1. With the logical test that is used here (i NE 0), this ensures that the loop is executed at least once. Within the loop, the user is asked to enter an integer, and the program prints the square of that integer. This process is repeated until the logical expression is false, that is, until the user enters 0. This example shows that WHILE loops are capable of more diverse control methods than simply counting.

Note that something within the WHILE loop *must* change the loop control variable (i in this case). Otherwise, the loop will execute forever. This is known as an *infinite loop*. Infinite loops can be interrupted with control-c.

Because it is necessary to update the loop variable as well as do something useful (which usually requires at least two statements), WHILE loops almost always use a block structure.

16.6   Other Control Structures

IDL includes several other kinds of control structures. These include REPEAT...UNTIL, CASE, and SWITCH statements. The REPEAT...UNTIL structure is similar to a WHILE loop, but it tests the loop condition at the *end* of the loop, rather than at the beginning. The CASE statement can be used to select one case from a list of possible cases. It is more convenient than IF...THEN...ELSE statements in some circumstances. The SWITCH statement is similar to the CASE statement, with the difference that if a case is found to be true, that case and all of the following cases in the list are executed. More information on these control structures can be found in *IDL Reference Guide*.

16.7   Summary

This chapter has covered the basics of IDL program control statements. Here are some suggestions for avoiding problems with control statements:

- Use END statements that match the control structure; that is, use ENDIF, ENDELSE, ENDFOR, ENDWHILE, and so on.

- Check your starting and ending values in FOR loops carefully. It is easy to be off by one at either end.

- Indent block statements for readability.

- Choose the control structure that best matches the problem at hand.

Part IV

GRAPHICS

Line Graphs

This chapter covers some of the options available when creating line graphs, including drawing multiple lines on a single graph and plotting multiple graphs on a single page.

17.1 IDL Commands for Plotting Line Graphs

Simple line graphs, and multiple plots per page, are created with the following commands and system variables:

- The PLOT procedure and its many keywords
- The OPLOT procedure
- The !P.MULTI system variable

17.2 Plotting Styles

17.2.1 Basic Line Graphs

The PLOT procedure has keywords that can be used to customize line graphs. Without any keywords, IDL produces a very basic plot with no labels or title.

See the PLOT procedure in *IDL Reference Guide*.

```
IDL> x = findgen(11)
IDL> y = sqrt(x)
IDL> plot, x, y
```

The result of this statement can be seen in Figure 17.1.

IDL will automatically choose scales for the abscissa and ordinate. A second curve can be plotted on the same graph with the OPLOT procedure (short for over-plot):

See the OPLOT procedure in *IDL Reference Guide*.

```
IDL> oplot, x, 2.0*y
```

When the graph was drawn by the PLOT command, the axes were scaled to fit the original data provided to PLOT. In this example, the data plotted by OPLOT

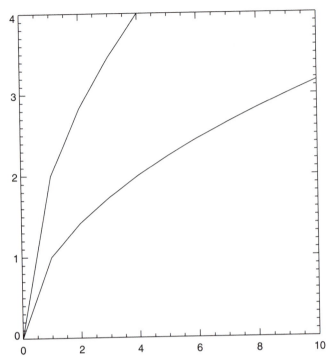

FIGURE 17.1   A simple line graph created with PLOT. The second line is over-plotted by using the OPLOT command. (LINEGRAPH3)

have a larger range than will fit on the graph that was drawn by PLOT. OPLOT *does not redraw the original graph*; instead, the curve is *clipped* to the existing plotting window. To correctly plot multiple curves within a single window, you need to determine the maximum and minimum values for the abscissa and ordinate for all of the graphs to be drawn before calling PLOT. Once you know those values, the range of the graph can be set with the XRANGE and YRANGE keywords.

17.2.2 Logarithmic Graphs

Log-linear, linear-log, and log-log plots can be created with the XLOG and YLOG keywords, which direct PLOT to use logarithmic scaling for the abscissa and ordinate, respectively. Figure 17.2 is an example of a log-log plot. Because the logarithm of zero is undefined, we omit the first element of the arrays x and y. The PSYM keyword is used to plot a marker at each of the data points (see the next section):

```
IDL> plot, x[1:10], y[1:10], /xlog, /ylog, psym = -4
```

As you can see, with log-log scaling the square root function becomes linear. Notice that markers plotted close to the edges of the plot box are clipped to the plotting rectangle. To distinguish different lines on the graph, different

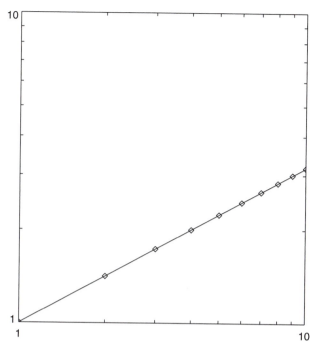

FIGURE 17.2   A log-log graph of $y = \sqrt{x}$ created with PLOT. (LINEGRAPH4)

plotting symbols, line styles, and colors can be used. The relevant keywords are discussed in the next two sections.

17.2.3 Plotting Symbols

The default style for PLOT is to connect the pairs of x and y values by a solid line without plotting any markers. To plot markers without connecting the dots, use the PSYM keyword with a positive value. IDL includes eight standard plotting symbols (including no symbol) plus one that can be defined by the user. See Figure 17.3 and Table 17.1.

```
IDL> plot, x, y
IDL> for i = 1, 7 do oplot, x, y/i, psym = i
```

To plot symbols *and* connect them with line segments, use a negative value for PSYM (Figure 17.4):

```
IDL> plot, x, y
IDL> for i = 1, 7 do oplot, x, y/i, psym = -i
```

Because symbol 3 plots the smallest possible dot for the current graphics device, PSYM = -3 looks the same as PSYM = 0. Positive values of PSYM are useful for scatterplots.

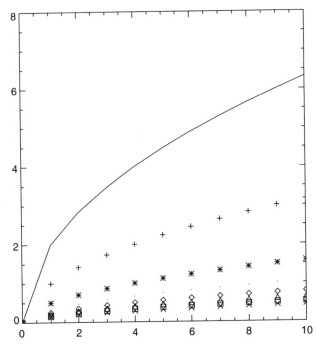

FIGURE 17.3   Built-in plotting symbols. PSYM = 0 connects each pair of points, but plots no symbol. The other curves (PSYM = 1 to PSYM = 7) are drawn without lines connecting the symbols. As this figure demonstrates, graphs can be difficult to interpret when symbols are plotted on top of each other. (LINEGRAPH5)

TABLE 17.1   IDL plotting symbols specified by the PSYM keyword.

Value	Plotting Symbol
0	no symbol
1	plus sign (+)
2	asterisk (*)
3	period (.)
4	diamond
5	triangle
6	square
7	X
8	user-defined. See USERSYM procedure in *IDL Reference Guide*.

17.2.4 Line Styles

An alternative to using plotting symbols to distinguish multiple curves is to use different line styles. IDL provides six different line styles, listed in Table 17.2 (Figure 17.5).

```
IDL> plot, x, y
IDL> for i = 1, 5 do oplot, x, y/i, linestyle = i
```

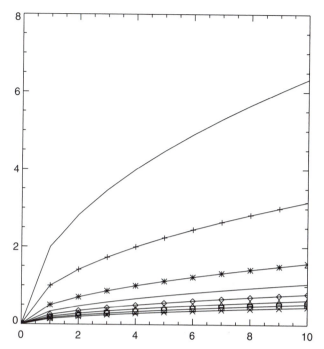

FIGURE 17.4   Built-in plotting symbols. In this case, the symbols in each curve are connected by solid lines. (LINEGRAPH6)

TABLE 17.2   IDL line styles specified by the LINESTYLE keyword.

Index	Linestyle
0	Solid
1	Dotted
2	Dashed
3	Dash Dot
4	Dash Dot Dot
5	Long Dashes

It is possible to combine line styles and plotting symbols (Figure 17.6):

```
IDL> plot, x, y
IDL> for i = 1, 5 do oplot, x, y/i, linestyle = i, psym = -i
```

17.3   Titles and Labels

A scientific graph is not complete without proper labels (Figure 17.7):

```
IDL> plot, x, y, title = 'Square-root function', $
IDL>     xtitle = 'x', ytitle = 'y', $
IDL>     subtitle = 'You can have a subtitle too.'
```

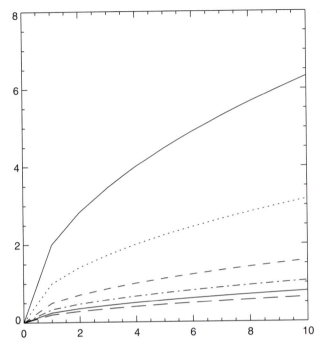

FIGURE 17.5   Built-in line styles. (LINEGRAPH7)

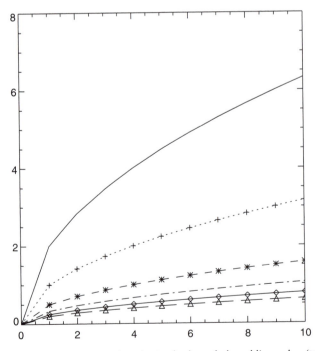

FIGURE 17.6   These curves are plotted using both symbols and line styles. (LINEGRAPH8)

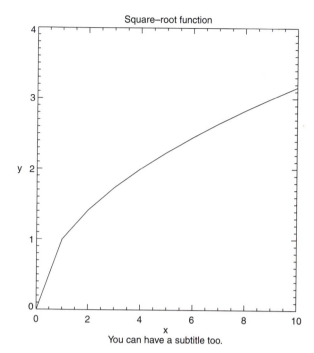

FIGURE 17.7   Titles for the graph and axes are added with the TITLE, XTITLE, YTITLE, and SUBTITLE keywords. (LINEGRAPH9)

You will often want to create the labels ahead of time and store them in variables:

```
IDL> title = 'Square-root function'
IDL> xtitle = 'x'
IDL> ytitle = 'y'
IDL> plot, x, y, title = title, xtitle = xtitle, ytitle = ytitle
```

17.4 Axes

By default, the PLOT procedure selects a range for each axis that is large enough to include all of the data with "nice" upper and lower limits. Each axis is divided into intervals with major and minor tick marks. Labels are displayed for each major tick mark. You can override the defaults for each of these properties and define each axis to have exactly the style that you want. You might do this, for example, when you are plotting multiple related graphs and you want all of them to have the same scales.

The following examples show two plots of the same data. The first (Figure 17.8) uses the default for all axis parameters:

```
IDL> x  = -90.0 + 5.0*findgen(37)
IDL> y  =  28.0 - (0.09*x)^2
IDL> plot, x, y
```

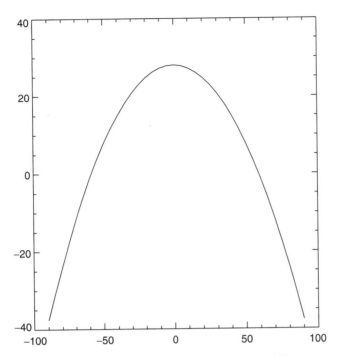

FIGURE 17.8   Example in which all axis parameters are set to their defaults. (LINEGRAPH10)

In this case, the abscissa represents latitude and has values ranging from $-90°$ to $90°$. When IDL automatically scales the abscissa, it chooses limits of ±100. Because latitude is always in the range $[-90°, +90°]$, the resulting graph is incorrect.

In the next example, shown in Figure 17.9, the axis parameters are specified explicitly:

```
IDL> plot, x, y, $
        title  = 'Annual-Mean Temperature', $
        xtitle = 'Latitude (degrees)', $
        xstyle = 1, $
        xrange = [-90.0, 90.0], $
        xticks = 6, $
        xminor = 3, $
        ytitle = 'Temperature (K)', $
        ystyle = 1, $
        yrange = [-40.0, 30.0], $
        yticks = 7, $
        yminor = 2
```

The XSTYLE keyword indicates that the range of the abscissa should be set to exactly the range specified by the XRANGE keyword (-90 to $+90$). The number of major and minor tick marks are set to appropriate values (XTICKS and XMINOR). The range and tick marks for the ordinate are specified similarly. Titles are provided for the axes and the graph.

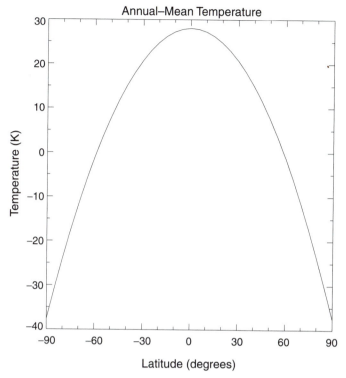

FIGURE 17.9   In this graph the axis parameters are set explicitly so that each axis has the correct range and tick spacing. (`LINEGRAPH11`)

17.5   Multiple Plots Per Page

IDL makes it easy to plot multiple graphs on a single page, like panes in a window.

Plot characteristics can be changed by using the IDL system variable `!P`. `!P` is a structure that contains a variety of variables that are used to control plot characteristics, such as background color, line thickness, line style, and so on. Multiple plots per page are controlled by `!P.MULTI`. `!P.MULTI` is a five-element array of long integers. For most purposes, you should need to set only two of the values of `!P.MULTI`: the number of columns and rows of panes on a page. To start a new plotting page with two columns and three rows of panes, set

See Graphics System Variables procedure in IDL Reference Guide.

```
!P.MULTI = [0, 2, 3, 0, 0]
```

By default, IDL starts plotting in the upper left pane and automatically advances across each row as calls are made to `PLOT`, `CONTOUR`, and so on. The other elements of `!P.MULTI` are used to set the current plotting pane, to change the plotting order (that is, to plot by columns rather than rows), and to stack plots in the Z dimension. An example of a graph using a 2 × 2 arrangement can be seen in Figure 3.4.

The values in !P.MULTI are preserved until they are explicitly reset or the plotting device is changed. Therefore, when you have finished plotting a page with multiple plots, do not forget to set !P.MULTI back to zero!

```
!P.MULTI = 0
```

17.6 Summary

This chapter covers the basics of customizing line graphs using keywords with the PLOT and OPLOT commands:

- The plotting symbol is specified with the PSYM keyword.

- Lines connecting the plot symbols are turned on by making PSYM negative.

- The line style is specified with the LINESTYLE keyword.

- Axis scaling is controlled separately for each axis with the (XYZ)STYLE, (XYZ)RANGE, (XYZ)TICKS, and (XYZ)MINOR keywords.

Contour and Surface Plots

This chapter shows how to make contour and surface plots.

18.1 IDL Commands and Keywords

The following IDL commands and keywords are used for making contour and surface plots:

- CONTOUR procedure
- SURFACE procedure
- SHADE_SURF procedure

18.2 Contour Plots

Contour plots are one way to graphically represent the values of a function of two variables, such as $z(x, y)$. Familiar examples of contour plots are topographic maps used for outdoor activities. *Contours* or *isopleths* are lines that connect points of equal value (equal altitude in the case of a topographic map). Figure 18.1 illustrates the concept of contour plots.

Contour plots are drawn with the CONTOUR procedure. CONTOUR takes three positional parameters, z, x, and y, which can take several different forms. In this chapter we will cover only the simplest form, where z is a two-dimensional array, z(nx, ny). If x and y are omitted, CONTOUR will create independent coordinates x = 0, 1, ..., nx-1 and y = 0, 1, ..., ny-1. Generally, you will want to provide x and y coordinate arrays to correctly scale the plot axes.

See the CONTOUR procedure in *IDL Reference Guide*.

CONTOUR can also produce contour plots for irregularly distributed data, which is discussed in Chapter 24.

CONTOUR has many optional keyword parameters that enable you to control almost every aspect of the plot. CONTOUR-specific keywords are principally used to control properties of the contour lines (contour value, color, line width, line style, and labeling). Additionally, CONTOUR accepts most of the keywords accepted by PLOT.

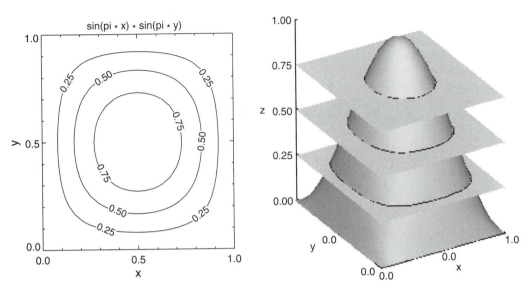

FIGURE 18.1 Contour plot of the function $z(x, y) = \sin(\pi x) \sin(\pi y)$. Contours are drawn at $z = 0.25, 0.5$, and 0.75. The right-hand panel illustrates that the contours are defined by the intersections between the surface $z = \sin(\pi x) \sin(\pi y)$ and the surfaces $z = 0.25, 0.5$, and 0.75. (CONTOUR1)

The following program illustrates some of the options available with CONTOUR keywords. The resulting plot is shown in Figure 18.2.

```
PRO CONTOUR2

COMPILE_OPT IDL2                      ;Set compiler options

WINDOW, XSIZE = 600, YSIZE = 600      ;Open graphics window
!P.MULTI = [0, 2, 2, 0, 0]           ;2 x 2 plot panes


nx = 25                               ;Number of x-grid points
ny = 25                               ;Number of y-grid points
x  = FINDGEN(nx)/(nx-1)               ;Compute 1-D x-coordinates
y  = FINDGEN(ny)/(ny-1)               ;Compute 1-D y-coordinates
xx = REBIN(x, nx, ny, /SAMPLE)        ;Expand x-coordinates to 2-D
yy = REBIN(REFORM(y, 1, ny), $        ;Expand y-coordinates to 2-D
        nx, ny, /SAMPLE)
z  = SIN(!PI*xx) * SIN(!PI*yy)        ;Compute z

CONTOUR, z, $                         ;All defaults
   TITLE = 'All defaults'


CONTOUR, z, x, y, $                   ;Coordinates provided
   TITLE = 'x and y coords'
```

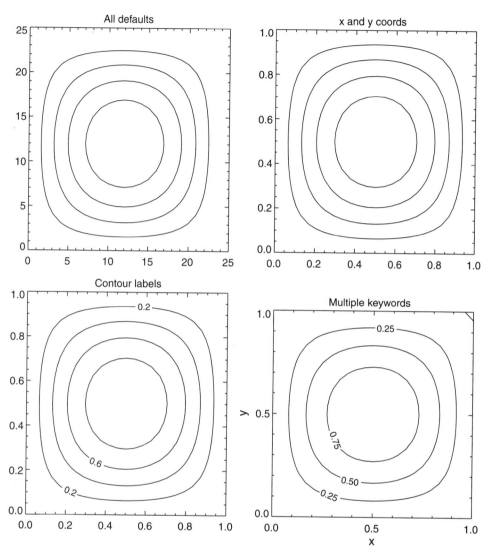

FIGURE 18.2 Contour plot of the function $z(x, y) = \sin(\pi x) \sin(\pi y)$ illustrating some of the options available with the CONTOUR procedure. (CONTOUR2_PS)

```
CONTOUR, z, x, y, /FOLLOW, $           ;Contour labels
   TITLE = 'Contour labels'

CONTOUR, z, x, y, /ISOTROPIC, $        ;Plot contour graph
   LEVELS   = 0.25*FINDGEN(20), $      ;Specify contour levels
   C_LABELS = REPLICATE(1, 20), $      ;Label all contour levels
   TITLE    = 'Multiple keywords', $
   XTITLE   = 'x', $
   XSTYLE   = 1, $
   XRANGE   = [0.0, 1.0], $
   XTICKS   = 2, $
```

```
    XMINOR   = 5, $
    YTITLE   = 'y', $
    YSTYLE   = 1, $
    YRANGE   = [0.0, 1.0], $
    YTICKS   = 2, $
    YMINOR   = 5

!P.MULTI = 0                              ;Reset !P.MULTI

END
```

The example program CONTOUR2 illustrates a good way to develop a program that uses a complex procedure such as CONTOUR. Begin by using the defaults, and then add keywords as needed to produce the plot that you desire.

Contouring programs work best with *smooth* data. The following program illustrates what happens when you try to contour noisy data. The resulting plots are shown in Figure 18.3.

```
PRO CONTOUR3

COMPILE_OPT IDL2                         ;Set compiler options

WINDOW, XSIZE = 400, YSIZE = 400         ;Open graphics window
!P.MULTI = [0, 2, 2, 0, 0]               ;2 x 2 panes

... create z-array (see CONTOUR2)

seed  = 17                               ;Pseudorandom number seed
noise = RANDOMN(seed, nx, ny)            ;Compute noise

CONTOUR, z +  0.01*noise, /FOLLOW, $     ;Plot 1
   TITLE = 'Very weak noise'
CONTOUR, z +  0.10*noise, /FOLLOW, $     ;Plot 2
   TITLE = 'Weak noise'
CONTOUR, z +  1.00*noise, /FOLLOW, $     ;Plot 3
   TITLE = 'Moderate noise'
CONTOUR, z + 10.00*noise, /FOLLOW, $     ;Plot 4
   TITLE = 'Strong noise'

!P.MULTI = 0                             ;Reset !P.MULTI

END
```

As this illustrates, CONTOUR works best for smooth functions. In the third and fourth plots (moderate and strong noise), the shape of the underlying function z becomes increasingly difficult to discern.

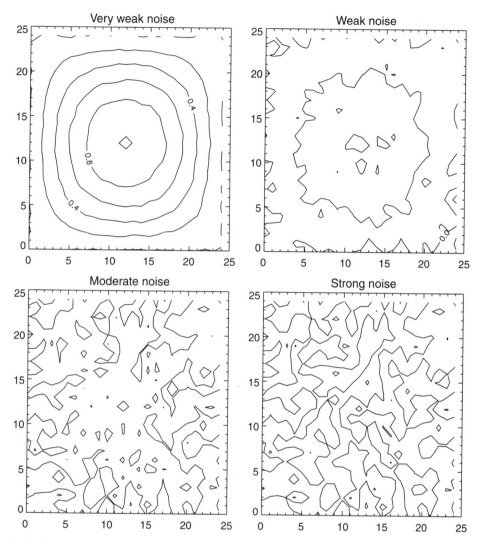

FIGURE 18.3   Contour plot of the function $z(x, y) = \sin(\pi x) \sin(\pi y) + R$, where R is a random normal variable, illustrating how noise affects the graphs produced by CONTOUR. (CONTOUR3_PS)

18.3   Surface Plots

A second method for plotting a function of two variables is what is commonly referred to as a *wire-mesh* plot. IDL can draw wire-mesh plots using the SURFACE procedure. The following program repeats the previous plots of noisy data using the SURFACE procedure. The resulting plots are shown in Figure 18.4.

See the SURFACE procedure in *IDL Reference Guide*.

```
PRO SURFACE1

COMPILE_OPT IDL2                        ;Set compiler options
```

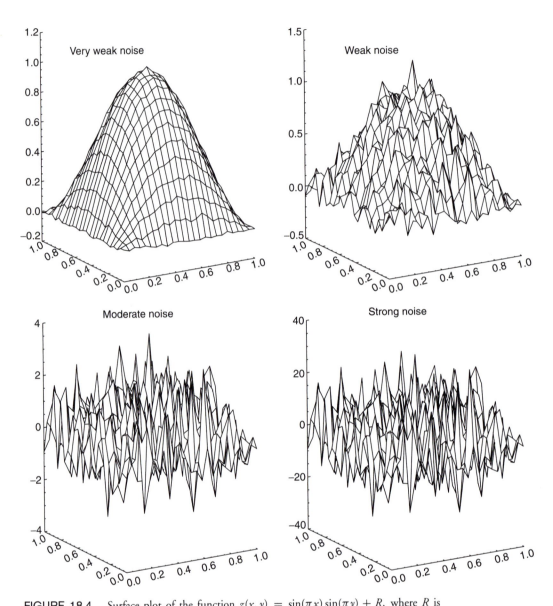

FIGURE 18.4   Surface plot of the function $z(x, y) = \sin(\pi x) \sin(\pi y) + R$, where R is a random normal variable, illustrating how noise affects the graphs produced by SURFACE. (SURFACE1_PS)

```
WINDOW, XSIZE = 400, YSIZE = 400     ;Open graphics window
!P.MULTI = [0, 2, 2, 0, 0]           ;2 x 2 panes


... create z-array (see CONTOUR1)


seed  = 17                           ;Pseudorandom number seed
noise = RANDOMN(seed, nx, ny)        ;Compute noise
```

```
SURFACE, z +  0.01*noise, x, y, $  ;Plot 1
   TITLE = 'Very weak noise'
SURFACE, z +  0.10*noise, x, y, $  ;Plot 2
   TITLE = 'Weak noise'
SURFACE, z +  1.00*noise, x, y, $  ;Plot 3
   TITLE = 'Moderate noise'
SURFACE, z + 10.00*noise, x, y, $  ;Plot 4
   TITLE = 'Strong noise'

!P.MULTI = 0                           ;Reset !P.MULTI

END
```

Surface plots can be better than contour plots for noisy data. Comparing Figure 18.4 with 18.3, you can at least get a feel for the shape of the function z when it is shown as a surface. SURFACE has keyword parameters to control the viewing angles of the plot.

Surface plots do have disadvantages compared to contour plots. For one thing, part of the surface plot is almost always hidden. For another, with contour plots you can usually estimate numerical values of z, which is considerably more difficult with wire mesh plots.

18.4   Shaded Surface Plots

A third method for plotting a function of two variables is a smooth *rendered* surface, which can be plotted with the SHADE_SURF procedure. A third version of the noisy plots is shown in Figure 18.5.

See the SHADE_SURF procedure in *IDL Reference Guide.*

```
PRO SHADE_SURF1

COMPILE_OPT IDL2                       ;Set compiler options

WINDOW, XSIZE = 400, YSIZE = 400       ;Open graphics window
!P.MULTI = [0, 2, 2, 0, 0]             ;2 x 2 panes

... create z-array (see CONTOUR1)

seed  = 17                             ;Create pseudorandom numbers
noise = RANDOMN(seed, nx, ny)          ;Compute noise

SHADE_SURF, z +  0.01*noise, x, y, $  ;Plot 1
   TITLE = 'Very weak noise'
SHADE_SURF, z +  0.10*noise, x, y, $  ;Plot 2
   TITLE = 'Weak noise'
```

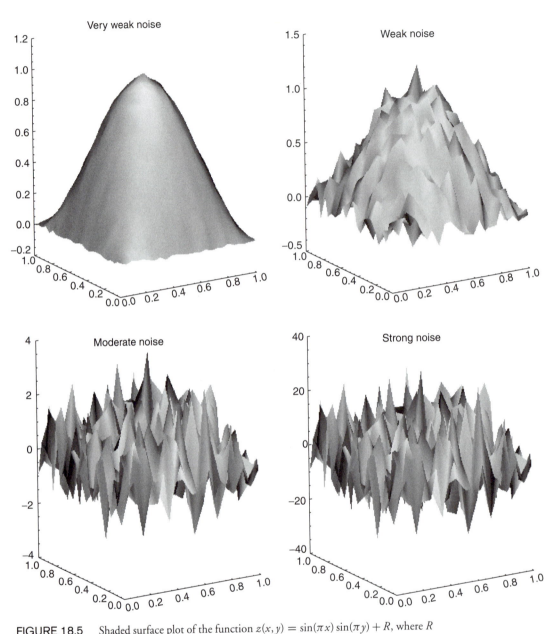

FIGURE 18.5   Shaded surface plot of the function $z(x, y) = \sin(\pi x)\sin(\pi y) + R$, where R is a random normal variable, illustrating how noise affects the graphs produced by SHADE_SURF. (SHADE_SURF_1_PS)

```
SHADE_SURF, z +  1.00*noise, x, y, $   ;Plot 3
   TITLE = 'Moderate noise'
SHADE_SURF, z + 10.00*noise, x, y, $   ;Plot 4
   TITLE = 'Strong noise'

!P.MULTI = 0                           ;Reset !P.MULTI


END
```

The XSURFACE procedure can be used to interactively rotate SURFACE and SHADE_SURF plots.

18.5 Summary

This chapter has covered the basics of plotting contour, surface, and shaded surface plots using CONTOUR, SURFACE, and SHADE_SURF:

- When using these plotting routines, start by using the default options. Gradually add options to get the final plot you desire. Some trial and error is often necessary to get all of the details of contour and surface plots correct.

Mapping

This chapter shows how to plots maps using IDL. Mapping the spherical Earth onto a flat surface requires compromises. Different map *projections* can preserve directions, distances, areas, or shapes, but not all four simultaneously. This chapter contains examples of map projections that are commonly used to plot Earth-referenced data.[1]

19.1 IDL Commands and Keywords

The following IDL commands and keywords are used for drawing maps and setting up the mapping transformation:

- `MAP_SET` procedure
- `MAP_GRID` procedure
- `MAP_CONTINENTS` procedure

19.2 Drawing Maps

19.2.1 Setting Up the Map Projection

IDL can plot maps using a wide variety of map projections. Once the mathematical transformation for the map projection is set up, data can be superimposed on the maps using contours, images, or symbols. The available map projections are listed in Table 19.1.

The map projection is selected with the `MAP_SET` procedure. `MAP_SET` can take three optional, positional parameters, `POLAT`, `POLON`, and `ROT`. The first two parameters specify the latitude and longitude of the point on the Earth's surface that is mapped to the center of the map. The third parameter specifies the rotation of the map around that point. Some projections have additional keywords associated with them to set specific properties of those projections.

See the `MAP_SET` procedure in *IDL Reference Guide.*

`MAP_SET` can also draw latitude-longitude grids and various boundary data on the maps (continental outlines, rivers, etc.). These options are controlled

---

1   The U.S. Geological Survey has a web page illustrating many different map projections at `http://erg.usgs.gov/isb/pubs/MapProjections/projections.html`

TABLE 19.1   Map projections available in IDL and keywords.

Name	Keyword
Aitoff	/AITOFF
Albers equal-area conic	/ALBERS
Azimuthal equidistant	/AZIMUTHAL
Lambert conformal conic	/CONIC
Cylindrical equidistant	/CYLINDRICAL
Gnomonic	/GNOMIC
Goode's homolosine	/GOODESHOMOLOSINE
Hammer-Aitoff equal area	/HAMMER
Lambert azimuthal equal area	/LAMBERT
Mercator	/MERCATOR
Miller cylindrical	/MILLER_CYLINDRICAL
Mollweide	/MOLLWEIDE
Orthographic	/ORTHOGRAPHIC
Robinson pseudo-cylindrical	/ROBINSON
Satellite	/SATELLITE
Sinusoidal	/SINUSOIDAL
Stereographic	/STEREOGRAPHIC
Transverse Mercator	/TRANSVERSE_MERCATOR

with MAP_SET keywords. Alternatively, grids and boundaries can be added in separate steps by using the MAP_GRID and MAP_CONTINENTS procedures after the map projection is established by MAP_SET. These procedures allow you to control the order in which data, boundaries, and grids are drawn. Among other things, this permits boundaries and grids to be superimposed on top of data, such as satellite images.

See the MAP_GRID and MAP_CONTINENTS procedures in *IDL Reference Guide*.

Some map projections can display the entire globe, whereas others can display only a portion of the globe. When plotting complete global data, two useful projections are the cylindrical equidistant and Hammer projections. The Mercator projection should generally be avoided because it leads to large distortions at high latitudes and is incapable of plotting data near the poles.

19.2.2   Cylindrical Equidistant Projection

The cylindrical equidistant projection is particularly simple. Longitude is plotted on the abscissa and latitude on the ordinate. Both scales are linear. Figure 19.1 shows four examples of cylindrical equidistant projections. The title of each map gives the values of POLAT, POLON, and ROT used. The MAP_SET calls used to create each map are given below. The complete program used to create Figure 19.1 is MAP_CYLINDRICAL_PS.

```
MAP_SET,  0.0,  0.0, /CYLINDRICAL, /CONTINENTS, $
   TITLE = 'POLAT = 0.0, POLON =  0.0, ROT = 0.0'

MAP_SET,  0.0, 90.0, /CYLINDRICAL, /ISOTROPIC, /CONTINENTS, $
   /ADVANCE, /NOBORDER, /GRID, GLINESTYLE = 0, $
   TITLE = 'POLAT = 0.0, POLON = 90.0, ROT = 0.0'
```

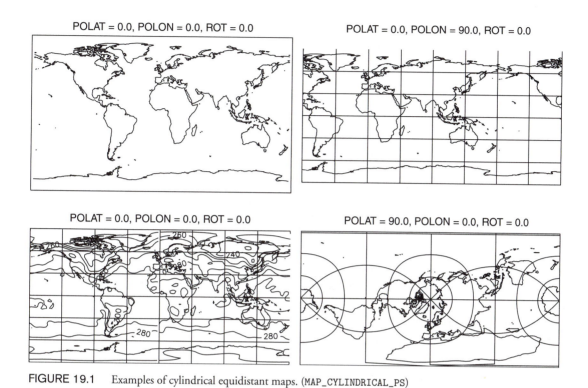

FIGURE 19.1 Examples of cylindrical equidistant maps. (`MAP_CYLINDRICAL_PS`)

```
MAP_SET, 0.0,    0.0, /CYLINDRICAL, /ISOTROPIC, /CONTINENTS, $
   /ADVANCE, /NOBORDER, /GRID, GLINESTYLE = 0, $
   TITLE = 'POLAT =  0.0, POLON =    0.0, ROT = 0.0'
CONTOUR, T.values[*,*,0], T.x.values, T.y.values, $
   /OVERPLOT, /FOLLOW, LEVELS = 200.0 + 10.0*FINDGEN(20)

MAP_SET, 90.0,   0.0, /CYLINDRICAL, /ISOTROPIC, /CONTINENTS, $
   /ADVANCE, /NOBORDER, /GRID, GLINESTYLE = 0, $
   TITLE = 'POLAT = 90.0, POLON =    0.0, ROT = 0.0'
```

In each case, the projection type is specified with the /CYLINDRICAL keyword. If the /ISOTROPIC keyword is omitted, as in the first example, MAP_SET *stretches* the projection to fill the available space. This can lead to inconsistency between the horizontal and vertical scales. Including the /ISOTROPIC keyword ensures that the horizontal and vertical scales are the same. (For most map projections, it is unusual *not* to include the /ISOTROPIC keyword.)

These examples illustrate that the center of the map can be adjusted with the POLON parameter. Normally, for a cylindrical equidistant projection, POLAT is set to 0. If not, as in the lower right panel of Figure 19.1, the projection can look rather odd (although it is perfectly valid).

Normally, MAP_SET behaves like PLOT or CONTOUR. When called, it erases the current window or starts a new page. In these examples, we are using the !P.MULTI system variable to plot four maps per page. In order to cause MAP_SET to advance to the next pane without erasing the previous plots, the /ADVANCE keyword is used. This keyword is necessary only if you are using !P.MULTI.

For some reason known only to RSI, MAP_SET draws a rectangular border around each map, *slightly larger* than the map area. The border can be omitted by using the /NOBORDER keyword. As you can see in the examples, IDL sometimes has problems drawing latitude-longitude gridlines at the edges of maps. Adding the /HORIZON keyword helps, but does not solve the problem in all cases. The only good solution that I have found for cylindrical equidistant projections is to draw the boundary directly using the PLOTS procedure. MAP_SET also does not label gridlines in a very attractive manner. Once again, the only solution is to directly label grid lines using XYOUTS, rather than using the built-in labelling options in MAP_SET.

The cylindrical equidistant projection exaggerates areas at higher latitudes, although not as severely as the Mercator projection. One advantage of the cylindrical equidistant projection is that it is easy to read values at a particular latitude and longitude. This is illustrated in the lower-left panel of Figure 19.1, in which the surface air temperature (in K) on January 1, 2001 is contoured atop the map. The contours are drawn using the CONTOUR procedure with the /OVERPLOT keyword. /OVERPLOT tells CONTOUR to not erase the screen and to draw the contours using the existing coordinate system (the map projection in this case).

19.2.3 Hammer Equal-Area and Conic Projections

An alternative global projection that does not distort areas at high latitudes is the Hammer equal-area projection. Examples of the Hammer projection are given in three of the panels of Figure 19.2. (The complete program to create these maps is MAP_HAMMER_PS.)

```
MAP_SET, /HAMMER, /ISOTROPIC, /HORIZON, $
   TITLE = 'POLAT =  0.0, POLON =   0.0, ROT = 0.0'
MAP_CONTINENTS, FILL = 1, COLOR = COLOR_24(192)
MAP_GRID, LATDEL = 30, LONDEL = 90, GLINESTYLE = 0

MAP_SET,  0.0, -90.0, /HAMMER, /ISOTROPIC, /HORIZON, $
    /NOBORDER, /ADVANCE, $
   TITLE = 'POLAT =  0.0, POLON = -90.0, ROT = 0.0'
MAP_CONTINENTS, COLOR = COLOR_24(192), FILL = 1
CONTOUR, T.values[*,*,0], T.x.values, T.y.values, /OVERPLOT, $
   /FOLLOW, LEVELS = 200.0 + 10.0*FINDGEN(20)
MAP_GRID, LATDEL = 30, LONDEL = 90, GLINESTYLE = 0
```

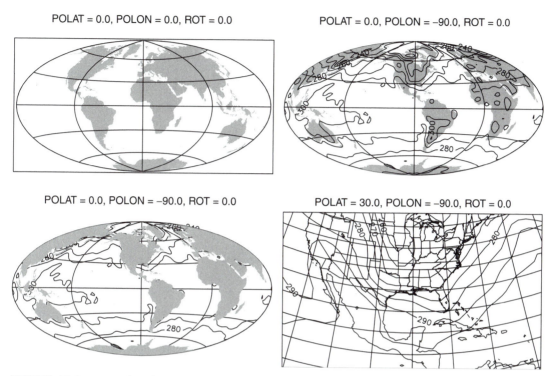

FIGURE 19.2 Examples of Hammer equal-area (top and lower left) and conic map projections. (MAP_HAMMER_PS)

```
MAP_SET,  0.0, -90.0, /HAMMER, /ISOTROPIC, /HORIZON, $
   /NOBORDER, /ADVANCE, $
   TITLE = 'POLAT =  0.0, POLON = -90.0, ROT = 0.0'
CONTOUR, T.values[*,*,0], T.x.values, T.y.values, /OVERPLOT, $
   /FOLLOW, LEVELS = 200.0 + 10.0*FINDGEN(20)
MAP_GRID, GLINESTYLE = 0, LATDEL = 30, LONDEL = 90
MAP_CONTINENTS, COLOR = COLOR_24(192), FILL = 1

MAP_SET,  30.0, -90.0, /CONIC, SCALE = 1.0E8, /ISOTROPIC, $
   /GRID, GLINESTYLE = 0, /CONTINENTS, /USA, /ADVANCE, $
   TITLE = 'POLAT = 30.0, POLON = -90.0, ROT = 0.0'
CONTOUR, T.values[*,*,0], T.x.values, T.y.values, /OVERPLOT, $
   /FOLLOW, LEVELS = 200.0 + 5.0*FINDGEN(30)
```

This example also shows how to plot filled continents, rather than simply outlining the continental boundaries. The filled continents are generated by setting FILL = 1 and COLOR = COLOR_24(192) (light gray) in MAP_CONTINENTS. (COLOR_24 is not a built-in IDL routine. It is included with the example programs for this book. For more information on using color, see Chapter 21.)

The lower left panel illustrates what can happen if the data, the continents, and the grids are not plotted in the correct order. Here, the filled continents obscure the data and grid lines.

The lower right panel in Figure 19.2 is an example of a *conic* projection. As the name suggests, conic projections project the spherical Earth onto a cone, which can then be cut and laid flat without stretching. Conic projections are frequently used for regional maps. They minimize the distortion of the map by projecting onto a surface that is tangent to Earth's surface near the region of interest.

19.2.4 Azimuthal-Equidistant Projection

In atmospheric and oceanic applications, we often want to plot maps of either the northern or southern hemisphere, usually to focus on data in the middle and high latitudes. There are several types of *polar* projections to choose from. Two that are frequently used are the azimuthal-equidistant and orthographic projections. Examples of the azimuthal-equidistant projection are given in Figure 19.3. (The calls to the CONTOUR procedure that are used to plot the temperature contours are omitted in the IDL listing below. The full program can be found in MAP_AZIMUTHAL_PS.)

```
MAP_SET,  90.0, 0.0,   0.0, /AZIMUTHAL, /ISOTROPIC, $
   LIMIT = [0.0, -180.0, 90.0, 180.0], /CONTINENTS, $
   /GRID, GLINESTYLE = 0, LATDEL = 30, LONDEL = 90, $
   TITLE = 'POLAT =  90.0, POLON = 0.0, ROT =   0.0'

MAP_SET,  90.0, 0.0, -90.0, /AZIMUTHAL, /ISOTROPIC, $
   LIMIT = [0.0, -180.0, 90.0, 180.0], /CONTINENTS, $
   /GRID, GLINESTYLE = 0, LATDEL = 30, LONDEL = 90, $
   /NOBORDER, /ADVANCE, $
   TITLE = 'POLAT =  90.0, POLON = 0.0, ROT = -90.0'

MAP_SET, -90.0, 0.0,   0.0, /AZIMUTHAL, /ISOTROPIC, $
   LIMIT = [-90.0, -180.0, 0.0, 180.0], /CONTINENTS, $
   /GRID, GLINESTYLE = 0, LATDEL = 30, LONDEL = 90, $
   /NOBORDER, /ADVANCE, $
   TITLE = 'POLAT = -90.0, POLON = 0.0, ROT =   0.0'

MAP_SET, -90.0, 0.0,  90.0, /AZIMUTHAL, /ISOTROPIC, $
   LIMIT = [-90.0, -180.0, 0.0, 180.0], /CONTINENTS, $
   /GRID, GLINESTYLE = 0, LATDEL = 30, LONDEL = 90, $
   /NOBORDER, /ADVANCE, $
   TITLE = 'POLAT = -90.0, POLON = 0.0, ROT =  90.0'
```

The LIMIT keyword is used to specify the area of the globe to be plotted. The four elements of the LIMIT array specify the minimum latitude, minimum

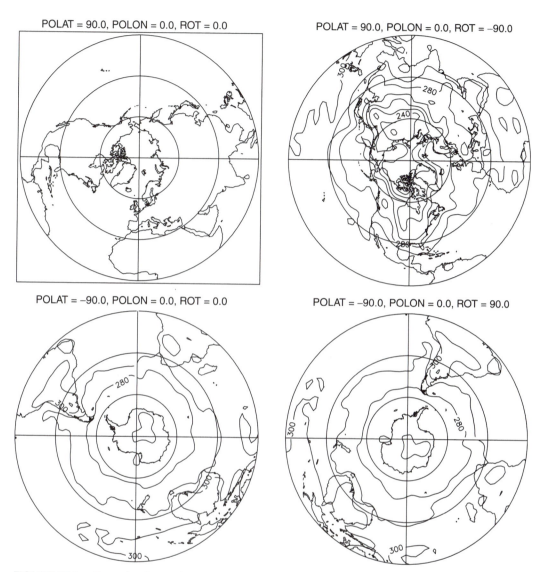

FIGURE 19.3   Examples of azimuthal-equidistant maps. Three of the maps include contours displaying the surface temperature field on January 1, 2001 in Kelvins. (MAP_AZIMUTHAL_PS)

longitude, maximum latitude, and maximum longitude of the area to be plotted.

The /ISOTROPIC keyword is required for azimuthal projections (unless the plotting area happens to be exactly square). These examples illustrate the use of the ROT parameter to orient the map as desired, for European or American audiences, for example.

Notice that the latitude circles are equally spaced in the azimuthal-equidistant projection. The azimuthal-equidistant projection is essentially the same as a standard two-dimensional polar coordinate system. The angular coordinate is longitude, and the radial coordinate is the colatitude (angle measured from the pole). This projection distorts areas to some degree, but makes it possible to see the entire hemisphere, including the tropics.

19.2.5 Orthographic Projection

The other polar projection illustrated here is the orthographic projection.
Examples of the orthographic maps are given in Figure 19.4. (The calls
to the CONTOUR procedure that are used to plot the temperature contours
are omitted in the IDL listing below. The full program can be found in
MAP_ORTHOGRAPHIC_PS.)

```
MAP_SET,  90.0, 0.0,   0.0, /ORTHOGRAPHIC, /ISOTROPIC, $
   /GRID, GLINESTYLE = 0, /CONTINENTS, $
   LIMIT = [0.0, -180.0, 90.0, 180.0], LATDEL = 30, LONDEL = 90, $
   TITLE = 'POLAT =  90.0, POLON = 0.0, ROT =   0.0'
```

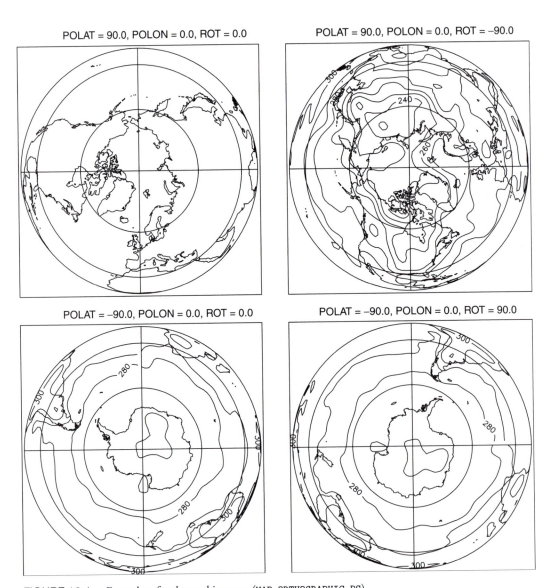

FIGURE 19.4   Examples of orthographic maps. (MAP_ORTHOGRAPHIC_PS)

```
MAP_SET,  90.0, 0.0, -90.0, , /ORTHOGRAPHIC, /ISOTROPIC, $
   /GRID, GLINESTYLE = 0, /CONTINENTS, /ADVANCE, $
   LIMIT = [0.0, -180.0, 90.0, 180.0], LATDEL = 30, LONDEL = 90, $
   TITLE = 'POLAT =  90.0, POLON = 0.0, ROT = -90.0'

MAP_SET, -90.0, 0.0,   0.0, /ORTHOGRAPHIC, /ISOTROPIC, $
   /GRID, GLINESTYLE = 0, /CONTINENTS, /ADVANCE, $
   LIMIT = [-90.0, -180.0, 0.0, 180.0], LATDEL = 30, LONDEL = 90, $
   TITLE = 'POLAT = -90.0, POLON = 0.0, ROT =   0.0'

MAP_SET, -90.0, 0.0,  90.0, /ORTHOGRAPHIC, /ISOTROPIC, $
   /GRID, GLINESTYLE = 0, /CONTINENTS, /ADVANCE, $
   LIMIT = [-90.0, -180.0, 0.0, 180.0], LATDEL = 30, LONDEL = 90, $
   TITLE = 'POLAT = -90.0, POLON = 0.0, ROT =  90.0'
```

Note that in the orthographic projection the latitude circles are closer together near the equator. This projection is not suitable for viewing the tropics, but works well for regions poleward of about 30° latitude. A third polar projection that is sometimes used is the stereographic projection. It can provide better display of lower latitude regions when a polar projection is desired. Usage is very similar to azimuthal and orthographic projections.

19.3   Contour Plots on Maps

A common use of maps is to plot contour maps of geophysical quantities. Figure 19.5 shows northern and southern hemisphere maps of surface temperature.

```
MAP_SET,  90.0, 0.0, -90.0, TITLE = 'Surface Temperature (K)', $
   /AZIMUTHAL, /ISOTROPIC, LIMIT = [0.0, -180.0, 90.0, 180.0], $
   /NOBORDER, /ADVANCE
MAP_CONTINENTS, COLOR = COLOR_24(192), FILL = 1
CONTOUR, T.values[*,*,0], T.x.values, T.y.values, $
   /OVERPLOT, /FOLLOW, LEVELS = 200.0 + 5.0*FINDGEN(20)
MAP_GRID, GLINESTYLE = 0, LATDEL = 30, LONDEL = 90

MAP_SET, -90.0, 0.0,  90.0, TITLE = 'Surface Temperature (K)', $
   /AZIMUTHAL, /ISOTROPIC, LIMIT = [-90.0, -180.0, 0.0, 180.0], $
   /NOBORDER, /ADVANCE
MAP_CONTINENTS, COLOR = COLOR_24(192), FILL = 1
CONTOUR, T.values[*,*,0], T.x.values, T.y.values, $
   /OVERPLOT, /FOLLOW, LEVELS = 200.0 + 5.0*FINDGEN(20)
MAP_GRID, GLINESTYLE = 0, LATDEL = 30, LONDEL = 90
```

The order in which maps, contours, and gridlines are drawn can be important. In these examples, the map projection is defined with MAP_SET, then

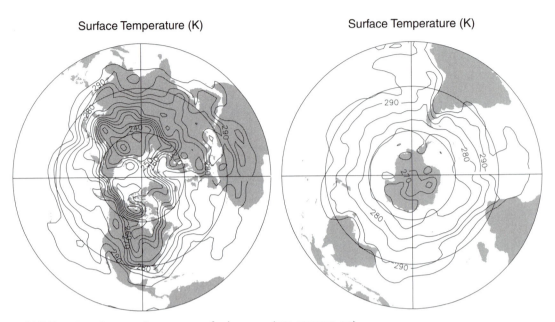

FIGURE 19.5   Contours drawn on top of polar maps. (`MAP_CONTOUR_PS`)

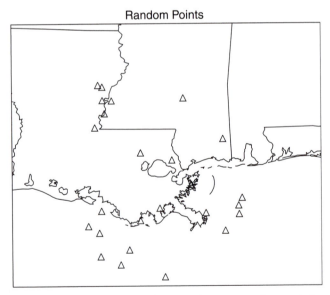

FIGURE 19.6   This map illustrates the use of `PLOTS` to plot symbols on a map.
(`MAP_PLOTS_PS`)

continents are drawn with MAP_CONTINENTS. Next, data are drawn with CONTOUR, and finally the grid lines are drawn with MAP_GRID. This ensures that the continents do not cover (obscure) the data or grid lines.

19.4 Other Plots on Maps

Maps can also be used to plot point data. Figure 19.6 shows 25 randomly distributed points plotted on a local map.

```
MAP_SET,  30.0, -90.0, TITLE = 'Random Points', $
   /CONIC, SCALE = 5.0E6, /ISOTROPIC, /HIRES, /USA
PLOTS, x, y, PSYM = 5, SYMSIZE = 2
```

Markers are plotted by using the PLOTS command. PLOTS is similar to the PLOT command, but it does not draw axes or set up the plotting transformation. It assumes that the plotting coordinates have already been defined.

See the PLOTS procedure in *IDL Reference Guide.*

19.5 Summary

This chapter covers the basics of plotting data on maps using MAP_SET, MAP_GRID, MAP_CONTINENTS, and CONTOUR or PLOTS.

Printing Graphics

This chapter shows you how to send graphics output to a printer or file.

20.1   IDL Commands and Keywords

The following IDL commands and keywords are used to direct graphics output to the PS (PostScript) or PRINTER devices:

- SET_PLOT procedure

- PS_ON procedure

- PS_OFF procedure

- DEVICE procedure

- DIALOG_PRINTERSETUP function

- PRINTER_ON procedure

- PRINTER_OFF procedure

20.2   Device Drivers

Each time you issue an IDL graphics command, IDL sends the appropriate graphics instructions to intermediate software called a *device driver*, which translates the IDL instructions into commands that the current device can understand. The device drivers available in IDL are described in *IDL Graphics Devices* in *IDL Reference Guide*. When you start IDL, the graphics device is set to the default device for your system. For Unix and Mac OS X systems it is the X-Windows (X) device. For Windows systems it is WIN. Issuing the PLOT command causes a window to automatically appear on your screen and a line graph to be drawn.

> See the X and WIN devices in *IDL Reference Guide*.

To print graphics output, you must select the device driver for a *hardcopy device*, typically a printer, before running the graphics commands. The device is selected with the SET_PLOT command. Once the device is selected, the DEVICE procedure can be used to control the various options for the device,

> See the SET_PLOT and DEVICE procedures in *IDL Reference Guide*.

such as paper size, font, and so on. IDL includes device drivers for a number of different output devices. This chapter discusses the basics of two of those devices: the PS (PostScript) and PRINTER devices. PostScript is a language developed by Adobe, Inc. specifically for printing graphics. Because many printers can understand the PostScript language, the PRINTER device can also be used to generate PostScript output.

See the PS and PRINTER devices in *IDL Reference Guide.*

In an ideal world it would be easy to write an IDL graphics program that worked with any graphics device. In reality, each graphics device has capabilities or limitations that do not translate well to other devices. Some devices are black-and-white only, some use 8-bit color, some use 24-bit color, and so on. To make attractive graphical output on different devices, often you must customize your graphics programs for each graphics device you use. In most cases this is a straightforward task. To keep things simple, we will not cover all of the features of the PS and PRINTER devices in this chapter. For example, we will not use PostScript fonts with the PS device or Truetype fonts with the PRINTER device. Instead, we will use the default built-in IDL fonts (also called *vector fonts* or *Hershey fonts*). For more information on customizing graphics, see the books by Gumley and Fanning listed in the bibliography.

20.3 The PostScript Device

The PS device driver creates a file that contains graphics commands in the PostScript language. PostScript is widely used to print text and graphics on laser printers and other hardcopy devices. To create PostScript output, you select the PS device, issue IDL graphics commands, close the PS device, and then send the PostScript file to a printer. You can also save the file for later printing or editing.

An important advantage of PostScript output is the variety of software tools that can work with PostScript files. Some are commercial software; some are freeware or shareware. For example, there are software tools to convert PostScript files to Portable Document Format (PDF) files. PDF files can be viewed with the free Adobe Acrobat Reader software and are commonly used to send graphics electronically. Adobe Illustrator (and other drawing programs) can be used to open and edit PostScript files interactively. This is very convenient when you need to make changes to an IDL graph to make it suitable for publication or presentation.

With a few exceptions, the figures in this book were generated using standard IDL graphics commands and the PS device driver. In a few cases the PostScript files were opened in Adobe Illustrator and modified slightly. The PostScript files were then converted to PDF files and imported directly into the book. Depending on your software and printing requirements, other workflows with PostScript files are possible. The result is high-quality output that can be easily used with other programs, including standard word processing programs such as Microsoft Word.

20.3.1 Using the PS Device

The PS device has a sometimes confusing set of options that are controlled with the DEVICE command. To ease the process of using the PS device, two procedures are included with the example programs: PS_ON and PS_OFF. These programs are simplified versions of the PSON and PSOFF procedures described in *Practical IDL Programming* by Gumley. The original procedures by Gumley can be downloaded from http://www.gumley.com.

IDL graphics programs are usually written so that the default behavior is to draw graphics in a window on the screen using the X or WIN device. An optional keyword is used to tell the program to send the graphics output to a PostScript file instead. The example program below, taken from Chapter 17, shows how to use the PS_ON and PS_OFF procedures:

```
PRO LINEGRAPH3, PS = ps

;+
; Name:
;       LINEGRAPH3
; Purpose:
;       Plots a simple line graph and optionally saves a PostScript file.
; Calling sequence:
;       LINEGRAPH3
; Inputs:
;       None.
; Output:
;       Line graph and optional PostScript file.
; Keywords:
;       PS : If set, save the PostScript output to linegraph3.ps.
; Author and history:
;       Kenneth P. Bowman, 2004.
;-

COMPILE_OPT IDL2                             ;Set compiler options

xsize  = 4.0                                 ;Width of graphic
ysize  = 4.0                                 ;Height of graphic
dpi    = 100                                 ;Screen dots per inch
margin = 0.1                                 ;Margins of graphic

IF KEYWORD_SET(ps) THEN BEGIN
   psfile = !Bowman + 'ps/linegraph3.ps'     ;PostScript file name
   PS_ON, FILENAME = psfile, MARGIN = margin, $  ;Set device to PostScript
      PAGE_SIZE = [xsize, ysize], /INCHES
ENDIF ELSE BEGIN
   WINDOW, XSIZE = dpi*xsize, YSIZE = dpi*ysize   ;Open graphics window
ENDELSE
```

```
x = FINDGEN(11)                        ;Abscissa
y = SQRT(x)                            ;Ordinate
PLOT, x, y                             ;Draw line graph
OPLOT, x, 2.0*y                        ;Overplot second line

IF KEYWORD_SET(ps) THEN PS_OFF         ;End PostScript output

END
```

The first four lines of the program define the size of the graphics window and the printed output. If the PS keyword is *not* set, like this,

```
IDL> linegraph3
```

a screen window is opened. In this case the window size is 400 × 400 pixels, as specified by the XSIZE and YSIZE keywords of the WINDOW procedure. A simple line graph is drawn in the window using PLOT and OPLOT. Because the PS keyword is not set, the PS_OFF procedure is not called at the end of the program.

If the PS keyword *is* set, like this,

```
IDL> linegraph3, /ps
Starting PS output to /Users/bowman/idl/bowman/ps/linegraph3.ps
PS output ended.
```

the device is switched to PS by the PS_ON procedure. The keyword parameters of PS_ON allow you to specify the name of the PostScript output file, the size of the output page, the margin size, the units, and other options. See the PS_ON program file for details. As before, the program draws a simple line graph. Before exiting, the PS device is closed and the previous device is restored by calling the PS_OFF procedure. In this example the PostScript output is written to the file name stored in the variable psfile. If no file name is provided, the PostScript output is written to the file idl.ps in your current directory (usually your home directory).

Using the PS device for color output is covered in Chapter 21.

20.4 The PRINTER Device

In addition to the PS device, IDL also supports the PRINTER device, which can interact directly with printers connected to your computer or network. Before IDL can use a printer, your computer must know how to talk to it. Follow the instructions that came with your printer, refer to the operating system documentation, or see your system administrator for help configuring a printer at the operating system level.

Once your computer is aware of a printer, the next step is to set up your PRINTER device inside IDL. Details of configuring printers within IDL are found in *Printing in IDL* in *Using IDL*.

20.4.1 Setting Up the PRINTER Device for Windows

On Windows systems, IDL interacts with the standard operating system printing facilities. For more information about configuring printers under Windows, see the Windows documentation.

20.4.2 Setting Up the PRINTER Device for Mac OS X and Unix

On Unix and Mac OS X systems, IDL uses the Xprinter technology from Bristol Systems. The following is an outline of how to configure a printer to create a PostScript file as output. You can also use the PRINTER device to send output directly to an available printer. Additional information on configuring printers can be found in *Using IDL*.

In the following instructions the printer is assumed to be named myprinter. You should replace myprinter with the name of your printer wherever it is used. The first step in using the PRINTER device is to make IDL aware of that printer. This is done with the DIALOG_PRINTERSETUP function. As the name indicates, DIALOG_PRINTERSETUP displays an interactive dialog box that allows you to configure your printer. To set up your printer, enter the following command (make sure X-Windows is running first):

See the DIALOG_PRINTERSETUP procedure in *IDL Reference Guide*.

```
IDL> r = DIALOG_PRINTERSETUP()
```

This function requires no arguments, so no arguments are provided between the parentheses.

DIALOG_PRINTERSETUP opens a dialog box that allows you to configure your printer. The organization of DIALOG_PRINTERSETUP is rather difficult to follow. The procedure below works for me, but I cannot guarantee that it will work on all systems. If you have problems, see the documentation for DIALOG_PRINTERSETUP.

1. At the top, select **Printer Specific**. Click the **Install** button in the lower right.

2. In the new (second) dialog box that appears, select **Add Printer**. A third dialog box appears.

3. From the list on the left side, select **Generic PostScript Printer**.

4. Click **Define New Port**, which opens a fourth dialog box.

5. Click the **Spooler** button at the bottom of the dialog; select myprinter =lp -d myprinter.

6. Click **Add-Replace**, then **Dismiss**.

7. From the list on the right side, select `myprinter =lp -d myprinter`.

8. In the third dialog box, click **Add Selected**, followed by **Dismiss**. The third dialog box closes.

9. You should now see something like **Generic PostScript Printer on** `myprinter` in the list of printers.

10. Click on that line to highlight it, then click the **Dismiss** button.

11. Finally, in the first dialog box click the **Options** button. This opens a dialog box with a list of pop-up menus.

12. Open the first menu and select the printer that you just added. Click **OK** and then **OK** again to close the first dialog box.

You can use the `DIALOG_PRINTJOB` function to control compression, scaling, and the number of copies printed with the `PRINTER` device. It is used in a similar fashion to the `DIALOG_PRINTERSETUP` function:

```
IDL> r = DIALOG_PRINTJOB()
```

20.4.3 Using the `PRINTER` **Device**

As with the PS device, the `PRINTER` device has a number of options. To simplify the process of using the `PRINTER` device, two procedures are included with the example programs: `PRINTER_ON` and `PRINTER_OFF`. These procedures are based on `PRINTON` and `PRINTOFF` from Liam Gumley's book, *Practical IDL Programming*. The original procedures by Gumley can be downloaded from `http://www.gumley.com`.

The `PRINTER_ON` procedure switches from the current device to `PRINTER`. `PRINTER_OFF` sends the output to the selected printer and switches back to the original device. The following example program illustrates how to send output to the `PRINTER` device. This program is the previous example (`LINEGRAPH3`) modified to use the `PRINTER` device.

```
PRO LINEGRAPH3_PRINTER, PRINTER = printer

;+
; Name:
;       LINEGRAPH3_PRINTER
; Purpose:
;       Plots a simple line graph and prints the output
;       using the PRINTER device.
; Calling sequence:
;       LINEGRAPH3_PRINTER
; Inputs:
;       None.
```

```
;  Output:
;       Line graph and optional PRINTER output.
;  Keywords:
;       PRINTER : If set, use the currently configured PRINTER device.
;  Author and history:
;       Kenneth P. Bowman, 2004.
;-


COMPILE_OPT IDL2                              ;Set compiler options

xsize  = 4.0                                  ;Width of graphic
ysize  = 4.0                                  ;Height of graphic
dpi    = 100                                  ;Screen dots per inch
margin = 0.1                                  ;Margins of graphic

IF KEYWORD_SET(printer) THEN BEGIN
   PRINTER_ON, MARGIN = margin, /INCHES, $    ;Set device to PostScript
      PAGE_SIZE = [xsize, ysize]
ENDIF ELSE BEGIN
   WINDOW, XSIZE = dpi*xsize, YSIZE = dpi*ysize ;Open graphics window
ENDELSE

x = FINDGEN(11)                               ;Abscissa
y = SQRT(x)                                   ;Ordinate
PLOT, x, y                                    ;Draw line graph
OPLOT, x, 2.0*y                               ;Overplot second line

IF KEYWORD_SET(printer) THEN PRINTER_OFF      ;End PostScript output

END
```

To execute the program and have the graphics output go to the screen, simply enter

```
IDL> linegraph3_printer
```

To execute the program and have the graphics output go to the printer, enter

```
IDL> linegraph3_printer, /printer
Starting PRINTER output.
PRINTER output ended.
```

The PRINTER device does not allow you to specify the output file name. If you have configured the PRINTER device to create a PostScript file, the output is written to xprinter.out in your current directory. Before viewing the file, you may need to change the file suffix from .out to .ps.

Using the PRINTER device for color output is covered in Chapter 21.

20.5   Some Limitations of the PRINTER and PS Devices

The PRINTER and PS device drivers provided by RSI have a few limitations.

The PS driver can handle 24-bit (truecolor) images (bitmaps), but not truecolor vector graphics (lines, markers, etc.) Vector graphics are limited to 8-bit colors (256 different colors). In addition, the PostScript device cannot rotate PostScript fonts properly in three-dimensional plots, such as those created by SURFACE. If you need high-quality fonts in 3-D graphs, use the DEVICE command to select the Truetype fonts.

The PostScript output produced by the PRINTER device driver *can* produce 24-bit color for vector graphics. It cannot, however, use PostScript fonts. It uses Truetype fonts instead. Truetype fonts are available that are very similar to many PostScript fonts. Output sent from the PRINTER device directly to a PostScript printer appears nearly identical to equivalent output from the PS device. Problems can arise, however, if you try to edit a PostScript file generated by the PRINTER device in a program like Adobe Illustrator. Because the fonts are not true PostScript fonts, they are actually rendered as collections of polygons. These polygons are vector graphics, and cannot be edited directly like text composed of PostScript fonts.

20.6   Summary

IDL has a number of graphics device drivers to create printed output. The most commonly used are the PS and PRINTER devices.

- The PS_ON procedure can be used to switch the output to the PS (PostScript) device. When the graphics are complete, the PS_OFF procedure is used to send the output to the selected printer and switch back to the previous output device (typically the terminal screen).

- The PRINTER device is configured using the DIALOG_PRINTERSETUP and DIALOG_PRINTJOB functions. Printers must be available to the operating system before they can be configured with DIALOG_PRINTERSETUP.

- The PRINTER_ON procedure can be used to switch the output to the PRINTER device. When the graphics are complete, the PRINTER_OFF procedure is used to send the output to the selected printer and switch back to the previous output device (typically the terminal screen).

- Options for the various devices are set with the DEVICE command.

20.7   Exercises

1. Run the LINEGRAPH3 procedure to test PostScript output.

2. Run the LINEGRAPH3_PRINTER procedure to test that your printer is set up correctly.

Color and Image Display

Color graphics are simple in principal, but can be complicated in practice due to differences among various color output devices. This chapter explains the basics of 8- and 24-bit color graphics in IDL.

21.1 IDL Commands and Keywords

The following IDL commands are used to create and display color graphics:

- COLOR_CONVERT procedure

- DEVICE procedure

- TVLCT procedure

- LOADCT procedure

- XLOADCT procedure

- TV procedure

- TVSCL procedure

- TVRD procedure

21.2 Color Basics

21.2.1 Pixels

Virtually every computer graphics device creates an image by dividing the display region into a grid of pixels (short for picture elements). Current computer monitors (video displays) range in size from small (640×480 pixels) to large (more than 2000×1600 pixels). Display technology continues to improve in both size and resolution.

Printers, on the other hand, whether color or black-and-white, generally start at 300 *dpi* (dots-per-inch) and range up to several thousand dpi. The total number of pixels (dots) on a page depends on the size of the paper that the printer can handle. Even a low-resolution (300 dpi) printer can print more dots on a standard-size page than the number of pixels on the best current monitors.

To display a graph or image, the pixels that represent each graphical element (line, polygon, etc.) must be set to the appropriate colors. This process is called *rasterization*. Generally, rasterization is handled by the graphics device driver, and the user does not have to worry about things at the level of individual pixels. An exception is the display of *bitmapped* or *raster images*, which are already rasterized into pixels. The display of images is covered later in this chapter.

21.2.2 The RGB Color System

To create a color image, each pixel of your computer screen can emit a combination of red, green, and blue light (hence the name RGB). By combining the correct intensities of those three colors, any desired color can be displayed in each pixel on the screen.[1] This method of creating color is referred to as the *RGB* or *additive* color system.

For the convenience of the computer (not the user), the intensity of each of the three color components is allowed to vary in integral steps between 0 and 255. Therefore, the intensity of each color component can be specified by using 1 byte of computer memory. Because each byte is composed of 8 bits, this color resolution is referred to as 24-bit color. Each of the three color components can have 256 different values, so the number of possible colors that can be displayed in a single pixel is $256 \times 256 \times 256 = 2^{24} = 16,777,216$. Of course, a single pixel can display only one color at a time. Table 21.1 lists the combinations of red, green, and blue intensities that produce some common colors.

The red, green, and blue *primary colors*, and the mixtures used to create other colors, are not the same as the primary colors you learned when finger-painting. On the computer screen, combining red and green produces yellow.

TABLE 21.1   Common colors in terms of their RGB components.

Color	Red	Green	Blue
black	0	0	0
white	255	255	255
red	255	0	0
green	0	255	0
blue	0	0	255
yellow	255	255	0
magenta	255	0	255
cyan	0	255	255
gray (50%)	128	128	128

---

1   This is true within the limits of the display's ability to emit the component colors, which depends on the type and quality of the display.

With paint pigments, on the other hand, mixing blue and yellow produces green. This difference occurs because, on paper, colors are created by *absorption* of some colors and *reflection* of others, rather than *emission* of component colors. Because colored paints and inks create color by *absorbing* some wavelengths, this color system is referred to as *subtractive* color. The process of mixing subtractive colors is fundamentally different from that for additive color. Color printers generally add varying amounts of *four* different-colored inks (cyan, magenta, yellow, and black) to produce the full range of colors. Cyan is light blue, while magenta is a reddish purple. The black ink is necessary to produce darker colors and good quality grays. This is often referred to as the CMYK color system.

Fortunately, you do not need to deal directly with the CMYK color system. In IDL, all colors can be specified using the RGB system. For printed output, RGB colors are automatically converted to CMYK colors by the printer's device driver. Without expending considerable effort, however, you cannot expect the printed colors to *exactly* match the colors on the screen.

21.2.3 The HSV Color System

Mixing RGB components to create desired colors can be a frustrating, trial-and-error process. Fortunately, other more intuitive color schemes are available. My personal favorite is the hue-saturation-value (HSV) system.[2] The HSV system can be thought of as a color wheel. An example of an HSV color wheel is shown in Figure 21.1. The program used to create Figure 21.1 (HSV_WHEEL_PS) is included with this book. HSV_WHEEL_PS displays the image on the screen and optionally writes the image to a PostScript file. A similar program that creates a PNG file is also included (HSV_WHEEL_PNG).

The *hue*, which determines the color, is specified by the angle around the color wheel in degrees. Angles are measured clockwise from the up direction, so 0° is red, 60° is yellow, 120° is green, 180° is cyan, 240° is blue, and 300° is magenta.

You can think of the *saturation* as the amount of colored pigment of a particular hue that is added to a can of white paint. On the color wheel, saturation is indicated by the radial distance from the center, which ranges from 0 to 1. A saturation of 0 is located at the center, and indicates that *no* pigment has been added. If the saturation is 0, the color is always white (or gray if the *value* is less than 1) regardless of the hue. Moving radially outward at a given hue gradually increases the saturation of the color. For example, a hue of 0 and a saturation of 0.5 produces pink.

The *value* parameter can be thought of as adding black pigment to the paint. A value of 1 indicates *no* black pigment. As the value decreases toward 0, the color becomes darker. If the value is 0, the color is black, regardless of the hue or saturation. A complete color wheel for a value of 0.5 is shown in Figure 21.2.

---

2   This is also sometimes referred to as the hue-saturation-brightness (HSB) system.

FIGURE 21.1   Example of a color wheel created using the HSV color system. In this case the value v is set to 1.0. Also see this figure in the color plates section. (HSV_WHEEL_PS)

FIGURE 21.2   Example of a color wheel created using the HSV color system. In this case the value v is set to 0.5. Also see this figure in the color plates section. (HSV_WHEEL_PS)

The IDL COLOR_CONVERT procedure can be used to convert an HSV color specification into RGB intensities (or vice versa). The RGB intensities can then be used to specify colors in your IDL programs. When converting from HSV to RGB, the calling sequence is:

See the COLOR_CONVERT procedure in *IDL Reference Guide.*

```
COLOR_CONVERT, h, s, v, r, g, b, /HSV_RGB
```

Here are some examples of converting HSV coordinates to RGB intensities:

```
IDL> color_convert, 0.0, 1.0, 1.0, r, g, b, /hsv_rgb      ;red
IDL> print, r, g, b
 255   0   0
IDL> color_convert, 0.0, 0.5, 1.0, r, g, b, /hsv_rgb      ;pink
IDL> print, r, g, b
 255 127 127
IDL> color_convert, 0.0, 1.0, 0.5, r, g, b, /hsv_rgb      ;dark red
IDL> print, r, g, b
 127   0   0
IDL> color_convert, 180.0, 1.0, 1.0, r, g, b, /hsv_rgb    ;cyan
IDL> print, r, g, b
   0 255 255
```

21.3   24-Bit Devices

Some IDL graphics devices support *24-bit* color. This means that each pixel of the device has (at least) 3 bytes of memory to store the red, green, and blue intensities of the RGB components (or the equivalent for a CMYK device). The available 24-bit devices include most video displays, the PRINTER device, and the POSTSCRIPT device (for bitmapped images only). Because 24-bit displays are capable of displaying realistic images, they are referred to within IDL as *truecolor* displays.

Newer personal computers and workstations usually have 24-bit color video displays. The memory required to store the RGB components for each pixel of the display is special-purpose memory located on the computer's *graphics* or *video card.* To determine whether your computer display supports 24-bit color, use the HELP command with the /DEVICE keyword, as shown here:

```
IDL> help, /device
Available Graphics Devices: CGM HP LJ NULL PCL PRINTER PS REGIS TEK X Z
Current graphics device: X
    Server: X11.0, The XFree86 Project, Inc, Release 40300000
    Display Depth, Size: 24 bits, (1152,768)
    Visual Class: TrueColor (4)
    Bits Per RGB: 8 (8/8/8)
    Physical Color Map Entries (Emulated / Actual): 256 / 256
    Colormap: Private, 16777216 colors.  Translation table: Enabled
```

```
    Graphics pixels: Decomposed,          Dither Method: Ordered
    Write Mask: 16777215 (decimal) ffffff (hex)
    Graphics Function: 3 (copy)
    Current Font: <default>,     Current TrueType Font: <default>
    Default Backing Store: Req from Server.
```

The first line after the HELP command lists the available graphics devices. The X in the list of devices indicates that the X-Windows device is available on this computer. If you are using the Windows version of IDL, you should see an available WIN device instead of X. The WIN and X devices have similar capabilities. In this chapter we discuss only the X and WIN devices, which are used to display graphics on your computer screen, and the PRINTER and PS (PostScript) devices, which are used for printing.

The output from the HELP command above shows that the computer in the example is currently using the X device. The screen size is 1152×768 pixels. Each pixel has 24 bits of depth associated with it, making it a truecolor device. Furthermore, each color component has 8 bits of depth (256 intensity levels per component), which gives a total of 16,777,216 colors. Not all X or WIN devices will support 24-bit color. Use the HELP command to determine your computer's capabilities.

Running the HSV_WHEEL_PS procedure on this computer produces a window containing the color wheel shown in Figure 21.1.

If the device is changed to PRINTER, then HELP gives the following:

```
IDL> set_plot, 'printer'
IDL> help, /device
Available Graphics Devices: CGM HP LJ NULL PCL PRINTER PS REGIS TEK X Z
Current graphics device: PRINTER
    Printer : HP Color LaserJet PS
    Orientation: Portrait
    Scale Factor: 1
    Resolution: 300 dots per inch
    Font: -adobe-courier-medium-r-normal--0-0-300-300-m-0-iso8859-1,
    TrueType Font: <none>
    Size (X,Y): (17.78,12.7) cm., (7,5) in.
    Offset (X,Y): (1.905,12.7) cm., (0.75,5) in.
```

In this case, the PRINTER device has been configured to use an HP color laser printer.

Setting the device to PS produces the following information. Some details, such as available fonts, are omitted.

```
IDL> set_plot, 'ps'
IDL> device, /color, bits_per_pixel = 8
IDL> help, /device
Available Graphics Devices: CGM HP LJ NULL PCL PRINTER PS REGIS TEK X Z
Current graphics device: PS
```

```
File: <none>
Mode: Portrait, Non-Encapsulated, EPSI Preview Disabled, Color Enabled
Offset (X,Y): (1.905,12.7) cm., (0.75,5) in.
Size (X,Y): (17.78,12.7) cm., (7,5) in.
Scale Factor: 1
Font Size: 12
Font Encoding: AdobeStandard
Font: Helvetica      TrueType Font: <default>
# bits per image pixel: 8
```

Because the PS device does not automatically have color turned on, the DEVICE command is used to enable color and set the color depth to 8 bits per pixel. This is done automatically by the PS_ON procedure described in Chapter 20. *The PostScript device driver provided by RSI has a very important limitation*: Bitmapped images sent to the PS device (using the TV command) can use 24-bit color, but ordinary line graphics, such as those produced by the PLOT command, can use only 8-bit color (discussed in the next section). If you need to use full 24-bit color to display graphics other than bitmapped images, the PRINTER device can be used to produce PostScript output.

See the DEVICE procedure in *IDL Reference Guide*.

21.3.1 Specifying 24-Bit Colors

Most IDL graphics commands, such as PLOT and CONTOUR, include a COLOR keyword to set the main color of the graph. Some procedures, such as CONTOUR, have separate keywords to specify the colors of specific graphical elements (text, contour lines, etc.). If your current graphics device supports 24-bit color, you can specify any of more than 16 million possible colors for each color-related keyword. Rather than passing three separate values (the R, G, and B intensities) for each color, the three components are combined into a single 32-bit integer. Three of the four bytes that make up the integer are used for the component values. The first byte is used for the red component, the second for the green, and the third for the blue. The three components can be combined into a LONG integer with the simple arithmetic operation

```
color = r + 256*(g + 256*b)
```

where r, g, and b are component intensities between 0 and 255. To avoid having to write (and remember) this formula, the COLOR_24 function will convert the R, G, and B components into an integer.

```
FUNCTION COLOR_24, r, g, b

; NAME:
;       COLOR_24
; PURPOSE:
;       Convert r, g, and b color value(s) to 24-bit color
;       values.  R, g, and b should be integers in the
;       range [0, 255].  If not, they are converted to LONGs
```

```
;       and then truncated to that range. R, g, and b can
;       be three scalars or three arrays of equal dimension.
;
;       If g and b are omitted and r is a numerical
;       expression, then r is assumed to represent a
;       grayscale value.  That is, the g and b values are
;       set equal to r.
;
;       This function also includes a set of predefined
;       colors that can be selected by name.  If g and b
;       are omitted and r is a STRING expression, COLOR_24
;       attempts to find a color with that name in the
;       predefined table of colors.  If the current device
;       is not a 24-bit device (such as the PS device),
;       COLOR_24 assumes that LOAD_BASIC_COLORS has been
;       called to load the predefined colors into the color
;       table.
; CATEGORY:
;       Color calculations.
; CALLING SEQUENCE:
;       color = COLOR_24(r, g, b) for 24-bit color
;       color = COLOR_24(r)       for 24-bit grayscale
;       color = COLOR_24('name')  for pre-defined color
; INPUT:
;       r   : red value(s).    r is converted to LONG and
;             truncated to the range [0, 255]
;       g   : green value(s).  g is converted to LONG and
;             truncated to the range [0, 255]
;       b   : blue value(s).   b is converted to LONG and
;             truncated to the range [0, 255]
;
;       r   : string containing the name of a predefined color
; OUTPUT:
;   Scalar or array of 24-bit color value(s) of type LONG.
; MODIFICATION HISTORY:
;   K. Bowman, 2004.


COMPILE_OPT IDL2                               ;Set compile options

IF (N_PARAMS() EQ 1L) THEN BEGIN               ;Find a predefined color
    IF (SIZE(r, /TNAME) EQ 'STRING') THEN BEGIN   ;Look for name in table
        IF (!D.N_COLORS NE 256^3) THEN BEGIN      ;Use indexed color
            CASE STRUPCASE(r) OF
                'BLACK'  : RETURN,  0
                'WHITE'  : RETURN,  1
                'RED'    : RETURN,  2
                'GREEN'  : RETURN,  3
```

```
        'BLUE'    : RETURN,  4
        'YELLOW'  : RETURN,  5
        'MAGENTA' : RETURN,  6
        'CYAN'    : RETURN,  7
        'GRAY0'   : RETURN,  8
        'GRAY10'  : RETURN,  9
        'GRAY20'  : RETURN, 10
        'GRAY30'  : RETURN, 11
        'GRAY40'  : RETURN, 12
        'GRAY50'  : RETURN, 13
        'GRAY60'  : RETURN, 14
        'GRAY70'  : RETURN, 15
        'GRAY80'  : RETURN, 16
        'GRAY90'  : RETURN, 17
        'GRAY100' : RETURN, 18
        ELSE      : BEGIN
                    MESSAGE, 'Color ' + r + $
                      ' is not defined.', /CONTINUE
                    RETURN, 0
                  END
    ENDCASE
  ENDIF ELSE BEGIN                        ;Use 24-bit color
    CASE STRUPCASE(r) OF
        'BLACK'   : RETURN, COLOR_24(  0,   0,   0)
        'WHITE'   : RETURN, COLOR_24(255, 255, 255)
        'RED'     : RETURN, COLOR_24(255,   0,   0)
        'GREEN'   : RETURN, COLOR_24(  0, 255,   0)
        'BLUE'    : RETURN, COLOR_24(  0,   0, 255)
        'YELLOW'  : RETURN, COLOR_24(255, 255,   0)
        'MAGENTA' : RETURN, COLOR_24(255,   0, 255)
        'CYAN'    : RETURN, COLOR_24(  0, 255, 255)
        'GRAY0'   : RETURN, COLOR_24(  0,   0,   0)
        'GRAY10'  : RETURN, COLOR_24( 25,  25,  25)
        'GRAY20'  : RETURN, COLOR_24( 51,  51,  51)
        'GRAY30'  : RETURN, COLOR_24( 76,  76,  76)
        'GRAY40'  : RETURN, COLOR_24(102, 102, 102)
        'GRAY50'  : RETURN, COLOR_24(127, 127, 127)
        'GRAY60'  : RETURN, COLOR_24(153, 153, 153)
        'GRAY70'  : RETURN, COLOR_24(178, 178, 178)
        'GRAY80'  : RETURN, COLOR_24(204, 204, 204)
        'GRAY90'  : RETURN, COLOR_24(229, 229, 229)
        'GRAY100' : RETURN, COLOR_24(255, 255, 255)
        ELSE      : BEGIN
                    MESSAGE, 'Color ' + r + $
                      ' is not defined.', /CONTINUE
                    RETURN, 0
                  END
```

```
      ENDCASE
    ENDELSE
  ENDIF ELSE BEGIN                              ;Assume gray
    g = r
    b = r
  ENDELSE
ENDIF

RETURN,       ((0 > LONG(r)) < 255) + $        ;Convert to 24-bit color
       256*(((0 > LONG(g)) < 255) + $
       256* ((0 > LONG(b)) < 255))

END
```

For added flexibility, COLOR_24 can be used in several different ways. The first is to provide three arguments: the individual r, g, and b components. The arguments can be scalars or arrays of equal size. The output matches the size of the input. Before computing the 24-bit color value, the component intensities are converted to LONGs and clipped to the range 0 to 255; that is, if the intensity of any component is less than zero, the intensity is set to zero. If the intensity is greater than 255, it is set to 255. The second way to use COLOR_24 is to pass a single value or array. If the single argument is numerical, it is assumed to contain gray levels between 0 and 255. In this case, the g and b components are set equal to r. If the single argument is a string or an array of strings, the strings are assumed to be the *names* of colors. A limited set of named color definitions is included in the procedure (the colors in Table 21.1 plus some gray values). You can add other color definitions as desired.

The examples below show how to use 24-bit color keywords for some simple plots. This example draws the entire plot in red:

```
IDL> plot, findgen(10), findgen(10)^2, color = color_24('red')
```

To plot the graph axes using the default color and the graph data using a different color, use the following.

```
IDL> plot, findgen(10), findgen(10)^2, /nodata
IDL> oplot, findgen(10), findgen(10)^2, color = color_24('green')
```

To draw colored contour lines, use the C_COLOR keyword of the CONTOUR command:

```
IDL> contour, dist(50), c_color = color_24('blue')
```

The color of individual contour lines can be set by passing an array of colors with the C_COLOR keyword.

21.3.2 24-Bit Images

The following examples illustrate how to display images on a 24-bit display. For convenience, a two-dimensional array of floating-point numbers is created with the DIST function. This array is plotted in Figures 3.3 and 3.4 using other display methods.

```
IDL> z = dist(400)
IDL> window, xsize = 400, ysize = 400
IDL> tv, z
IDL> print, min(z), max(z)
      0.00000      282.843
IDL> print, byte(max(z))
   26
```

The first line above creates the 400×400 array z using the DIST function. The second opens a display window of the proper size to display z as an image. The next line displays z in the window using the TV procedure. The resulting image is shown in Figure 21.3 (upper left). TV automatically converts the floating-point values in z to BYTE type. As a result, values close

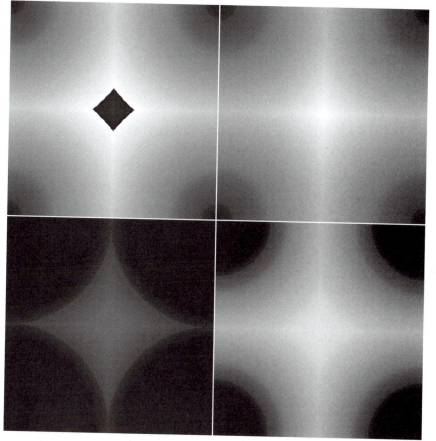

FIGURE 21.3   Examples of different images. Top left: image without scaling. Top right: image with automatic scaling by TVSCL. Bottom left: scaled image loaded into the red channel only. Bottom right: identical scaled images loaded into both the red and green channels. Also see this figure in color in the color plates section. (IMAGE1)

to the center of the array z, which are greater than 255, wrap around to values between 0 and 26. The center pixels appear black, but are actually very dark gray.

To properly display all of the values in z, they must first be scaled into the appropriate range [0, 255]. You can scale the values explicitly like this:

```
IDL> tv, 255*z/max(z)
```

or you can do it by using the BYTSCL procedure:

```
IDL> tv, bytscl(z)
```

The resulting image is shown in Figure 21.3 (upper right). BYTSCL scales the actual data into the appropriate range with the following transformation

$$z_{output} = N \frac{z - z_{min}}{z_{max} - z_{min}}, \tag{21.1}$$

where N is the number of entries in the color table and z_{min} and z_{max} are the minimum and maximum values of the array z. The value of N is stored in the system variable !D:

```
IDL> print, !d.table_size
         256
```

For most devices this value is at least 256; but older video displays may have smaller color tables. This value is *not* the total number of colors that can be displayed. In this case, the device is a 24-bit display and there are possible colors:

```
IDL> print, !d.n_colors
       16777216
```

Although the display in the example supports 24-bit color, the array z has only a single byte value for each pixel. It does not contain separate red, green, and blue color information. By default, TV uses the same value for the R, G, and B intensities for each pixel; that is, it loads the same image into the red, green, and blue *channels* of the display. The resulting image is shades of gray. To load the image into a single color channel, the CHANNEL keyword is used:

```
IDL> erase
IDL> tv, bytscl(z), channel = 1
```

Because channel 1 is the red channel, the resulting image ranges from black to red (Figure 21.3, lower left). The ERASE statement is necessary to clear (zero) the green and blue channels. If only a single channel is written, TV does not automatically erase the other channels.

Loading z into channel 2 changes the colors to shades of yellow (Figure 21.3, lower right). The red and green intensities are equal in each pixel, with the blue intensity set to zero. Adding red and green gives yellow.

```
IDL> tv, bytscl(z), channel = 2
```

You can easily create a true 24-bit color image with more than 256 different colors by using the HSV color system:

```
IDL> h = 240.0*rebin(findgen(400), 400, 400, /sample)/400.0
IDL> s = transpose(rebin(findgen(400), 400, 400, /sample)/400.0)
IDL> v = replicate(1.0, 400, 400)
IDL> color_convert, h, s, v, r, g, b, /hsv_rgb
IDL> tv, r, channel = 1
IDL> tv, g, channel = 2
IDL> tv, b, channel = 3
```

The three different image planes can also be combined into a truecolor image and displayed with a single call to TV by using the following array notation and the TRUE keyword:

```
IDL> tv, [ [[r]], [[g]], [[b]] ], true = 3
```

The result is shown in the upper left panel of Figure 21.4. In this image, the hue varies from 0.0 (red) at the left edge of the image to 240.0 (blue) at the right edge. The saturation varies from 1.0 (fully saturated) at the top edge to 0.0 (unsaturated) at the bottom. The value is 1.0 everywhere in the image. Separate plots of the hue and saturation are shown in the lower panels of Figure 21.4.

21.3.3 Reading Images from the Screen

Images can be read from the video display by using the TVRD function. By default, TVRD will read the entire contents of the current graphics window into a BYTE array. When using a 24-bit display, you can specify which dimension should be the color dimension or *interleave* dimension. If your window has $ni \times nj$ pixels, the resulting image can be dimensioned $3 \times ni \times nj$ (TRUE = 1), $ni \times 3 \times nj$ (TRUE = 2), or $ni \times nj \times 3$ (TRUE = 3). The choice of interleave dimension is up to you, but be aware that some output file types require that the image be interleaved over a particular dimension. To read an image from the screen to be written as a PNG file, for example, TRUE should be set to 1:

```
IDL> image = tvrd(true = 1)
IDL> help, image
IMAGE               BYTE      = Array[3, 400, 400]
```

FIGURE 21.4   A 24-bit color image created using the HSV color system. The hue is shown by itself in the lower left panel. The saturation is shown in the lower right. The saturation, which ranges from 0 to 1, is scaled in the image from 0 to 255. The value for all of three images is equal to 1. Also see this figure in the color plates section. (IMAGE2)

The BYTE variable image is a $3 \times 400 \times 400$ array containing the R, G, and B values of each pixel.

21.3.4   Writing Images to Files

IDL supports writing to a variety of standard image file types, including BMP, GIF, JPEG, PICT, PNG, PPM, and TIFF. My personal preference is PNG images. The PNG standard is open and freely usable. It can handle both 8- and 24-bit images. Its lossless compression scheme is quite efficient, and many popular programs can display PNG files, including most web browsers.

To write the array image above to a PNG file use the WRITE_PNG function:

```
IDL> write_png, 'image.png', image
```

Chapter 22 shows how to read PNG files with the READ_PNG function. Imag files of different types can also be written and read interactively with the DIALOG_WRITE_IMAGE and DIALOG_READ_IMAGE functions.

21.4 8-Bit Devices

Eight-bit color is largely a holdover from times when video memory was expensive. Instead of storing 24 bits of color information for each pixel (3 bytes), 8-bit devices store only 8 bits (1 byte). As a result, only $2^8 = 256$ different colors can be displayed on the screen at a time. Generally even fewer colors are available to an IDL program because some colors must be reserved to draw window borders, menus, the cursor, and the like. Despite these drawbacks, there are situations in which 8-bit color must be used. One instance is when drawing three-dimensional graphics using the Z (Z-buffer) device. Another is when drawing line graphs with the PS device. This section briefly covers how to use 8-bit color devices.

Although 8-bit devices can display only 256 colors on the screen at a time, those colors can usually be selected from the full palette of 24-bit colors. Color selection is accomplished by using a color lookup table, sometimes referred to as a CLUT or CT. Each pixel of the display device has a single byte of memory associated with it. The value of each byte is used to look up a triplet of red, green, and blue intensities in an RGB color table. An example of a possible color table is shown in Table 21.2. The first five entries in the table are black, white, red, green, and blue. If this table was loaded in an 8-bit device, a pixel with a value of 3 would appear as bright green.

The contents of the color table can be loaded or retrieved with the TVLCT procedure. Before using an 8-bit color table on a 24-bit device, you need to turn off *decomposed* color (separate R, G, and B values) with the following command:

See the TVLCT procedure in *IDL Reference Guide.*

```
IDL> device, decomposed = 0
```

To load the values in Table 21.2 into the first five elements of the current device's color table, use the following commands:

```
IDL> r = [   0, 255, 255,   0,   0]
IDL> g = [   0, 255,   0, 255,   0]
IDL> b = [   0, 255,   0,   0, 255]
IDL> tvlct, r, g, b
```

The three arrays of intensities for the R, G, and B components are loaded in the color table starting at index 0. Additional parameters and keywords can

TABLE 21.2   Part of an 8-bit color table.

Index	R	G	B
0	0	0	0
1	255	255	255
2	255	0	0
3	0	255	0
4	0	0	255
.			
.			
.			

be used to load values at any point in the tables and to use the HLS (hue-lightness-saturation) or HSV color systems. To switch from 8-bit color back to decomposed color on a 24-bit capable device use DEVICE, DECOMPOSED = 1.

IDL includes some predefined color tables that can be loaded with the LOADCT or XLOADCT procedures. For example,

See the LOADCT and
XLOADCT procedures in
IDL Reference Guide.

```
IDL> LOACT, 0
```

will load the three color component tables (R, G, and B) with (0, . . . , 255), which gives a linear gray scale. The XLOADCT command provides an interactive interface to view and select from the available predefined color tables.

To get the current values of the color tables, use the GET keyword like this:

```
IDL> TVLCT, r, g, b, /GET
```

The arrays r, g, and b contain the component intensities associated with each index value.

An advantage of 8-bit over 24-bit displays is that the colors displayed on the screen can be changed by changing only the color tables. You need not redraw the graphics on the screen. The limitations of 8-bit color and the complications of using color tables, however, mean that 24-bit color is preferable in most circumstances.

21.5 Printing Color Output

The preferred method for producing printed output is usually to produce a PostScript file. A PostScript file can be sent directly to a PostScript printer, or the file can be modified, if necessary, with other software programs, such as Adobe Illustrator. The PS and PRINTER devices will both produce PostScript output. The devices are similar in most ways, but have some important differences. Files produced by the PS device can contain 24-bit color bitmapped images, but only 8-bit color is supported for line graphics. The PRINTER device supports 24-bit color for both images and line graphics. The PS device can create plots with PostScript fonts, whereas the PRINTER device uses Truetype fonts. When printed, the appearance of the two kinds of fonts is quite similar, but only PostScript fonts can be edited easily in programs like Illustrator.

The example program HSV_WHEEL_PS illustrates how to make PostScript files containing 24-bit color images with the PS device. If the PS keyword is set in HSV_WHEEL_PS, the device is switched to PS and a PostScript file containing the image of the color wheel is created.

As noted earlier, 24-bit color does not work with the PS device and commands such as PLOT and CONTOUR. If you only need a small number of colors, however, the PS device does support 8-bit color for vector graphics. Calling the LOAD_BASIC_COLORS procedure after starting the PS device will load a set of basic colors into the bottom part of the 8-bit color table. The COLOR_24 function will correctly look up that set of colors by name. You can load additional

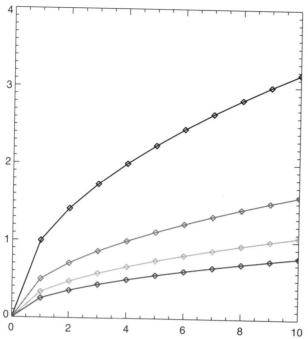

FIGURE 21.5   Example of using 8-bit color with the PLOT command and the PS device. Also see this figure in the color plates section. (LINEGRAPH12)

colors into the color table and reference them by index number. An example of 8-bit color plotting with the PS device is shown in Figure 21.5.

An example program (RGB_PLOT_PRINTER) is included to show how to use 24-bit color with nonimage graphics (programs like PLOT and CONTOUR) and the PRINTER device. RGB_PLOT_PRINTER plots a set of randomly located points. The color of the points depends on their location. The red component intensity is proportional to the x value, whereas the green intensity is proportional to the y value. As a result, points in the lower left part of the plot have low intensities of both components and tend toward black. Points in the lower right have large red intensities but small green intensities and so appear red. Points in the upper left have large green intensities but small red intensities and so appear green. Finally, points in the upper right have large red and green intensities that, when mixed, appear yellow. The output from RGB_PLOT_PRINTER is shown in Figure 21.6. In this case the PRINTER device has been configured to use an HP color laser printer and send the output to a file.

21.6 Summary

This chapter has covered the basics of using 24- and 8-bit color in IDL. Because the interaction between color and the various devices can be complicated, several IDL authors have written general purpose image display routines that automatically handle different bit depths (8 and 24) and different devices

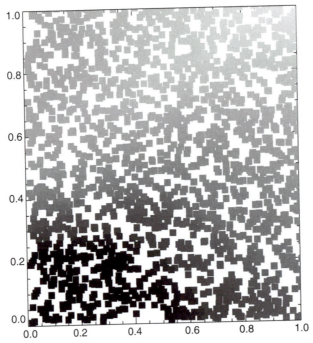

FIGURE 21.6   Example of using 24-bit color with the PLOT command and the PRINTER device. Also see this figure in color plates section. (RGB_PLOT_PRINTER)

(video displays and printers). These include the IMDISP program in Liam Gumley's book, *Practical IDL Programming* and several image display routines available from David Fanning's web site (http://dfanning.com).

Users interested in advanced image processing should consult the manual *Image Processing in IDL* that is provided by RSI as part of the IDL documentation and the other books recommended in Chapter 2.

If you wish to develop your own color and image display programs, the following procedures are useful:

- COLOR_CONVERT procedure. COLOR_CONVERT can be used to convert color intensities among the different color systems (RGB, HSV, and HLS).

- DEVICE procedure. The DEVICE procedure has a large number of keywords that are used to control the behavior of the various graphics devices.

- TVLCT procedure. TVLCT is used to load a color table to an 8-bit device, or to read the current color table.

- LOADCT procedure. LOADCT allows the user to select and load a variety of predefined 8-bit color tables.

- XLOADCT procedure. XLOADCT allows the user to interactively view, select, and load a variety of predefined 8-bit color tables.

Animation

This chapter shows how to create animations using XINTERANIMATE.

22.1 IDL Commands and Keywords

The following IDL commands are used to create and display animations:

- XINTERANIMATE procedure
- READ_PNG procedure
- WRITE_PNG procedure

22.2 Background

Like a motion picture, computers can create the illusion of motion (animation) by rapidly displaying a sequence of still images. Fast computers with properly designed programs can actually create each frame quickly enough so that the result is perceived as smooth motion. Many computer games work this way, updating the display of a scene in real time as the user interacts with the game. These programs take advantage of modern computer graphics cards (video cards) to handle much of the processing required to display each image. These video cards are designed to display three-dimensional (*rendered*) graphics at very high speed.

For scientific applications, however, several factors can slow the graphics display process. First, data often must be read from disk storage, and disks are *much* slower than computer memory. Second, a scientific graph may require substantial amounts of computation to create the graph. Finally, on Unix and Mac OS X systems, IDL uses the X-Windows system to display graphics. X-Windows is not designed primarily for speed. If you try to create animations by repeatedly drawing graphics to the screen, the results are usually jerky, irregular motion.

Because of these limitations, animations are better produced by drawing and storing each of the complete images that make up an animation sequence in computer memory. These images can then be sent to the screen quickly using standard image display methods.[1] Even using X-Windows, most graphics systems can load images quickly enough to produce smooth animation.

22.3 Using XINTERANIMATE

22.3.1 Creating an Animation

IDL includes a procedure, XINTERANIMATE, for creating and displaying animations using the technique of storing all of the complete images in memory.

The following three steps are used to create an animation using XINTERANIMATE:

See the XINTERANIMATE procedure in *IDL Reference Guide*.

1. Call XINTERANIMATE once to set up the animation. The essential information required here includes the size of the animation window (height and width in pixels) and the number of *frames* or images in the animation. This information is used to allocate a block of memory in which all of the individual frames are stored.

2. Draw each frame. Each frame is drawn individually and then loaded into memory by calling XINTERANIMATE once for each frame. Normally, this step is done inside a loop.

3. Run the animation. A final call to XINTERANIMATE starts the animation and makes interactive controls (buttons and sliders) available. The controls allow you to change the speed and direction of the animation and close the animation window when finished.

The following example shows how to create an animation with XINTERANIMATE:

```
PRO ANIMATE

;+
; Name:
;       ANIMATE
; Purpose:
;       Create a sample animation sequence.
; Calling sequence:
;       ANIMATE
; Inputs:
;       None.
```

---

1 IDL *can* display three-dimensional rendered graphics using the built-in IDL *Object Graphics* system. On most computers, Object Graphics uses the processing power of the computer's video card. The Object Graphics system is best suited for applications in which three-dimensional visualization of surfaces or volumes is required. Object Graphics are not discussed in this book. For ordinary scientific graphs, the *Direct Graphics* system with its many available devices and plotting functions is usually preferred.

```
; Output:
;       Interactive animation sequence.
; Keywords:
;       None.
; Author and history:
;       Kenneth P. Bowman, 2004.
;-

COMPILE_OPT IDL2                           ;Set compile options

xsize    = 300                             ;Width of window
ysize    = 300                             ;Height of window
nframes  =  20                             ;Number of frames
speed    =   5                             ;Animation speed

np       = 1000                            ;Number of points
x        = FINDGEN(np)/np                  ;Create x-coordinate
y        = SIN(2.0*!Pi*x)                  ;Function to plot

WINDOW, XSIZE = xsize, YSIZE = ysize, $    ;Create pixmap
   /PIXMAP
!P.BACKGROUND = COLOR_24('white')          ;Set background to white
IF (!D.N_COLORS EQ 256^3) THEN bpp = 3 $   ;Bytes per pixel
                          ELSE bpp = 1
PRINT, 'Memory required : ', $             ;Memory requirements
   (xsize*ysize*nframes*bpp)/(2.0^20), ' MB'

XINTERANIMATE, /SHOWLOAD, $                ;1) Initialize animator
   SET = [xsize, ysize, nframes], $
   TITLE = 'Animation Demo 1'

FOR n = 0, nframes-1 DO BEGIN              ;Create each frame
   PLOT, x, SHIFT(y, n*(np/nframes)), $    ;Plot graph
      COLOR = 0, PSYM = 3
   image = TVRD(TRUE = 3)                  ;Read image from pixmap
   XINTERANIMATE, IMAGE = image, FRAME = n ;2) Copy image to animator
ENDFOR

XINTERANIMATE, speed                       ;3) Run animation

!P.BACKGROUND = 0                          ;Set background to black

END
```

XINTERANIMATE creates a window that includes the graphics display area
and several control buttons and sliders. A sample window is shown in
Figure 22.1.

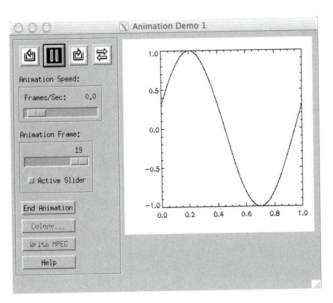

FIGURE 22.1   The XINTERANIMATE window. (Screen capture)

22.3.2 Animating Files

You can use the basic framework provided above in the ANIMATE program
for different approaches to animation. For example, if you have a series of
previously created images stored as files in a directory, you can create an
animation by using the animation program below, which is very similar to the
previous example:

```
PRO ANIMATE_FILES, indir


;+
; Name:
;       ANIMATE_FILES
; Purpose:
;       Animate existing created PNG files.
; Calling sequence:
;       ANIMATE_FILES, indir
; Inputs:
;       indir : path to input directory.
; Output:
;       Interactive animation sequence.
; Keywords:
;       None.
; Author and history:
;       Kenneth P. Bowman, 2004.
;-


COMPILE_OPT IDL2                              ;Set compile options
```

```
IF (N_ELEMENTS(indir) EQ 0) THEN $
   indir = !Bowman + 'data/animation/'      ;Default input directory

file = FILE_SEARCH(indir + '*', $           ;Find all files in indir
   COUNT = nframes)
IF (nframes EQ 0) THEN $
   MESSAGE, 'No files found in ' + indir

status = QUERY_PNG(file[0], info)           ;Get frame size
xsize  = info.dimensions[0]                 ;Width of graphic window
ysize  = info.dimensions[1]                 ;Height of graphic window
speed  =   5                                ;Initial animation speed

IF (!D.N_COLORS EQ 256^3) THEN bpp = 3 $    ;Bytes per pixel
                          ELSE bpp = 1
PRINT, 'Memory required : ', $              ;Memory requirements
   (xsize*ysize*nframes*bpp)/(2.0^20), ' MB'

XINTERANIMATE, /SHOWLOAD, $                  ;1) Initialize animator
   SET = [xsize, ysize, nframes], $
   TITLE = 'Animation Demo 1'

FOR n = 0, nframes-1 DO BEGIN               ;Create each frame
   image = READ_PNG(file[n])                ;Read image from file
   XINTERANIMATE, IMAGE = image, FRAME = n  ;2) Copy image to animator
ENDFOR
)
XINTERANIMATE, speed                        ;3) Run animation

END
```

In this example, each image frame is read from a file, rather than being created within the program. The program finds all of the files in the directory indir and loads them into the animator. In this case, the files are assumed to be PNG files.[2] PNG is a widely used, high-quality, lossless, open source library for storing graphic image files. PNG files can be written and read in IDL by using the WRITE_PNG and READ_PNG functions. To ensure that the files are loaded in the correct order, they should be given sequential names like frame.000, frame.001, and so on. All of the images in the files are assumed to have the same height and width. (ANIMATE_FILES could be modified to check that the file sizes all match.)

See the XINTERANIMATE procedure in *IDL Reference Guide*.

IDL can also read other graphic format types, including JPEG, TIFF, PICT, and BMP.

See the various READ_ procedures in *IDL Reference Guide*.

---

2   PNG stands for Portable Network Graphics *or* PNG's Not GIF.

22.3.3 Saving Your Animation

If you or your institution has purchased a license for the MPEG video file format, you can use XINTERANIMATE to save your animation in MPEG format. If you do not have a license, the **Write MPEG** button is grayed out. The MPEG standard was primarily designed for storing video signals (that is, movies) in digital format. Unless properly used, MPEG video of scientific graphics can look very bad. You may need to experiment with the MPEG compression settings to achieve a satisfactory result. If you do not have an MPEG license, you can still save the individual images (using WRITE_PNG, for example) and use an external program to convert the sequence of individual images into various video formats.

22.4 Summary

This chapter has covered the basics of creating and running animations with XINTERANIMATE. Animations can be created as part of the program or stored in image files in various formats, such as GIF, JPEG, or PNG. Animations created with XINTERANIMATE are stored in computer memory, so the length of the animation is limited by the amount of available memory.

22.5 Exercises

1. Use XINTERANIMATE along with CONTOUR, SURFACE, or SHADE_SURF to plot an animation of the function

$$z(x, y, t) = z_0 \cos\left(\frac{2\pi t}{\tau}\right) \sin(\pi x) \sin(\pi y)$$

over one complete period τ.

Part V

APPLICATIONS

23

Statistics and Pseudorandom Numbers

This chapter covers the basics of computing statistics and generating pseudo-random numbers using IDL.

23.1 IDL Commands and Keywords

The following IDL commands are used for statistical problems:

- RANDOMU function
- RANDOMN function
- HISTOGRAM function
- MEAN function
- VARIANCE function
- STDEV function
- SKEWNESS function
- KURTOSIS function
- MOMENT function
- MIN function
- MAX function
- MEDIAN function
- CORRELATE function
- A_CORRELATE function
- C_CORRELATE function
- M_CORRELATE function
- P_CORRELATE function
- R_CORRELATE function

23.2 Pseudorandom Numbers

23.2.1 Background

There are many applications for which it is useful to be able to generate *random numbers*. You might wish, for example, to simulate a process that you know contains random elements. There are a number of common ways to generate random numbers. For example, if you roll a pair of dice, the physical processes involved (the collisions and tumbling of the dice) are so complicated that it is impossible to predict the outcome. If the dice are not loaded, the probability that any given side will end up on top should be the same. Therefore, a single die can be used to generate a series of random integers between 1 and 6. In a sequence of many rolls, the proportion of each side that ends up on top will tend toward one-sixth, and each roll is independent of previous and following rolls (that is, they are uncorrelated).

A computer, on the other hand, should always give the same result when carrying out the same calculation (unless the computer is broken!). As a result, it is difficult to use a computer to generate truly random numbers.[1] To get around this limitation, methods have been developed to generate what are called *pseudorandom numbers*. A good pseudorandom number generation algorithm will produce numbers with the desired distribution (such as uniform or normal) and the right statistical properties (such as no serial correlation).

To generate a sequence of pseudorandom numbers, the pseudorandom number algorithm must start with a numerical value called a *seed*. A good way to select a relatively random number for the seed is to use the computer's system clock. Unless you run the program many times, the precise instant at which you start a calculation should be a nearly random event. If you wish to be able to repeat the calculation with the same set of random numbers, the seed can be stored and used again.

Once the seed is selected, the pseudorandom number generation algorithm applies a moderately complicated nonlinear mathematical operation to the seed. The resulting value is then used as the seed for the next number in the sequence. If properly designed, the algorithm should generate a sequence of numbers that has the same statistical properties as a sequence of true random numbers.

A little thought will show that this approach cannot generate a truly random sequence of numbers. Because there are only a finite number of different floating-point numbers that can be represented with 32 bits, eventually the sequence will return to a previously calculated value. From that point on, the entire sequence will repeat. Designers of pseudorandom number generation algorithms use a number of clever ideas to ensure that the repeat period is very long. Even if the sequence does repeat, it may not matter for your particular

---

1   Special hardware devices can be purchased that use a physical noise source to generate true random numbers. There are even true random number generators available on the Web that your computer can contact to get a small set of random numbers.

application. Keep in mind, however, that these computer algorithms generate *pseudorandom numbers*, not true random numbers.

23.2.2 IDL Pseudorandom Number Functions

IDL originally had two functions that could be called to generate pseudorandom numbers: RANDOMU, which generates pseudorandom numbers uniformly distributed between 0 and 1, and RANDOMN, which generates normally distributed (Gaussian) pseudorandom numbers with a mean of 0 and standard deviation of 1. Both of these functions now include keywords that can be used to specify the distribution from which the pseudorandom numbers should be drawn, so either function can be used. The available distributions include the uniform, normal, binomial, gamma, and Poisson distributions. Both functions will return a single pseudorandom number or an array containing a sequence of pseudorandom numbers. You can specify the dimensions of the array using the function's arguments. If no dimensions are specified, a single scalar result is returned.

Here are some examples of short sequences of pseudorandom numbers:

```
IDL> x = randomu(seed, 5, 5)
IDL> print, x
     0.648501      0.334211      0.505953      0.652182      0.158174
     0.912751      0.257593      0.810990      0.267308      0.188872
     0.237323      0.312265      0.551604      0.944883      0.673464
     0.613302     0.0874299      0.782052      0.374534     0.0799968
     0.581460      0.433864      0.459824      0.634644      0.182057
IDL> print, seed
   791874665     390964491    1775310458    2051248307    1009066971     350453954
  1376904518    1787724064    1787857450     928973326    1710094693    1048576392
   909535867    2004054417     578950449     974237040    1586606552     495713212
   780717323    1172613062     710221238    1122306036     791874665    1123704022
    82658645     763960694     780458725    1278106473     505076188     332487872
  1282223531     834638471     650304515     851438674             0             0
```

In this case we have generated uniformly distributed pseudorandom numbers (equal probability of lying anywhere between 0 and 1). The first argument of the function is the seed. If the variable seed is undefined, as it is in this case, IDL uses the system clock to create the seed. The following two arguments specify the size of the output array, 5×5 in this case. Printing the output array shows 25 numbers between 0 and 1. If we print the value of seed, we see that it is not in fact a single number, but an array of integers. The multiple elements of the seed are used to improve the statistical properties of the algorithm. Be careful not to modify the values of the seed variable. Its only use is to be passed to a subsequent call to the RANDOMU function. Because the seed is based on the system clock at the time this program was run, if you try this calculation, you should see a different set of output numbers.

You can do some basic checks of the statistical properties of this function by generating a large number of pseudorandom numbers and plotting the distribution of values. Use the HISTOGRAM function to calculate the number of values that fall within a set of equal-sized bins:

```
IDL> x = randomu(seed, 100000)
IDL> h = histogram(x, min = 0.0, binsize = 0.01)
IDL> plot, h
```

A fancier version of the resulting plot is shown in Figure 23.1. As expected, the number of values within each bin is close to, but not exactly equal to, 1000.

We can similarly generate normally distributed (Gaussian) pseudorandom numbers:

```
IDL> x = RANDOMN(seed, 100000)
IDL> h = HISTOGRAM(x, MIN = -5.0, BINSIZE = 0.1, NBINS = 100)
IDL> plot, h
```

Because normally distributed numbers can be less than 0 or greater than 1, we set the limits of the histogram bins using the MIN, BINSIZE, and NBINS keywords. A fancier version of the resulting plot is shown in Figure 23.2.

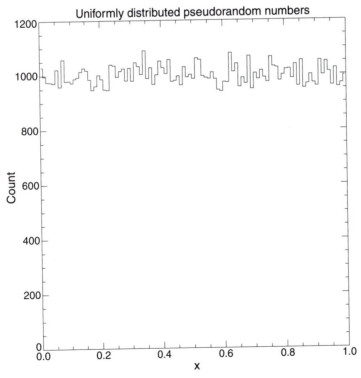

FIGURE 23.1   Histogram of a set of 100,000 uniformly distributed pseudorandom numbers. The bin size is 0.01, so each bin should contain approximately 1000 numbers. (RANDOM1)

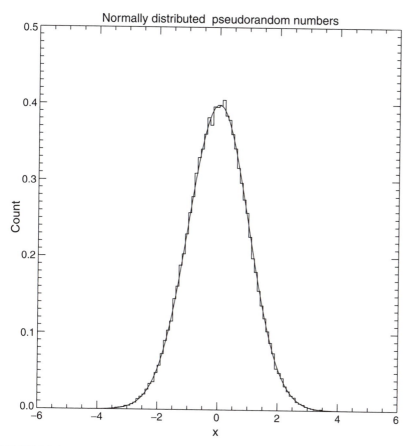

FIGURE 23.2   Histogram of a set of 100,000 normally distributed pseudorandom numbers. The bin size is 0.1. A theoretical normal distribution with a mean of 0 and a standard deviation of 1 is over-plotted on the histogram (smooth curve). The results are normalized so that the area under the curves is equal to 1. (RANDOM2)

The BINOMIAL, GAMMA, and POISSON keywords can be used with either RANDOMU or RANDOMN to generate pseudorandom numbers from those distributions.

23.3   Basic Statistics

The MEAN, STDEV, VARIANCE, SKEWNESS, and KURTOSIS functions can be used to compute basic descriptive statistics. These quantities can also be computed by using the MOMENT function. The following example shows how these functions work. We start with an array of 10 pseudorandom numbers:

```
IDL> x = randomn(seed, 10)
IDL> print, x
      2.52840      0.913887     -0.277393      -1.66645      0.591064
      0.525165     -1.93741      1.28269     -0.0126883     -0.433611
IDL> print, mean(x)
      0.151365
```

If any of the values in the array are NaNs, the result is an NaN

```
IDL> x[3] = !values.f_nan
IDL> print, x
      2.52840      0.913887     -0.277393           NaN      0.591064
     0.525165      -1.93741       1.28269    -0.0126883     -0.433611
IDL> print, mean(x)
         NaN
```

unless the NAN keyword is used:

```
IDL> print, mean(x, /nan)
     0.353345
```

If all of the values are NaNs

```
IDL> x[*] = !values.f_nan
IDL> print, x
         NaN           NaN          NaN          NaN          NaN
         NaN.          NaN          NaN          NaN          NaN
IDL> print, mean(x, /nan)
         NaN
```

the result is also NaN. The DOUBLE keyword can be used to ensure that all internal calculations are carried out using double precision arithmetic. It is generally a good idea to use the DOUBLE keyword unless you have a specific reason not to. The other statistical functions work in a similar manner. Additional functions can compute the mean absolute deviation (MEANABSDEV), the minimum value (MIN), the maximum value (MAX), and the median (MEDIAN).

The MOMENT function returns all four moments (mean, variance, skewness, and kurtosis) in a single array. It also accepts the NAN and DOUBLE keywords.

All of the statistical functions described above calculate statistics for the entire input array. If you need to compute statistics over just one dimension, you can use the TOTAL function, as the following example illustrates for rows and columns of a 2-D array:

```
IDL> x = randomn(seed, 4, 3)
IDL> print, x
     -1.65983       1.31386      0.333662     -1.42991
    -0.708080      0.493735       1.06967     -0.668656
    -0.237232     -0.223428       1.62977     -0.627912
IDL> print, transpose(total(x, 1)/4)
    -0.360556
    0.0466679
     0.135298
IDL> print, total(x, 2)/3
    -0.868382      0.528056       1.01103     -0.908827
```

In the first example, which sums across the rows (the first dimension), the TRANSPOSE function is used to print the results in a column for consistency with the input array.

23.4 Regression and Correlation

If two variables, x and y, are related by the linear relationship

$$y_i = a + bx_i + \epsilon_i, \qquad (23.1)$$

where ϵ_i is a random variable, the coefficients a and b can be computed by using *linear regression*. To demonstrate linear regression, we compute a set of random variables and use the REGRESS procedure to calculate a, b, and the correlation coefficient r:

```
IDL> n = 100
IDL> x = randomn(seed, n)
IDL> y = x + 0.5* randomn(seed, n)
IDL> b = regress(x, y, const = a, correlation = r, /double)
IDL> plot, x, y, psym = 1
IDL> oplot, [-4.0, 4.0], [a - b*4.0, a + b*4.0]
IDL> print, a, b[0], r[0]
      0.051745942        1.0281032        0.87449634
```

The results are plotted in Figure 23.3. The OPLOT command plots the linear fit calculated by REGRESS. As shown in the example, REGRESS will optionally compute the correlation coefficient r. Because REGRESS can also compute multiple linear regressions, b and r are returned as arrays, even when they contain only one element.

IDL also has specialized procedures to compute correlations, cross-correlations, and autocorrelations. These include CORRELATE (correlation coefficients), A_CORRELATE (autocorrelations), C_CORRELATE (cross-correlations), M_CORRELATE (multiple correlations), P_CORRELATE (partial correlations), and R_CORRELATE (rank correlations). Here is an example that uses the random variables from above:

```
IDL> print, correlate(x, y, /double)
      0.87449634
```

23.5 Curve Fitting

Linear regression is the simplest case of the general problem of *curve fitting*. The REGRESS procedure is able to compute multiple linear regressions against

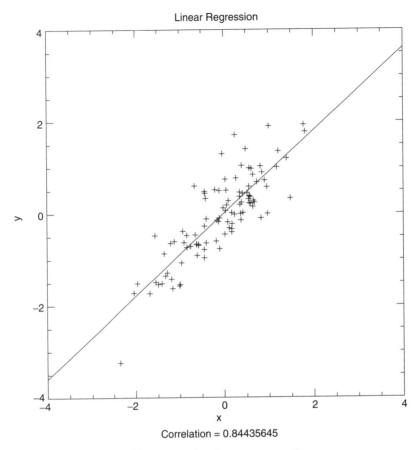

FIGURE 23.3   Example of linear regression. (LINEAR_REGRESS)

arbitrary functions, and can be used for polynomial curve fitting, for example. IDL has a number of other procedures and functions that can be used
to apply various curve fitting methods, including nonlinear curve fitting
algorithms, such as CURVEFIT and SVDFIT.[2]

23.6   Significance Tests

IDL has functions that can compute a number of the statistical functions that
are needed to evaluate statistical significance. These include the Gaussian, χ^2,
F, and t distributions, and the cutoff values of those distributions. For more
information, see the *IDL Reference Guide*. For a list of the available procedures
and functions, see the **IDL Quick Reference**.

---

2   A robust, general-purpose, curve fitting program MPFIT is available from Craig B.
     Markwardt on the World Wide Web. It can be found by searching the web or the IDL
     newsgroup comp.lang.idl-pvwave.

23.7 Summary

This chapter covers basic descriptive statistics and pseudorandom number generation in IDL. IDL has built-in functions to handle many descriptive statistics and significance testing problems. IDL also includes functions to generate pseudorandom numbers from a variety of different distributions.

24

Interpolation

A problem that often arises in data analysis is *interpolation*, that is, estimating the value of a function between points at which the function is known. This chapter presents several simple interpolation examples using the built-in IDL interpolation functions.

24.1 IDL Commands and Keywords

The following built-in IDL functions can be used to interpolate data:

- INTERPOL function
- BILINEAR function
- INTERPOLATE function
- TRIANGULATE function
- TRIGRID function

24.2 Background

Given a function that is tabulated at a finite set of points, *interpolation* is the problem of estimating the value of the function at locations *between* the tabulated points. *Extrapolation* is the problem of estimating the value of the function *outside* the range of tabulated points. To interpolate or extrapolate, the tabulated values are used to construct an *interpolating function*. The interpolating function is often a piecewise polynomial of relatively low order, typically linear, quadratic, or cubic, although other kinds of functions can be used. In order to be considered interpolation, as opposed to *curve fitting*, the interpolating function should pass *exactly* through the tabulated points.

IDL includes several built-in functions to do interpolation using various kinds of interpolating functions. These include INTERPOL and INTERPOLATE.

24.3 1-D Interpolation

The IDL function INTERPOL can do several different kinds of one-dimensional interpolation, specifically *linear*, *quadratic*, and *cubic spline* interpolation.

Here is a quick demonstration of how to use INTERPOL. Annotated versions
of the resulting graphs are plotted in Figure 24.1.

```
IDL> x = findgen(6)
IDL> y = [0.1, 0.9, 0.2, 0.8, 0.3, 0.7]
IDL> xx = 5.0*findgen(26)/25
IDL> yy = interpol(y, x, xx)
IDL> plot, x, y, psym = -4, symsize = 2
IDL> oplot, xx, yy, psym = -1
```

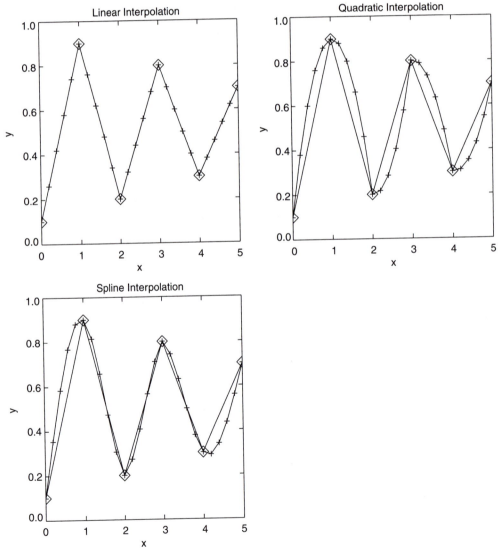

FIGURE 24.1   Examples of 1-D interpolation using linear interpolation (top left), quadratic
interpolation (top right), and spline interpolation (bottom left). (INTERPOLATE1)

This example starts by creating a regularly spaced, independent coordinate x and an oscillatory set of dependent values y. The coordinates of the tabulated points do not have to be regularly spaced, but they must be monotonic (that is, in either increasing or decreasing order of x). The variable xx contains the coordinates of the points that we want to interpolate *to*. These points do not need to be monotonic. The interpolated values (yy) are computed using the INTERPOL function. By default, INTERPOL uses linear interpolation. Finally, the original points (x, y) are plotted and the interpolated points (xx, yy) are overplotted. The resulting graph is the upper left panel of Figure 24.1. The original data points are indicated by diamonds, the interpolated values by pluses. As expected for a piecewise linear interpolating function, the interpolated values lie on straight lines connecting the tabulated points.

To use a quadratic interpolating function, add the QUADRATIC keyword:

```
IDL> yy = interpol(y, x, xx, /quadratic)
IDL> plot, x, y, psym = -4, symsize = 2
IDL> oplot, xx, yy, psym = -1
```

The result is plotted in the upper right panel of Figure 24.1. Because quadratic interpolation requires *three* data points to construct the pieces of the interpolating function, there are two possible choices for the points to be used to interpolate each segment. Either choice will be *asymmetric*. In part due to this asymmetry, interpolating functions of *odd* order are usually preferred (linear, cubic, etc.). In this case, you can see that although the interpolating function passes through the tabulated points, it has kinks at the tabulated points and looks obviously different on either side of those points.

Splines are interpolating functions that are specifically designed to be smooth. Setting the SPLINE keyword tells INTERPOL to use cubic splines, which ensures that the interpolating function and its first and second derivatives are continuous everywhere, including the tabulated points.

```
IDL> yy = interpol(y, x, xx, /spline)
IDL> plot, x, y, psym = -4, symsize = 2
IDL> oplot, xx, yy, psym = -1
```

The resulting interpolated points are shown in the lower left panel of Figure 24.1. Note that the extrema of the interpolated values do not coincide with the tabulated points.

As you can see, interpolation schemes of different order have different characteristics that need to be taken into account when selecting an interpolation method. Higher order does not necessarily mean better!

24.4 Bilinear Interpolation

IDL includes two primary functions for doing two-dimensional interpolation. The simpler of the two is BILINEAR, which, as the name suggests, performs *bilinear interpolation.* Bilinear interpolation is often used to interpolate two-dimensional gridded data between similar data grids (from the corners of a rectangular grid to the centers of the grid boxes, for example) or when a fast, simple interpolation scheme is sufficient.

The concept of bilinear interpolation is illustrated in Figure 24.2. Tabulated values of a function z are assumed to be available on a two-dimensional grid, indicated by black dots. The grid does not need to be regular (evenly spaced), but the grid lines do need to be perpendicular; that is, the x-coordinates of the grid points depend only on i, and the y-coordinates depend only on j.

The desired quantity is the value $\hat{z}$ at the point $(\hat{x}, \hat{y})$, which is indicated by the red circle. Applying the ideas of linear interpolation to this two-dimensional problem suggests two possible approaches. One is to interpolate first in the x-direction to get values at the locations marked by the filled red squares. Then interpolate in the y-direction to get $\hat{z}$. The second approach would be to interpolate first in the y-direction to get values at the locations marked by the open red squares. Then interpolate in the x-direction to get $\hat{z}$. This ambiguity suggests that one might get different answers depending on the order in which the calculation is done. In fact, comparing the two approaches reveals that, due to the linearity of the method, the two approaches give the same answer. (The algorithm is

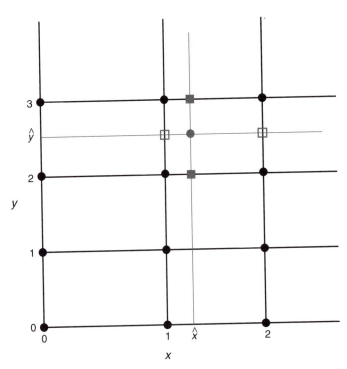

FIGURE 24.2   Schematic illustrating the concept of bilinear interpolation. Also see the color version of this figure in the color plates. (Not IDL)

usually implemented by computing *weights* w so that, when $\hat{x}$ lies between x_i and x_{i+1} and $\hat{y}$ lies between y_j and y_{j+1}, the result can be written $\hat{z} = w_{i,j}\, z_{i,j} + w_{i+1,j}\, z_{i+1,j} + w_{i,j+1}\, z_{i,j+1} + w_{i+1,j+1}\, z_{i+1,j+1}$. The weights depend on $\hat{x}$ and $\hat{y}$.)

BILINEAR requires only three arguments and has no keywords. The user need only supply the 2-D array of tabulated data and the coordinates of the output grid ($\hat{x}$'s and $\hat{y}$'s). Here is a simple example that interpolates coarsely gridded values of the function $z(x, y) = \sin(\pi x)\sin(\pi y)$ to a finer grid. The original coordinates x and y both range from 0 to 1.

```
IDL> WINDOW, XSIZE = 600, YSIZE = 600
IDL> !P.MULTI = [0, 2, 2]
IDL> x_lo  = FINDGEN(5)/4
IDL> y_lo  = FINDGEN(5)/4
IDL> z_lo  = SIN(!PI*x_lo) # SIN(!PI*y_lo)
IDL> SURFACE, z_lo, x_lo, y_lo
```

The resulting surface plot is shown in the upper left panel of Figure 24.3. For comparison, a higher-resolution version of data is plotted in the upper right panel of Figure 24.3.

```
IDL> x_hi  = FINDGEN(17)/16
IDL> y_hi  = FINDGEN(17)/16
IDL> z_hi  = SIN(!PI*x_hi) # SIN(!PI*y_hi)
IDL> SURFACE, z_hi, x_hi, y_hi
```

The higher-resolution grid gives a much smoother picture of the underlying function. Finally, the low-resolution data are interpolated to the high-resolution grid by using BILINEAR. The coordinates used by BILINEAR are *grid coordinates*, which are based on the indices of the grid points. In this example, the grid coordinates range from 0 to 4 in both directions. Unlike grid *indices*, which are integers, the grid coordinates are floating-point values. In Figure 24.2, $\hat{x} \approx 1.25$, while $\hat{y} \approx 2.5$. The user must provide the grid coordinates to BILINEAR. BILINEAR computes the interpolated values, which are returned as a 2-D array.

```
IDL> z_int = BILINEAR(z_lo, 4*x_hi, 4*y_hi)
IDL> SURFACE, z_int, x_hi, y_hi
```

The result is shown in the lower left panel of Figure 24.3. As can be seen in the figure, there is a noticeable difference between the interpolated values and the high-resolution values. Because the sine function is a complex curve, the bilinear interpolating function cannot fully capture its curvature. As a result, the interpolated values have "facets" between the tabulated data points. This is a reminder that interpolation does not magically fill in between known data points; it only provides an estimate of the unknown values.

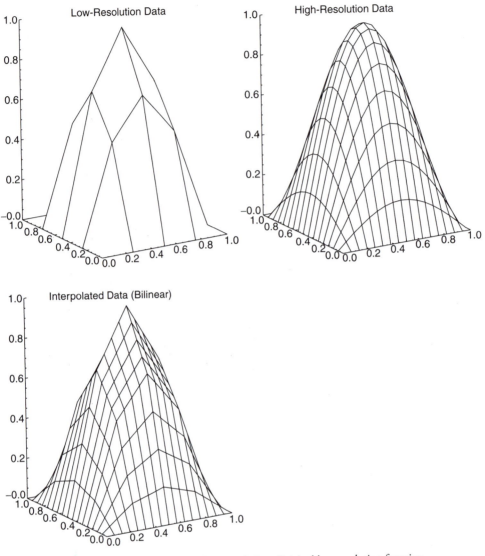

FIGURE 24.3   Examples of bilinear (2-D) interpolation. Original low-resolution function (top left), high-resolution version of original function (top right), original function interpolated to high-resolution grid (bottom left). (`BILINEAR1`)

24.5   **Higher Dimensions**

The IDL function INTERPOLATE will do one-, two-, and three-dimensional linear interpolation. It will also do *cubic convolution* on two-dimensional arrays. If you need to interpolate data with more than three dimensions, you may be able to use the built-in IDL functions on one or two dimensions at a time, or you may be forced to develop your own interpolation procedure. There are a great many different interpolation schemes that are not included in the IDL built-in functions. Before writing your own procedure, be sure to search the publicly available IDL libraries. Someone may have already done the work for you!

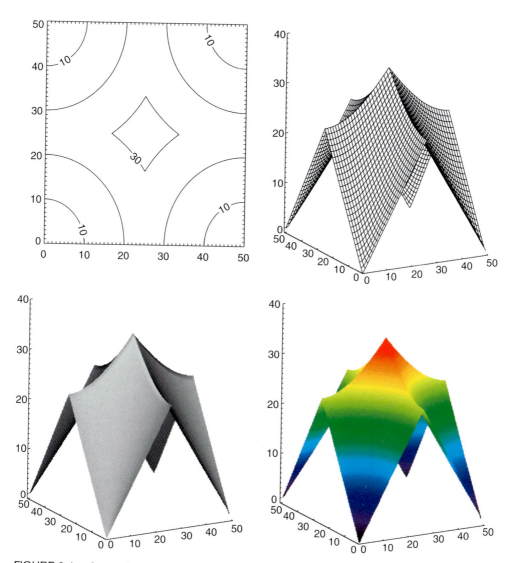

FIGURE 3.4   Some other types of graphics possible with IDL. (MULTIGRAPH)

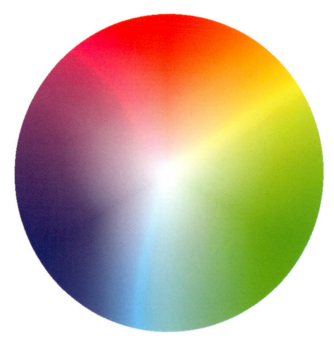

FIGURE 21.1   Example of a color wheel created using the HSV color system. In this case the value v is set to 1.0. (HSV_WHEEL_PS)

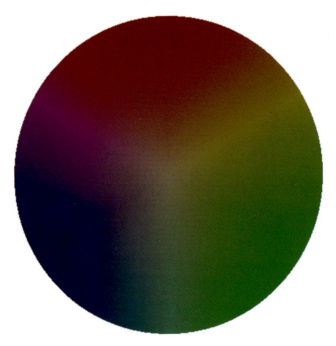

FIGURE 21.2   Example of a color wheel created using the HSV color system. In this case the value v is set to 0.5. (HSV_WHEEL_PS)

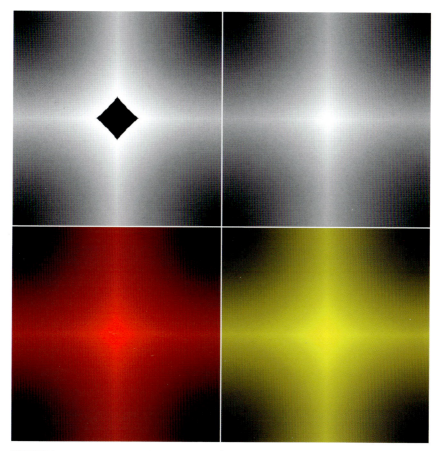

FIGURE 21.3   Examples of different images. Top left: image without scaling. Top right: image with automatic scaling by TVSCL. Bottom left: scaled image loaded into the red channel only. Bottom right: identical scaled images loaded into both the red and green channels. (IMAGE1)

FIGURE 21.4 A 24-bit color image created using the HSV color system. The hue is shown by itself in the lower left panel. The saturation is shown in the lower right. The saturation, which ranges from 0 to 1, is scaled in the image from 0 to 255. The value for all three images is equal to 1. (IMAGE2)

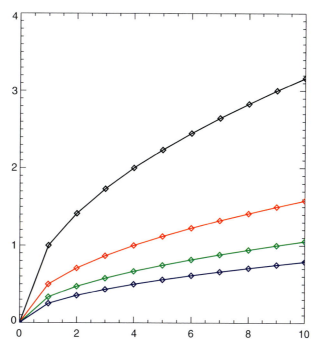

FIGURE 21.5   Example of using 8-bit color with the PLOT command and the PS device. (LINEGRAPH12)

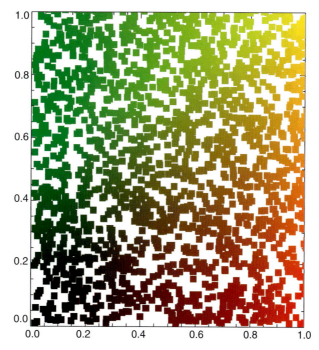

FIGURE 21.6   Example of using 24-bit color with the PLOT command and the PRINTER device. (RGB_PLOT_PRINTER)

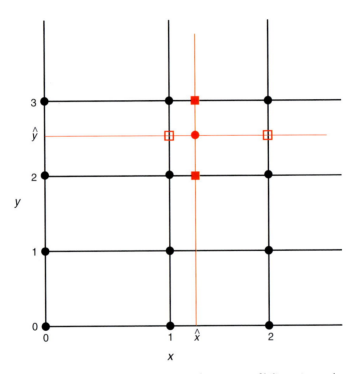

FIGURE 24.2   Schematic illustrating the concept of bilinear interpolation. (Not IDL)

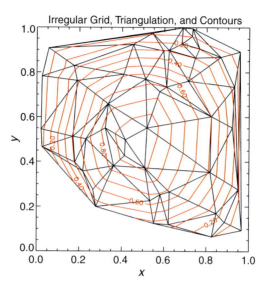

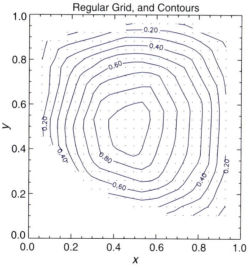

FIGURE 24.4   Examples of a 2-D triangular mesh created from irregularly gridded data by TRIANGULATE (top)
and the data interpolated to a regular rectangular grid
(bottom). (TRIANGULATE_PS)

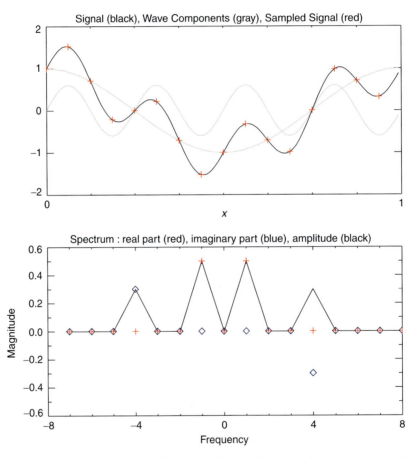

FIGURE 25.1   An example of a Fourier transform and spectrum for a signal composed of a pure cosine wave and a pure sine wave. (FOURIER1_PS)

24.6 Irregular Grids

IDL has several built-in tools for dealing with irregularly gridded data. Data can be considered to be irregularly gridded if they do not fit naturally into standard rectangular data arrays. An example of irregularly gridded data would be temperatures at major cities. The locations of cities do not fall onto a rectangular grid.

One useful approach to analyzing and displaying irregularly gridded data is *triangulation*. When a data set is triangulated, a network or mesh of triangles is constructed with the data points at the vertices of the triangles. The mesh of triangles defines a piecewise-planar interpolating function; that is, each triangle is a piece of a plane surface. Note that the mathematical form of the triangular surfaces (flat planes) is different from the bilinear functions used for interpolating rectangularly gridded data.[1]

Given the x and y coordinates of a set of irregularly distributed data points, the IDL procedure TRIANGULATE will construct a triangular mesh from those points (known as a Delaunay triangulation) and return a list of the indices of the vertices of each triangle. Constructing the triangular mesh requires only a single IDL command, but plotting the results is slightly more complicated than some other types of plots. Therefore, this process is demonstrated using the IDL script below. (The script is available in the file triangulate_script.pro in the script's directory.) The graphs produced by the script are shown in Figure 24.4.

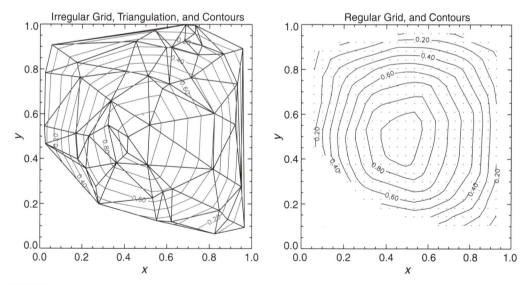

FIGURE 24.4   Examples of a 2-D triangular mesh created from irregularly gridded data by TRIANGULATE (left panel) and the data interpolated to a regular rectangular grid (right panel). Also see the color version of this figure in the color plates section. (TRIANGULATE_PS)

---

1   A rectangular grid could be converted to a triangular grid by drawing a diagonal through each rectangle of the grid. The triangles could then be used to construct an interpolating function for the data. Depending on which diagonal is chosen, however, the resulting triangles are generally different, which introduces ambiguity into the problem.

```
WINDOW, XSIZE = 800, YSIZE = 400              ;Open graphics window
!P.MULTI      = [0, 2, 1]                     ;Two graphics panes



;  PART 1 - Create irregular grid and display triangulation

n    = 50                                     ;Number of random points
seed = 47                                     ;Make result reproducible
x    = RANDOMU(seed, n)                       ;x-coords of irregular grid
y    = RANDOMU(seed, n)                       ;y-coords of irregular grid
z    = SIN(!PI*x)*SIN(!PI*y)                  ;Compute dependent variable

TRIANGULATE, x, y, tri                        ;Compute triangulation
ntri = (SIZE(tri))[2]                         ;Number of triangles

PLOT, x, y, PSYM = 3, $                        ;Plot data points
   TITLE  = 'Irregular Grid and Triangulation', $
   XTITLE = 'x', $
   YTITLE = 'y'
FOR i = 0, ntri-1 DO $                         ;Draw each triangle
   PLOTS, [x[tri[*,i]], x[tri[0,i]]], $
          [y[tri[*,i]], y[tri[0,i]]]
CONTOUR, z, x, y, TRIANGULATION = tri, $      ;Draw contours using triangles
   /OVERPLOT, /FOLLOW, $
   LEVELS = 0.1*FINDGEN(11), $
   COLOR  = COLOR_24('red')



;  PART 2 - Interpolate data to a regular grid and plot using CONTOUR

nx = 25                                       ;x-resolution of regular grid
ny = 25                                       ;y-resolution of regular grid
zz = TRIGRID(x, y, z, tri, $                  ;Interpolate to regular grid
        NX    = nx, NY    = ny, $             ;Resolution of output grid
        XGRID = xx, YGRID = yy, $             ;Coordinates of output grid
        MISSING = !VALUES.F_NAN)              ;Points outside triangles are
                                              ; set to NaN
CONTOUR, zz, xx, yy, /FOLLOW, $               ;Contour data on regular grid
   C_COLOR = COLOR_24('blue'), $
   LEVELS  = 0.1*FINDGEN(11), $
   TITLE   = 'Regular Grid and Contours', $
   XTITLE  = 'x', $
   YTITLE  = 'y'

xg = REBIN(           xx, nx, ny, /SAMPLE)    ;Make xx into 2-D grid
yg = REBIN(TRANSPOSE(yy), nx, ny, /SAMPLE)    ;Make yy into 2-D grid
```

```
i  = WHERE(FINITE(zz))              ;Find points within triangulation
PLOTS, xg[i], yg[i], PSYM = 3       ;Plot grid points within
                                     triangulation


!P.MULTI = 0                        ;Restore !P.MULTI
```

The first two lines of the script open a graphics window for two plots.

Next, the script creates an irregular grid of 50 data points by using the RANDOMU function to generate random x and y coordinates between 0 and 1. For the dependent variable z we use the same function as in the previous examples, $z(x, y) = \sin(\pi x) \sin(\pi y)$. The triangular mesh is computed using the TRIANGULATE procedure. The list of the indices of the vertices of the triangles is returned in the array tri, which is dimensioned $3 \times$ ntri, where ntri is the number of triangles needed to create the mesh. We use the SIZE function to get the number of triangles from the dimensions of tri.

Next, the data points are plotted (do not connect the dots!), and then, for each triangle, the three sides are drawn using the coordinates of the vertices of the triangles. Note that some triangles are nearly equilateral, whereas others are long and thin.

Given the irregularly gridded data and the list of triangles, the CONTOUR procedure will draw contour lines. These are drawn in red on top of the triangular mesh. Notice that the contours are straight lines within each triangle. This results from the fact that the contour segments are straight lines defined by the intersection of each triangle and the surfaces $z = \{0.0, 0.1, 0.2, \ldots, 1.0\}$. As you can see, although the function z is symmetric around the center of the plot box, the contours are not. Also, sizable parts of the box have no data points at all. This indicates that this set of 50 randomly distributed points is not sufficient to characterize this function well. Setting the IRREGULAR keyword to CONTOUR is equivalent to calling TRIANGULATE and then CONTOUR with the TRIANGULATION keyword.

If the only use of the data is to display contour plots, then the steps above are sufficient. In some cases, however, it is useful to interpolate the irregularly gridded data onto a regular grid. This can be done by using the TRIGRID function, which is demonstrated in the second part of the script.

The properties of the regular output grid can be specified by using various keywords of the TRIGRID function. Here we specify that the output grid be dimensioned 25×25. By default, the grid is created so that its rectangular border just includes all of the points of the mesh. The coordinates of the grid points are returned in the arrays xx and yy. Points that fall outside the boundary of the triangular mesh are set to NaN. Points inside are interpolated using the triangular mesh computed earlier by TRIANGULATE. If desired, points outside the mesh can be estimated by extrapolation, but the results are often unsatisfactory. The interpolated values on the regular grid are returned in the array zz.

The regularly gridded interpolated values are plotted in blue using a standard call to CONTOUR *without* the TRIANGULATE keyword. Finally, the locations of the regular grid points that fall within the triangular mesh (points with values that are not NaN) are drawn. Because contours are drawn differently on the irregular and regular grids, the two sets of contours are very similar, but not identical. You can see this by modifying the script triangulate.pro to overplot the two sets of contours on the same graph.

24.7 Summary

This chapter covers the basics of interpolation using the INTERPOL and BILINEAR functions. Displaying irregularly gridded data by using a triangular mesh, and interpolating to a regular grid are demonstrated using the TRIANGULATE and TRIGRID functions.

Fourier Analysis

This chapter shows how to use IDL to compute discrete Fourier transforms using the built-in IDL fast Fourier transform procedure FFT.

25.1 IDL Commands and Keywords

The following IDL command is used to compute forward and inverse Fourier transforms:

- FFT function and the INVERSE, DOUBLE, DIMENSION, and OVERWRITE keywords

25.2 Background

One of the most remarkable results in mathematics is the discovery by Fourier that any reasonably well-behaved function $f(x)$ can be represented as the sum of a (possibly infinite) set of sine and cosine functions. This discovery has had major theoretical and practical applications throughout mathematics and physical science. For example, Fourier transforms are useful for such diverse problems as solving differential equations, analyzing numerical methods, and filtering noise from a signal.

The use of Fourier transforms in data analysis was revolutionized in the middle of the twentieth century by the development of algorithms that allow fast, efficient numerical calculation of Fourier transforms. These algorithms are referred to as fast Fourier transforms (hence the name FFT). Because of their widespread use and potentially heavy computational requirements, many variations of the FFT algorithm have been developed for particular applications or computer systems. IDL includes a general-purpose fast Fourier transform algorithm that can be accessed via the built-in FFT function.

25.2.1 Basic Fourier Theory

See the FFT function in *IDL Reference Guide*.

There are a number of ways to develop the mathematical basis of Fourier theory. This section provides a short review of Fourier transforms aimed at the physical sciences and the computational use of fast Fourier transforms.

Consider an arbitrary function $f(x)$ that is defined on the finite interval $0 \leq x < L$. Although it is not essential, for simplicity we assume that f is smooth and continuous. The basic premise of the Fourier transform is that $f(x)$ can be represented as a sum of trigonometric functions:

$$f(x) = \sum_{k=0}^{\infty} \left[a_k \cos \left(\frac{2\pi kx}{L} \right) + b_k \sin \left(\frac{2\pi kx}{L} \right) \right]. \qquad (25.1)$$

The coefficients a_k and b_k are constants that depend on the function f. The index k is an integer that can be thought of as a frequency. It specifies the number of complete cycles of the cosine or sine functions per length L.

A particular coefficient, say a_m, can be found by multiplying Equation 25.1 by $\cos \left(\frac{2\pi mx}{L} \right)$ and integrating over the interval $[0, L]$:

$$\int_0^L f(x) \cos \left(\frac{2\pi mx}{L} \right) dx = \int_0^L \sum_{k=0}^{\infty} \qquad (25.2)$$

$$\left[a_k \cos \left(\frac{2\pi kx}{L} \right) + b_k \sin \left(\frac{2\pi kx}{L} \right) \right] \cos \left(\frac{2\pi mx}{L} \right) dx.$$

Reversing the order of the summation and integration and separating the cosine and sine terms gives:

$$\int_0^L f(x) \cos \left(\frac{2\pi mx}{L} \right) dx$$

$$= a_0 \int_0^L \cos \left(\frac{2\pi \cdot 0 \cdot x}{L} \right) \cos \left(\frac{2\pi mx}{L} \right) dx$$

$$+ a_1 \int_0^L \cos \left(\frac{2\pi \cdot 1 \cdot x}{L} \right) \cos \left(\frac{2\pi mx}{L} \right) dx$$

$$+ a_2 \int_0^L \cos \left(\frac{2\pi \cdot 2 \cdot x}{L} \right) \cos \left(\frac{2\pi mx}{L} \right) dx +$$

$$\vdots \qquad (25.3)$$

$$b_0 \int_0^L \sin \left(\frac{2\pi \cdot 0 \cdot x}{L} \right) \cos \left(\frac{2\pi mx}{L} \right) dx$$

$$+ b_1 \int_0^L \sin \left(\frac{2\pi \cdot 1 \cdot x}{L} \right) \cos \left(\frac{2\pi mx}{L} \right) dx$$

$$+ b_2 \int_0^L \sin \left(\frac{2\pi \cdot 2 \cdot x}{L} \right) \cos \left(\frac{2\pi mx}{L} \right) dx$$

$$\vdots$$

Similarly, the coefficients of the sine terms (the b_k's) are found by multiplying Equation 25.1 by $\sin\left(\frac{2\pi\,mx}{L}\right)$ and integrating over the interval $[0, L]$.

The key to the Fourier transform is evaluating the integrals on the right hand side of Equation 25.3. As it turns out, integrals of products of cosines and sines can be evaluated analytically. Because of the symmetry of the cosine and sine functions, integrating these products over an integral number of periods gives a very simple result:

$$\int_0^L \cos\left(\frac{2\pi\,kx}{L}\right)\cos\left(\frac{2\pi\,mx}{L}\right)dx = \begin{cases} 0 & : & k \neq m \\ L & : & k = m = 0 \\ L/2 & : & k = m \neq 0 \end{cases} \quad (25.4)$$

$$\int_0^L \sin\left(\frac{2\pi\,kx}{L}\right)\sin\left(\frac{2\pi\,mx}{L}\right)dx = \begin{cases} 0 & : & k \neq m \\ 0 & : & k = m = 0 \\ L/2 & : & k = m \neq 0 \end{cases} \quad (25.5)$$

$$\int_0^L \cos\left(\frac{2\pi\,kx}{L}\right)\sin\left(\frac{2\pi\,mx}{L}\right)dx = 0 \quad (25.6)$$

These are known as the orthogonality relations for the cosine and sine functions. If the frequencies are different ($k \neq m$) or the functions are different (that is, one function is a sine and the other a cosine), then the integrals vanish. If the frequencies are the same ($k = m$) and the functions are the same (both cosines or both sines), then the integrals evaluate to $L/2$, except for the special case where $k = m = 0$. When k and m are both zero, the integrals evaluate to L for the cosine case and 0 for the sine case.

Applying these rules to Equation 25.3 we see that *all of the integrals on the right hand side vanish except for one*: the integral containing the products of cosines with $k = m$ (that is, $\cos^2(\frac{2\pi\,kx}{L})$). Therefore,

$$\int_0^L \cos\left(\frac{2\pi\,kx}{L}\right)f(x)\,dx = a_k\frac{L}{2}. \quad (25.7)$$

(Remember that when $k = 0$ the integral evaluates on the right hand side to L, not $L/2$; see below.) Solving for a_k gives

$$a_k = \frac{2}{L}\int_0^L \cos\left(\frac{2\pi\,kx}{L}\right)f(x)\,dx. \quad (25.8)$$

A similar result holds for the sine coefficients (b_k's).

In general, the coefficients of the *Fourier series* can be computed by evaluating the following integrals. For $k = 0$:

$$a_0 = \frac{1}{L}\int_0^L f(x)\,dx \quad (25.9)$$

$$b_0 = 0 \quad (25.10)$$

and for $k \neq 0$:

$$a_k = \frac{2}{L} \int_0^L f(x) \cos\left(\frac{2\pi kx}{L}\right) dx \qquad (25.11)$$

$$b_k = \frac{2}{L} \int_0^L f(x) \sin\left(\frac{2\pi kx}{L}\right) dx \qquad (25.12)$$

In order to calculate each coefficient, one integral must be evaluated.

Calculating the coefficients a_k and b_k from $f(x)$ is referred to as *Fourier analysis*; that is, the function $f(x)$ is *analyzed* (split) into its *Fourier components*. This is also called a *forward Fourier transform*.

Computing the function $f(x)$ from the coefficients using Equation 25.1 is called the *Fourier synthesis* or *inverse Fourier transform*.

25.2.2 The Discrete Fourier Transform

The theory developed above is for *continuous* functions. Numerical data, on the other hand, consists of *discrete* values, f_j, $j = 0, 1, 2, \ldots, N - 1$. In this case, we could write

$$f_j = \sum_{k=0}^{N/2} \left[a_k \cos\left(\frac{2\pi kj}{N}\right) + b_k \sin\left(\frac{2\pi kj}{N}\right) \right]. \qquad (25.13)$$

where j/N can be thought of as a "coordinate" that ranges from 0 to 1. The difference from Equation 25.1 is that the dependent variable f_j is available only at a finite number of discrete points. For discrete data the "length" of the data record is taken to be N, the number of points in the record.

A theory for discrete data can be developed that is exactly analogous to that in the previous section for continuous functions. The Fourier transform in Equation 25.13 is referred to as a *discrete Fourier transform*. The coefficients of the Fourier series, a_k and b_k, are computed by evaluating sums, rather than integrals. The sums can be thought of as discrete approximations to the integrals in Equations 25.9, 25.10, 25.11, and 25.12.

Because real data series have a finite number of points, it is not necessary to have an infinite number of terms in the Fourier series. If a data series has N data points, only N terms are needed in the series. That is, $N/2$ cosine coefficients and $N/2$ sine coefficients together give a total of N coefficients. Thus, the total number of Fourier coefficients (a's and b's) is equal to the number of points in the data series.[1]

If you have N data points and wish to compute the Fourier transform, direct calculation of each coefficient (each sum) requires $\sim N$ operations

---

1   The sum written in Equation 25.13 has $N + 2$, coefficients, but two of the coefficients (b_0 and $b_{N/2}$) are always zero, leaving N nonzero coefficients.

(multiplications and additions). Calculating all N of the coefficients by directly evaluating the sums requires $\sim N^2$ operations. If your data series has 1000 points, for example, on the order of 1 million operations are required to compute the Fourier coefficients.

25.2.3   The Fast Fourier Transform (FFT)

The *fast Fourier transform* (FFT) is a highly efficient algorithm to compute the discrete Fourier transform and inverse transform. FFT algorithms are based on the realization that, due to the symmetries of the cosine and sine functions, many of the operations in the discrete Fourier transform are redundant. There are several properties of FFTs that are important to keep in mind. First, the FFT assumes that data samples are *equally spaced* in the independent coordinate. If the data points are not equally spaced, other methods, such as least-squares, must be used. Second, for an FFT to work correctly, there must not be any missing values. Again, if there are missing values, least-squares could be used to estimate the coefficients. Third, the number of operations required to compute the complete Fourier transform (all of the coefficients) using commonly available FFT algorithms is proportional to N times the sum of the prime factors of N (instead of the N^2 operations required for a straightforward discrete Fourier transform). This means that the best performance is achieved when N can be factored into many *small* prime factors. Thus, it is roughly five times faster to compute the Fourier transform of 64 points $(2 + 2 + 2 + 2 + 2 + 2 = 12)$, than 61 points (61 is prime). In fact, in the best case, where N is a power of 2, the Fourier transform can be completed using only $\sim N \cdot \log_2 N$ operations. For $N = 1024$, this gives an improvement over a plain discrete Fourier transform of about a factor of 100 (because $\log_2 1024 = 10$).

For all FFT algorithms, the speed of the transform depends on how well N can be factored. In general, FFTs are fast only when N can be factored into many small primes. The optimum choice is for N equal to a power of 2, but other values that have small prime factors will generally give reasonably good performance. What should you do if you have a data series with a length that is not highly factorable? There are several possibilities. One is to delete a small amount of data from one end or the other of the series to get a length that factors better. Another possibility is to *pad* the end of the series with zeroes to get a better length, such as a power of 2. Be cautious doing either of these until you have some experience with interpreting Fourier transforms and understand the implications of modifying the input data.

If there is a known periodicity in the data, then it is a good idea for the length of the series to be an integral number of multiples of that period. If you have hourly temperature data, for example (24 hours per day), you will be better off if your data series contains an integral number of days (integral multiple of 24), even if it means dropping some data at the beginning or end of the series.

25.3 The IDL FFT

25.3.1 Computing the Fourier Transform

Computing FFTs in IDL is very easy. The IDL FFT function can compute either forward or inverse transforms. The direction of the transform is set either by using the `direction` parameter of the FFT function or by using the INVERSE keyword.

Although computing the FFT is simple, using the results requires some care. There are two potentially confusing aspects to the Fourier coefficients calculated by the IDL FFT function. The first is the order in which the coefficients (a_k's and b_k's) are stored in the output array. The second is the fact that the IDL FFT is a general purpose FFT that works on *complex* numbers. Formally, the complex Fourier synthesis (inverse transform) performed by IDL is written

$$f_j = \sum_{k=0}^{N-1} g_k \, e^{i \frac{2\pi kj}{N}}, \tag{25.14}$$

while the Fourier analysis (forward transform) is

$$g_k = \frac{1}{N} \sum_{k=0}^{N-1} f_j \, e^{-i \frac{2\pi kj}{N}}. \tag{25.15}$$

In these equations, i represents $\sqrt{-1}$. In both equations, the coefficients (g_k and f_j) are complex numbers.

Often, the user wants only the Fourier transform of a *real* (FLOAT) array. IDL handles this by automatically converting the input array (either f or g) from FLOAT to COMPLEX, with the imaginary parts set to zero. It is important to remember that the output of FFT is *always* COMPLEX. This can introduce some minor additional complexity to your programs.

The best way to understand the organization of FFT output is to study an example. This section illustrates how IDL stores the array of complex coefficients that results from computing the transform and inverse transform of a real data series. The example function consists of a single cosine wave (amplitude 1.0, frequency 1) and a single sine wave (amplitude 0.6, frequency 4):

$$f_j = \cos\left(1 \cdot 2\pi \cdot \frac{j}{N}\right) + 0.6 \, \sin\left(4 \cdot 2\pi \cdot \frac{j}{N}\right). \tag{25.16}$$

```
PRO FOURIER1

;+
; Name:
;       FOURIER1
```

```
; Purpose:
;      Demonstrate a Fourier transform and inverse Fourier transform.
;      Plot the original function and the spectrum.
; Calling sequence:
;      FOURIER1
; Inputs:
;      None.
; Output:
;      Graphs of sample function and spectrum.
; Keywords:
;      None.
; Author and history:
;      Kenneth P. Bowman, 2004.
;-


COMPILE_OPT IDL2                              ;Set compiler options

n  = 16                                       ;Number of points in sampled function
x  = FINDGEN(n)/n                             ;Independent coordinate
f  = COS((2.0*!PI)*x)                         ;Compute function
      + 0.6*SIN((2.0*!PI)*4.0*x)

k  = [LINDGEN(n/2 + 1), $                     ;Compute frequencies
       REVERSE(-(1 + LINDGEN(n/2 - 1)))]

g  = FFT(f)                                   ;Compute Fourier transform
ff = FFT(g, /INVERSE)                         ;Compute inverse Fourier transform

;  Print results

PRINT, 'Original Function'
PRINT, '     j         x[j]          f[j]'
FOR j = 0, n-1 DO PRINT, j, x[j], f[j], FORMAT = "(I6, 2F12.3)"

PRINT
PRINT, 'Fourier Coefficients'
PRINT, '     n  k[n]       Real[n]      Imag[n]        Amp[n]'
FOR i = 0, n-1 DO PRINT, i, k[i], FLOAT(g[i]), IMAGINARY(g[i]), ABS(g[i]), $
   FORMAT = "2I6, 4F12.3)"

PRINT
PRINT, 'Resynthesized Function'
PRINT, '     j         x[j]       Real[j]      Imag[j]      Error[j]'
FOR j = 0, n-1 DO PRINT, j, x[j], FLOAT(ff[j]), IMAGINARY(ff[j]),
   ABS(ff[j]-f[j]), $ FORMAT = "(I6, 3F12.3, E12.3)"

END
```

Running FOURIER1 produces the following output. First, the original function
with 16 points is printed:

Original Function

j	x[j]	f[j]
0	0.000	1.000
1	0.062	1.524
2	0.125	0.707
3	0.188	-0.217
4	0.250	0.000
5	0.312	0.217
6	0.375	-0.707
7	0.438	-1.524
8	0.500	-1.000
9	0.562	-0.324
10	0.625	-0.707
11	0.688	-0.983
12	0.750	0.000
13	0.812	0.983
14	0.875	0.707
15	0.938	0.324

This is followed by the coefficients of the Fourier transform:

Fourier Coefficients

n	k[n]	Real[n]	Imag[n]	Amp[n]
0	0	-0.000	0.000	0.000
1	1	0.500	0.000	0.500
2	2	-0.000	-0.000	0.000
3	3	0.000	-0.000	0.000
4	4	0.000	-0.300	0.300
5	5	0.000	0.000	0.000
6	6	0.000	0.000	0.000
7	7	-0.000	0.000	0.000
8	8	-0.000	-0.000	0.000
9	-7	-0.000	-0.000	0.000
10	-6	0.000	-0.000	0.000
11	-5	0.000	-0.000	0.000
12	-4	0.000	0.300	0.300
13	-3	0.000	0.000	0.000
14	-2	-0.000	0.000	0.000
15	-1	0.500	-0.000	0.500

Look carefully at the table of coefficients. The first column is the array index
of each coefficient n. There are the same number of coefficients (16) as
there are points in the original series. The second column is the frequency
of each component in cycles per total length of the data series. Note that the

list includes both positive and negative frequencies. The largest frequency included is $N/2$ cycles per N points. This is known as the *Nyquist* frequency, and is the highest frequency that can be resolved given N input points.

The next two columns are the real and imaginary parts of the complex Fourier coefficients. The original signal consists of a cosine function with frequency 1 and amplitude 1 and a sine function with frequency 4 and amplitude 0.6. The coefficients of the cosine components of f are stored in the *real* part of the complex coefficients. Each cosine coefficient (a_k) is the sum of the two real parts for the pair of positive and negative frequencies k and $-k$. The sine coefficients are stored in the *imaginary* part of the complex coefficients. Each sine coefficient (b_k) is the sum of the *negative* of the imaginary part for frequency k and the imaginary part for frequency $-k$.

The last column is the amplitude (magnitude) of the complex coefficient for each frequencies (that is, $\sqrt{a_k^2 + b_k^2}$).

To check the result, the program resynthesizes the original signal using the complex coefficients and the inverse Fourier transform. The result is a complex array. In this case the original signal was real, so we are only interested in the real parts of the result. We see that the imaginary part is zero to within the roundoff error of a single-precision floating-point variable. The errors (differences between the original f and the resynthesized f) due to round-off error are negligible.

```
Resynthesized Function
    j          x[j]       Real[j]       Imag[j]       Error[j]
    0         0.000         1.000         0.000       0.000E+00
    1         0.062         1.524         0.000       1.846E-25
    2         0.125         0.707        -0.000       5.960E-08
    3         0.188        -0.217        -0.000       1.192E-07
    4         0.250         0.000         0.000       2.523E-08
    5         0.312         0.217        -0.000       8.941E-08
    6         0.375        -0.707         0.000       5.960E-08
    7         0.438        -1.524         0.000       1.192E-07
    8         0.500        -1.000         0.000       5.960E-08
    9         0.562        -0.324         0.000       5.960E-08
   10         0.625        -0.707        -0.000       5.960E-08
   11         0.688        -0.983        -0.000       1.549E-24
   12         0.750         0.000         0.000       2.523E-08
   13         0.812         0.983        -0.000       1.846E-25
   14         0.875         0.707         0.000       1.000E-24
   15         0.938         0.324         0.000       1.549E-24
```

A longer version of this example program (`fourier2.pro`) that also plots the original function and the spectrum is available in the `programs/` directory. The resulting output is shown in Figure 25.1. The top panel of the figure shows the original "continuous" function and the 16-point sampled function f used in the program (red pluses). The two individual components of the function are

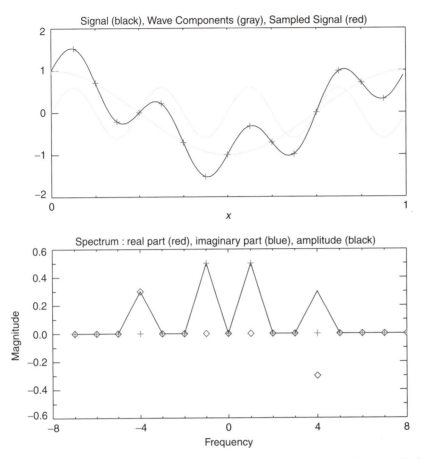

FIGURE 25.1   An example of a Fourier transform and spectrum for a signal composed of a pure cosine wave and a pure sine wave. Also see the color version of this figure in the color plates section. (FOURIER1_PS)

shown in gray. The lower panel shows the real (cosine) and imaginary (sine) parts of the complex Fourier coefficients. Note that for real input data the real parts are symmetric around zero ($\text{Real}(g(k)) = \text{Real}(g(-k))$), whereas the imaginary parts are antisymmetric ($\text{Im}(g(k)) = -\text{Im}(g(-k))$); that is, the coefficients of the negative frequencies are the complex conjugates of the coefficients of the corresponding positive frequencies. For real data it is not really necessary to plot the spectrum for both positive and negative frequencies. Given the coefficients for either the positive or negative frequencies, the complementary set can be found by simply taking the complex conjugate of the first.

Because IDL has only a general-purpose complex FFT, it is somewhat inefficient for Fourier transforms of real functions.[2]

---

2   Programs that use FFTs very heavily, and where computational time is a problem, can link to highly optimized, special-purpose FFTs written in Fortran or C. That topic is beyond the scope of this book.

25.3.2   Additional Properties and Keywords

IDL will automatically compute multidimensional Fourier transforms if the input array is multidimensional. Multidimensional FFTs are beyond the scope of this book, but if you need to compute multidimensional FFTs, I suggest that you develop a simple example like the one in the preceding section. The IDL demonstration program, which can be accessed by running demo at the IDL prompt, includes a demonstration of two-dimensional Fourier filtering of image data.

If you want to compute the Fourier transform of a multidimensional array in *only one dimension*, the DIMENSION keyword allows you to specify which dimension to transform. The first dimension is dimension 1, the second is dimension 2, and so on.

FFT will compute the Fourier transform using double-precision arithmetic if you specify the DOUBLE keyword.

If memory usage is a problem (for example, when computing the transform of a large multidimensional array), the OVERWRITE keyword can reduce memory usage by overwriting the input array with the output array. It is not sufficient to simply say:

```
a = FFT(a)
```

It is also necessary to include the OVERWRITE keyword.

```
a = FFT(a, /OVERWRITE)
```

To use OVERWRITE, the input array must be COMPLEX, not FLOAT.

25.4   Fourier Filtering

25.4.1   Filtering Methods

One of the many uses of the Fourier transform is *filtering*. Filtering is the process of reducing (or possibly amplifying) selected frequencies within a signal. Filtering can be done to a data series directly by using *convolution*.[3] This is usually referred to as filtering in the *time domain* or *space domain*, depending on the type of independent coordinate of the data series in question. For some applications, this *may* be the easiest and most efficient way to filter a data series. However, care must be taken when computing the filter weights and dealing with the ends of the data series to ensure that the results are correct. For example, the *running-mean* filter, which is commonly used to smooth data series, has complex spectral response characteristics that may change the data series in unexpected ways.

---

3   In IDL, convolution can be done with the CONVOL function.

Filtering can also be done using FFTs by:

1. computing the FFT of the data series in question,

2. multiplying the spectral coefficients by a frequency-dependent filter to reduce or amplify selected components, and

3. computing the inverse FFT to synthesize the filtered data series.

This process is usually referred to as *Fourier filtering* or filtering in the *spectral domain*. This approach may seem to involve a lot of extra work, because it requires both a transform and an inverse transform; but in fact, with the advent of the fast Fourier transform, Fourier filtering is often as fast as or faster than filtering in the time or space domain. In addition, it is easy to design a filter with precisely the spectral filtering properties desired; for example, a filter could be designed to pass a narrow band of frequencies and reject all others.

25.4.2   Types of Filters

Filters come in a wide variety of different types for different applications. Filters are commonly classified as low-pass, high-pass, or band-pass (other types can be defined). A low-pass filter passes the low-frequency components more or less unaltered, while reducing the high-frequency components. Similarly, a high-pass filter passes the high-frequency components, and a band-pass filter passes a selected band of frequencies. An *ideal filter* (demonstrated in the next section) passes a selected range of frequencies unaltered, while completely removing other frequencies. The ideal filter is essentially a step function of frequency (that is, either 0 or 1, depending on frequency).

Other mathematical functions, such as trigonometric or Gaussian functions, can be used to create filters that vary smoothly with frequency. The choice of filter depends on the application and the nature of the signal being filtered.

25.4.3   An Ideal Filter in IDL

The following program, FOURIER_FILTER1, implements an ideal filter using the IDL FFT function:

```
PRO FOURIER_FILTER1, type

;+
; Name:
;       FOURIER_FILTER1
; Purpose:
;       Demonstrate Fourier filtering and plot the original
;       and filtered functions.
; Calling sequence:
;       FOURIER_FILTER1
```

```
; Inputs:
;      type : String variable specifying the type of filter.
; Output:
;      Graphs of sample function with noise and filtered function.
; Keywords:
;      None.
; Author and history:
;      Kenneth P. Bowman, 2004.
;-

COMPILE_OPT IDL2                                    ;Set compiler options

IF (N_ELEMENTS(type) EQ 0) THEN TYPE = 'lowpass'   ;Default filter type

WINDOW, XSIZE = 600, YSIZE = 600                    ;Open graphics window

n   = 1024                                          ;Number of samples in signal
amp = 0.1                                           ;Noise amplitude
x   = FINDGEN(n)/n                                  ;Compute independent coordinate
f   = SIN(2.0*!PI* 2.0*x) + $                       ;Create synthetic signal
      SIN(2.0*!PI*16.0*x) + $
      amp*RANDOMN(3957, n)
k   = [LINDGEN(n/2 + 1), $                          ;Compute wavenumbers
          REVERSE(-(1 + LINDGEN(n/2 - 1)))]

filter = FLTARR(n)                                  ;Define filter array
CASE STRUPCASE(type) OF
   'LOWPASS'  : i = WHERE(ABS(k) LT  8, count)      ;Find low frequencies
   'HIGHPASS' : i = WHERE(ABS(k) GT 24, count)      ;Find high frequencies
   'BANDPASS' : i = WHERE((ABS(k) GT  8) AND $      ;Find band-pass frequencies
                     (ABS(k) LT 24), count)
   ELSE       : MESSAGE, 'Filter type must be specified.'
ENDCASE
IF (count EQ 0) THEN MESSAGE, 'Error creating filter'
filter[i] = 1.0                                     ;Create filter

ff = FLOAT(FFT(filter*FFT(f), /INVERSE))            ;Filter the signal

!P.MULTI = [0, 1, 2, 0, 0]                          ;Two plots per page
PLOT, x, f, $                                       ;Plot original signal
   TITLE  = 'Original signal', $
   XTITLE = 'x', $
   XMINOR = 1, $
   YTITLE = 'f', $
   YMINOR = 1
PLOT, x, ff, $                                      ;Plot filtered signal
   TITLE  = 'Filtered signal', $
```

```
    XTITLE = 'x', $
    XMINOR = 1, $
    YMINOR = 1
!P.MULTI = 0                                              ;Reset !P.MULTI

END
```

In this example, the input signal has 1024 points ($N = 1024$) and consists of two pure sine waves (frequencies of 2 and 16 cycles, respectively) plus a random component. The amplitude of the random component is 10% of

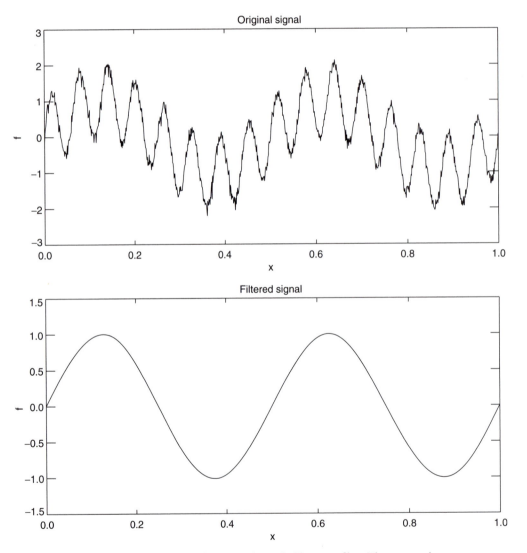

FIGURE 25.2   An example of Fourier filtering with an ideal low-pass filter. The top panel shows the original signal, and the bottom panel shows the filtered signal. The original signal consists of two pure harmonics and a random, white-noise background. Frequency components below the specified cutoff frequency are passed unaltered, and frequency components above the cutoff are set to zero. (FOURIER_FILTER1_PS)

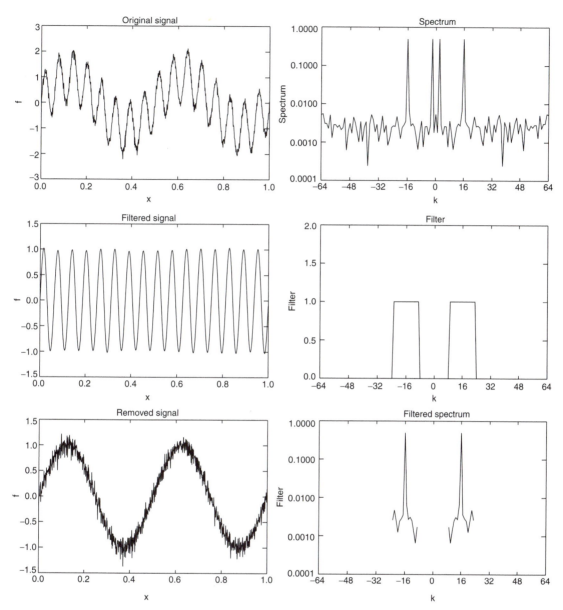

FIGURE 25.3 An example of Fourier filtering with an ideal band-pass filter. The left column shows the original signal, the signal after filtering, and part of the signal removed by the filter. The right column shows the spectrum of the original signal, the filter as a function of frequency, and the spectrum after filtering. The original signal consists of two pure harmonics and a random, white-noise background. Frequency components within the specified band are passed unaltered. All other frequency components are set to zero. (FOURIER_FILTER2_PS)

the amplitude of the two waves. The program creates the input signal and a filter with the specified cutoff frequency (or two frequencies in the case of the band-pass filter). The remaining steps are to transform the input signal, multiply the spectral coefficients by the filter, and inverse transform to create the filtered signal. These three operations are carried out by a single line of

IDL. Because the input signal is real (not complex), the output is converted to FLOAT. Finally, the program plots the original and filtered signals. The output is shown in Figure 25.2.

A slightly longer version of the filtering program, FOURIER_FILTER2_PS, is included with the example programs. In addition to the original and filtered signals, this version plots the part of the signal removed by the filter, the original spectrum, the spectral filter, and the filtered spectrum. The output is shown in Figure 25.3.

25.5 Summary

This chapter covers the basics of using the IDL fast Fourier transform (FFT).

- FFT. The IDL FFT function is a general-purpose complex fast Fourier transform. If your input signal is real, remember that the output from FFT is always complex.

25.6 Exercises

1. Compute the Fourier transform of a step function

$$f(x) = \begin{cases} 0: & x \le \frac{L}{2} \\ 1: & x > \frac{L}{2} \end{cases} \tag{25.17}$$

   and plot the complex spectrum.

2. Compute the Fourier transform of a purely imaginary function. How does the complex spectrum compare with that of a real function?

3. Compute the Fourier transform of a complex function.

4. Generate a random data series and filter it with either a low-pass or high-pass filter.

Appendix A

An IDL Style Guide

The style in which a program is written can have a major effect on how easy it is to read, understand, debug, and modify. The human visual system is very good at distinguishing *patterns* and *deviations from patterns*. Good visual clues (capitalization, indentation, alignment, etc.) make it much easier to grasp the structure of a program and locate errors.

There are many possible ways to present an IDL program with good style. Like other computer subjects (text editors, programming languages, PCs vs. Macs, and so on), programming-style discussions can become very heated. The guidelines that I present in this appendix are what I have discovered to work well through many years of experience programming in Fortran and IDL. They are not dogma. I suggest that you try to follow these guidelines closely, at least until you consider yourself to be well-skilled at IDL programming. The rules may seem both tedious and unnecessary, but believe me, time spent cleaning up your programs is not time wasted! It will save a much greater amount of time later when you are debugging and revising your code. After you have been programming for a few years, you can evolve your own style.

Some development environments, including the IDLDE and the emacs mode for IDL, will automatically color code the text of your programs (for example, comments are red, IDL reserved words are blue, and so on). I am not opposed to syntax coloring, but it is not a substitute for proper text layout and comments. At times, programs must be printed, and color printers are not always available. Some colors may show well on the screen but not on the printed page. Use syntax coloring in your development environment if it helps you to program, but write your programs as though syntax coloring were not available.

A.1 IDL Style Rules

Writing a program is like writing any other technical document. Plan to edit and correct your programs until they meet high standards for clarity, conciseness, and correctness.

A.1.1 Goals of the IDL Style Rules

The basic goals of the IDL style rules are:

■ to make the program easy to read, understand, debug, and modify.

■ to make the program as compact as possible. (This can reduce tedious scrolling while writing programs.)

A.1.2 Names and Reserved Words

■ IDL commands and reserved words should be all uppercase. A list of IDL reserved words is given at the end of this appendix.

■ Procedure and function names should be all uppercase.

■ Variable names should generally be lowercase. You can make exceptions if the standard symbols are normally uppercase, such as T for temperature. Remember that IDL is not case sensitive, so using t for time and T for temperature in the same program will not work!

■ Keep names as short as you can, but don't make them needlessly obscure. It makes sense for the variable containing a logical unit number for a file to be named ifile, not m. On the other hand, input_file_unit_number is probably overkill.

A.1.3 Spaces, Alignment, and Indentation

■ Indent, align, and space your code for readability.

■ Use single blank lines to separate related blocks of material. Avoid double blank lines; they make programs too long and lead to lots of scrolling up and down.

■ I find that a three-space indent is large enough for readability and small enough not to waste too much of a line. Set the tab width of your programming editor or environment to three spaces.

■ Use tabs, not spaces, to indent at the beginning of a line.[1]

■ Use spaces within a line and within multiple lines to align similar program structures.

■ Use tabs between the end of the IDL statement and a comment on the same line.

---

1   The example program files do not contain any tabs. This is done to allow the programs to be executed in IDL *and* imported directly into the text of this book without causing formatting problems.

- Put at least one space on each side of an equal sign. Line up the equal signs in contiguous blocks of program statements.

- Indent the inside lines of all blocks of code (IF blocks, FOR loops, etc.). Do not indent the first and last lines. Example:

```
FOR i = 0, n-1 DO BEGIN
    data[i] = READ_NETCDF(infile[i])
ENDFOR
```

- Indent continuation lines (hanging indent).

- Use nested indentation for nested structures, such as an IF block inside a FOR loop.

- Put the comment on the first line of a multiline statement.

- Align comments. Generally, you should align all comments within a single procedure. This makes the entire program into a two-column table with program statements in the left column and comments in the right. An occasional long program line with an unaligned comment is okay.

- Break statements into multiple lines so that you can align similar structures. In this example, the keywords of the PLOT command are aligned:

```
PLOT, x, y, $                          ;Plot y(x)
    TITLE  = 'Plot of x^' + STRTRIM(STRING(n), 2), $
    XTITLE = 'x', $
    YTITLE = 'y'
```

A.1.4 Comments

- Include a block of comments at the top of the procedure describing the procedure and its arguments. A standard layout for these comments can be found in the example program templates: PROGRAM_TEMPLATE and FUNCTION_TEMPLATE.

- Most statements should have a comment.

- I usually do not comment PRINT or MESSAGE statements. They are largely self-commenting.

- If you print your programs on standard paper using landscape orientation, you can have relatively long lines (including comments) without wrapping onto the next line.

- Usually you can avoid lines containing nothing but a comment, although you may occasionally want to label a block of statements in a longer program. Comments at the end of a line containing a command are usually sufficient.

A.2 Examples of Good and Bad Style

The following three examples show the same program with different styles. All three programs will work exactly the same. The computer doesn't care whether you include comments or not. The style rules are for the computer users—you and anyone else who uses your programs.

A.2.1 An Example of Bad Style

The example of bad style below has no comments, no spacing or alignment, and no apparent organization. Because everything is uppercase, there are no visual clues to help distinguish commands from variables. To decipher this program, you have to go through each line, one at a time.

```
PRO READ_NETCDF2,INFILE
COMPILE_OPT IDL2
IF (N_ELEMENTS(INFILE) EQ 0) THEN $
INFILE=!BOWMAN+'data/random.ncd'
IID= NCDF_OPEN(INFILE)
NCDF_VARGET,IID,'TIME',TIME
NCDF_VARGET,IID,'T',T
NCDF_VARGET,IID,'W',W
NCDF_ATTGET,IID,'TIME','LONGNAME',TIME_NAME
NCDF_ATTGET,IID,'TIME','UNITS',TIME_UNITS
NCDF_ATTGET,IID,'T','LONGNAME',T_NAME
NCDF_ATTGET,IID,'T','UNITS',T_UNITS
NCDF_ATTGET,IID,'W','LONGNAME',W_NAME
NCDF_ATTGET,IID,'W','UNITS',W_UNITS
NCDF_CLOSE,IID
TIME_NAME=STRING(TIME_NAME)
TIME_UNITS=STRING(TIME_UNITS)
T_NAME=STRING(T_NAME)
T_UNITS=STRING(T_UNITS)
W_NAME=STRING(W_NAME)
W_UNITS=STRING(W_UNITS)
B= REGRESS(W,T,YFIT= T_FIT,CONST= A,/DOUBLE)
!P.MULTI= [0,2,2,0,0]
PLOT,TIME,W,/YNOZERO,XTITLE= TIME_NAME + ' ('+TIME_UNITS+ )',$
YTITLE= W_NAME+' ('+W_UNITS+')'
PLOT,TIME,T,/YNOZERO,XTITLE= TIME_NAME+' ('+TIME_UNITS+')',$
YTITLE= T_NAME+' ('+T_UNITS + ')'
PLOT,W,T,PSYM=3,/YNOZERO,XTITLE= W_NAME+' ('+W_UNITS+')',$
YTITLE= T_NAME+' ('+T_UNITS+')'
OPLOT,[!X.CRANGE[0],!X.CRANGE[1]],[A + B[0]*!X.CRANGE[0],A + B[0]*!X.CRANGE[1]]
!P.MULTI= 0
END
```

A.2.2 An Example of Mediocre Style

This example of mediocre style does have comments, and it uses case to distinguish different elements, but it lacks breaks to show how the program is organized. Also, similar structures are not aligned well. This obscures the fact that many lines are doing the same operation on different variables.

```
PRO READ_NETCDF2, infile

;  This program reads a simple netCDF file and plots several graphs.

COMPILE_OPT IDL2  ;Set compile options

IF (N_ELEMENTS(infile) EQ 0) THEN $  ;Default input file
   infile = !Bowman + 'data/random.ncd'
iid = NCDF_OPEN(infile)        ;Open input file
NCDF_VARGET,iid,'Time',time                    ;Read time
NCDF_VARGET,iid,'T',T                          ;Read temperature
NCDF_VARGET,iid,'w',w                          ;Read vertical velocity
NCDF_ATTGET,iid,'Time','longname',time_name    ;Get long name of time
NCDF_ATTGET,iid,'Time','units',time_units      ;Get units of time
NCDF_ATTGET,iid,'T','longname',T_name          ;Get long name of T
NCDF_ATTGET,iid,'T','units',T_units            ;Get units of T
NCDF_ATTGET,iid,'w','longname',w_name          ;Get long name of w
NCDF_ATTGET,iid,'w','units',w_units            ;Get units of w
NCDF_CLOSE,iid                                 ;Close input file
time_name = STRING(Time_name)    ;Convert to string
time_units = STRING(Time_units)  ;Convert to string
T_name = STRING(T_name)          ;Convert to string
T_units = STRING(T_units)        ;Convert to string
w_name = STRING(w_name)          ;Convert to string
w_units = STRING(w_units)        ;Convert to string
b = REGRESS(w, t, YFIT = T_fit, CONST = a, /DOUBLE)   ;Compute linear regression
!P.MULTI = [0, 2, 2, 0, 0]   ;Multiple plots per page
PLOT, time, w, /YNOZERO, $  ;Plot w(t)
   XTITLE = time_name + ' (' + time_units + ')', $
   YTITLE = w_name + ' (' + w_units + ')'
PLOT, time, T, /YNOZERO, $  ;Plot T(t)
   XTITLE = time_name + ' (' + time_units + ')', $
   YTITLE = T_name + ' (' + T_units + ')'
PLOT, w, T, PSYM = 3, /YNOZERO, $  ;Plot T vs. w
   XTITLE = w_name + ' (' + w_units + ')', $
   YTITLE = T_name + ' (' + T_units + ')'
OPLOT, [!X.CRANGE[0], !X.CRANGE[1]], $  ;Plot linear fit
   [a + b[0]*!X.CRANGE[0], a + b[0]*!X.CRANGE[1]]
!P.MULTI = 0  ;Single plot per page

END
```

A.2.3   An Example of Good Style

This example of good style is well commented and organized into distinct
blocks of related statements. Because the comments are all aligned, it is easy
to read down the comments like a table and follow the flow of the program.
Some lines have been wrapped with the continuation character $ in order to
fit the program on the pages of this book.

```
PRO READ_NETCDF2, infile


;+
; Name:
;       READ_NETCDF2
; Purpose:
;       This program reads a simple netCDF file
;       and plots several graphs.
; Calling sequence:
;       READ_NETCDF2
; Inputs:
;       infile   : name of input file
; Output:
;       Plots of data from netCDF file.
; Keywords:
;       None.
; Author and history:
;       Kenneth P. Bowman, 2004.
;-


COMPILE_OPT IDL2                         ;Set compile options

IF (N_ELEMENTS(infile) EQ 0) THEN $      ;Default input file
    infile = !Bowman + 'data/random.ncd'


iid = NCDF_OPEN(infile)                  ;Open input file

NCDF_VARGET, iid, 'Time', time           ;Read time
NCDF_VARGET, iid, 'T',    T              ;Read temperature
NCDF_VARGET, iid, 'w',    w              ;Read vertical velocity

NCDF_ATTGET, iid, 'Time', 'longname', $  ;Get long name of time
    time_name
NCDF_ATTGET, iid, 'Time', 'units',    $  ;Get units of time
    time_units
NCDF_ATTGET, iid, 'T',    'longname', $  ;Get long name of T
    T_name
NCDF_ATTGET, iid, 'T',    'units',    $  ;Get units of T
    T_units
```

```
NCDF_ATTGET, iid, 'w',      'longname', $   ;Get long name of w
   w_name
NCDF_ATTGET, iid, 'w',      'units',    $   ;Get units of w
   w_units

NCDF_CLOSE, iid                             ;Close input file

time_name  = STRING(Time_name)              ;Convert to string
time_units = STRING(Time_units)             ;Convert to string
T_name     = STRING(T_name)                 ;Convert to string
T_units    = STRING(T_units)                ;Convert to string
w_name     = STRING(w_name)                 ;Convert to string
w_units    = STRING(w_units)                ;Convert to string

b = REGRESS(w, t, YFIT = T_fit, $           ;Linear regression
   CONST = a, /DOUBLE)

!P.MULTI = [0, 2, 2, 0, 0]                  ;Set plots per page

PLOT, time, w, /YNOZERO, $                  ;Plot w(time)
   XTITLE = time_name + ' (' + time_units + ')', $
   YTITLE = w_name + ' (' + w_units + ')'
PLOT, time, T, /YNOZERO, $                  ;Plot T(time)
   XTITLE = time_name + ' (' + time_units + ')', $
   YTITLE = T_name + ' (' + T_units + ')'

PLOT, w, T, PSYM = 3, /YNOZERO, $           ;Plot T vs. w
   XTITLE = w_name + ' (' + w_units + ')', $
   YTITLE = T_name + ' (' + T_units + ')'
OPLOT, [!X.CRANGE[0], !X.CRANGE[1]], $      ;Plot linear fit
   [a + b[0]*!X.CRANGE[0], a + b[0]*!X.CRANGE[1]]

!P.MULTI = 0                                ;Reset !P.MULTI

END
```

A.3 IDL Reserved Words

The words in Table A.1 are reserved in IDL for special purposes. You should not use these words for other purposes, such as variable names. You cannot, for example, use MOD as a variable name.

```
IDL> mod = 3

mod = 3
    ^
% Syntax error.
```

TABLE A.1   List of IDL reserved words.

AND	GE
BEGIN	GOTO
BREAK	GT
CASE	IF
COMMON	INHERITS
COMPILE_OPT	LE
CONTINUE	LT
DO	MOD
ELSE	NE
END	NOT
ENDCASE	OF
ENDELSE	ON_IOERROR
ENDFOR	OR
ENDIF	PRO
ENDREP	REPEAT
ENDSWITCH	SWITCH
ENDWHILE	THEN
EQ	UNTIL
FOR	WHILE
FORWARD_FUNCTION	XOR
FUNCTION	

Appendix B

Example Procedures, Functions, Scripts, and Data Files

B.1 Example Procedures, Functions, and Scripts

B.1.1 List of Procedures, Functions, and Scripts by Chapter

Table B.1 is a list of all of the procedures, functions, and scripts used in this book organized by chapter. If the file contains a procedure or function, the procedure or function name is given in uppercase. If the file contains a script, the name is given in lowercase. The actual file names are always lowercase, that is, the procedure ANIMATE is contained in the file animate.pro. The script add_arrays is contained in the file add_arrays.pro.

TABLE B.1   List of procedures, functions, and scripts by chapter.

Chapter or Appendix	Name	Type
3 - Interactive IDL	startup	startup script
	LINEGRAPH1	procedure
	LINEGRAPH2	procedure
	MULTIGRAPH	procedure
4 - IDL Scripts	log_plot	script
	LOG_PLOT_PS	procedure
	log_plot2	script
	LOG_PLOT2_PS	procedure
	exp_plot	script
	EXP_PLOT_PS	procedure
5 - Integer Constants and Variables	GRAYSCALE	procedure
7 - Using Arrays	add_arrays	script
	two_d_coords	script
	TWO_D_COORDS_PS	procedure
8 - Searching and Sorting	SEARCH_COMPARE	procedure
9 - Structures	named_structure	script
	WX_OB__DEFINE	procedure
	anonymous_structure	script
	hierarchical_structure	script

continued on next page

TABLE B.1   *continued*

Chapter or Appendix	Name	Type
11 - Reading Text	PLOT_POWER	procedure
	READ_LOG_TABLE	procedure
12 - Binary Files	WRITE_MY_BINARY	procedure
	READ_MY_BINARY	procedure
	READ_MY_BINARY2	procedure
13 - Reading NetCDF Files	READ_NETCDF1	procedure
	READ_NETCDF1_PS	procedure
	READ_NETCDF_2	procedure
	READ_NETCDF2_PS	procedure
14 - Writing NetCDF Files	WRITE_RANDOM_NETCDF	procedure
	WRITE_RANDOM_NETCDF2	procedure
15 - Procedures and Functions	PROCEDURE_TEMPLATE	procedure
	MYPRO	procedure
	MYSUB	procedure
	MYSIN	procedure
	MYSQUARE	function
	FUNCTION_TEMPLATE	function
17 - Line Graphs	LINEGRAPH3	procedure
	LINEGRAPH4	procedure
	LINEGRAPH5	procedure
	LINEGRAPH6	procedure
	LINEGRAPH7	procedure
	LINEGRAPH8	procedure
	LINEGRAPH9	procedure
	LINEGRAPH10	procedure
	LINEGRAPH11	procedure
18 - Contour and Surface Plots	CONTOUR1	procedure
	CONTOUR2	procedure
	CONTOUR2_PS	procedure
	CONTOUR3	procedure
	CONTOUR3_PS	procedure
	SURFACE1	procedure
	SURFACE1_PS	procedure
	SHADE_SURF1	procedure
	SHADE_SURF1_PS	procedure
19 - Mapping	MAP_CYLINDRICAL_PS	procedure
	MAP_HAMMER_PS	procedure
	MAP_AZIMUTHAL_PS	procedure
	MAP_ORTHOGRAPHIC_PS	procedure
	MAP_CONTOUR_PS	procedure
	MAP_PLOTS_PS	procedure
20 - Printing Graphics	PS_ON	procedure
	PS_OFF	procedure
	LINEGRAPH3	procedure
	PRINTER_ON	procedure
	PRINTER_OFF	procedure
	LINEGRAPH3_PRINTER	procedure

continued on next page

TABLE B.1 *continued*

Chapter or Appendix	Name	Type
21 - Color and Image Display	COLOR_24	function
	HSV_WHEEL_PNG	procedure
	HSV_WHEEL_PS	procedure
	IMAGE1	procedure
	IMAGE2	procedure
	LINEGRAPH12	procedure
	LOAD_BASIC_COLORS	procedure
	RGB_PLOT_PRINTER	procedure
22 - Animation	ANIMATE	procedure
	ANIMATE_FILES	procedure
23 - Statistics and Pseudorandom Numbers	RANDOM1	procedure
	RANDOM2	procedure
	LINEAR_REGRESS	procedure
24 - Interpolation	INTERPOLATE1	procedure
	BILINEAR1	procedure
	triangulate_script	script
	TRIANGULATE_PS	procedure
25 - Fourier Analysis	FOURIER1	procedure
	FOURIER1_PS	procedure
	FOURIER_FILTER1	procedure
	FOURIER_FILTER1_PS	procedure
	FOURIER_FILTER2_PS	procedure
Appendix A - IDL Style Guide	READ_NETCDF2_BAD	procedure
	READ_NETCDF2_MEDIOCRE	procedure

B.1.2 Alphabetical List of Procedures, Functions, and Scripts

Table B.2 is an alphabetical list of all of the procedures, functions, and scripts used in this book. If the file contains a procedure or function, the procedure or function name is given in uppercase. If the file contains a script, the name is given in lowercase. The actual file names are always lowercase; that is, the procedure ANIMATE is contained in the file animate.pro. The script add_arrays is contained in the file add_arrays.pro.

TABLE B.2 Alphabetical list of procedures, functions, and scripts used in this book.

Name	Type	Chapter or Appendix
add_arrays	script	7 - Using Arrays
ANIMATE	procedure	22 - Animation
ANIMATE_FILES	procedure	22 - Animation
anonymous_structure	script	9 - Structures
BILINEAR1	procedure	24 - Interpolation
COLOR_24	function	21 - Color and Image Display
CONTOUR1	procedure	18 - Contour and Surface Plots
CONTOUR2	procedure	18 - Contour and Surface Plots

continued on next page

TABLE B.2   *continued*

Name	Type	Chapter or Appendix
CONTOUR2_PS	procedure	18 - Contour and Surface Plots
CONTOUR3	procedure	18 - Contour and Surface Plots
CONTOUR3_PS	procedure	18 - Contour and Surface Plots
COORD__DEFINE	procedure	9 - Structures
exp_plot	script	4 - IDL Scripts
EXP_PLOT_PS	procedure	4 - IDL Scripts
FOURIER_FILTER1	procedure	25 - Fourier Analysis
FOURIER_FILTER1_PS	procedure	25 - Fourier Analysis
FOURIER_FILTER2_PS	procedure	25 - Fourier Analysis
FOURIER1	procedure	25 - Fourier Analysis
FOURIER1_PS	procedure	25 - Fourier Analysis
FUNCTION_TEMPLATE	function	15 - Procedures and Functions
GRAYSCALE	procedure	5 - Integer Constants and Variables
hierarchical_structure	script	9 - Structures
HSV_WHEEL_PNG	procedure	21 - Color and Image Display
HSV_WHEEL_PRINTER	procedure	21 - Color and Image Display
HSV_WHEEL_PS	procedure	21 - Color and Image Display
IMAGE1	procedure	21 - Color and Image Display
IMAGE2	procedure	21 - Color and Image Display
INTERPOLATE1	procedure	24 - Interpolation
LINEAR_REGRESS	procedure	23 - Statistics and Pseudorandom Numbers
LINEGRAPH1	procedure	3 - Interactive IDL
LINEGRAPH2	procedure	3 - Interactive IDL
LINEGRAPH3	procedure	17 - Line Graphs
LINEGRAPH3_PRINTER	procedure	20 - Printing Graphics
LINEGRAPH4	procedure	17 - Line Graphs
LINEGRAPH5	procedure	17 - Line Graphs
LINEGRAPH6	procedure	17 - Line Graphs
LINEGRAPH7	procedure	17 - Line Graphs
LINEGRAPH8	procedure	17 - Line Graphs
LINEGRAPH9	procedure	17 - Line Graphs
LINEGRAPH10	procedure	17 - Line Graphs
LINEGRAPH11	procedure	17 - Line Graphs
LINEGRAPH12	procedure	21 - Color and Image Display
LOAD_BASIC_COLORS	procedure	21 - Color and Image Display
log_plot	script	4 - IDL Scripts
LOG_PLOT_PS	procedure	4 - IDL Scripts
log_plot2	script	4 - IDL Scripts
LOG_PLOT2_PS	procedure	4 - IDL Scripts
MAP_AZIMUTHAL_PS	procedure	19 - Mapping
MAP_CONTOUR_PS	procedure	19 - Mapping
MAP_CYLINDRICAL_PS	procedure	19 - Mapping
MAP_HAMMER_PS	procedure	19 - Mapping
MAP_ORTHOGRAPHIC_PS	procedure	19 - Mapping
MAP_PLOTS_PS	procedure	19 - Mapping
MULTIGRAPH	procedure	3 - Interactive IDL
MYPRO	procedure	15 - Procedures and Functions
MYSIN	procedure	15 - Procedures and Functions
MYSQUARE	function	15 - Procedures and Functions
MYSUB	procedure	15 - Procedures and Functions
named_structure	script	9 - Structures
plot_power	script	7 - Using Arrays

continued on next page

TABLE B.2 *continued*

Name	Type	Chapter or Appendix
PRINT_OFF	procedure	20 - Printing Graphics
PRINT_ON	procedure	20 - Printing Graphics
PROCEDURE_TEMPLATE	procedure	15 - Procedures and Functions
PS_OFF	procedure	20 - Printing Graphics
PS_ON	procedure	20 - Printing Graphics
RANDOM1	procedure	23 - Statistics and Pseudorandom Numbers
RANDOM2	procedure	23 - Statistics and Pseudorandom Numbers
READ_LOG_TABLE	procedure	11 - Reading Text
READ_MY_BINARY	procedure	12 - Binary Files
READ_MY_BINARY2	procedure	12 - Binary Files
READ_NETCDF1	procedure	13 - Reading NetCDF Files
READ_NETCDF1_PS	procedure	13 - Reading NetCDF Files
READ_NETCDF2	procedure	13 - Reading NetCDF Files and Appendix A - IDL Style Guide
READ_NETCDF2_BAD	procedure	A - IDL Style Guide
READ_NETCDF2_MEDIOCRE	procedure	A - IDL Style Guide
READ_NETCDF2_PS	procedure	13 - Reading NetCDF Files
RGB_PLOT_PRINTER	procedure	21 - Color and Image Display
RGB_PLOT_PS	procedure	21 - Color and Image Display
SEARCH_COMPARE	procedure	8 - Searching and Sorting
SHADE_SURF1	procedure	18 - Contour and Surface Plots
SHADE_SURF1_PS	procedure	18 - Contour and Surface Plots
startup	startup script	3 - Interactive IDL
SURFACE1	procedure	18 - Contour and Surface Plots
SURFACE1_PS	procedure	18 - Contour and Surface Plots
TRIANGULATE_PS	procedure	24 - Interpolation
triangulate_script	script	24 - Interpolation
two_d_coords	script	7 - Using Arrays
TWO_D_COORDS_PS	procedure	7 - Using Arrays
WRITE_MY_BINARY	procedure	12 - Binary Files
WRITE_RANDOM_NETCDF	procedure	14 - Writing NetCDF Files
WRITE_RANDOM_NETCDF2	procedure	14 - Writing NetCDF Files
WX_OB__DEFINE	procedure	9 - Structures

B.2 Data Files

Table B.3 lists the data files used by the example programs in this book.

TABLE B.3 List of data files by chapter.

File Name	Programs	Chapter or Appendix
table.txt	READ_LOG_TABLE	11 - Reading Text
binary.dat	WRITE_MY_BINARY READ_MY_BINARY WRITE_MY_BINARY2	12 - Binary Files
random.ncdump random.ncd	output of ncdump utility RANDOM1	13 - Reading NetCDF Files

continued on next page

TABLE B.3   *continued*

File Name	Programs	Chapter or Appendix
	`READ_NETCDF1`	
	`READ_NETCDF1_PS`	
	`WRITE_RANDOM_NETCDF`	
	`WRITE_RANDOM_NETCDF2`	
`random2.ncd`	`RANDOM2`	
`flux/wc151_1810.ncd.ncd`	`READ_NETCDF2`	
	`READ_NETCDF2_PS`	
`NCEP/2001/ncep_20010101T00Z.ncd`	`MAP_CYLINDRICAL_PS`	19 - Mapping
	`MAP_HAMMER_PS`	
	`MAP_AZIMUTHAL_PS`	
	`MAP_ORTHOGRAPHIC_PS`	
	`MAP_CONTOUR_PS`	
`animation/frame.001.png`	`ANIMATE_PNG` and `ANIMATE2`	22 - Animation
`animation/frame.002.png`		
.		
.		
.		

Bibliography

Bohren, Craig F. and Bruce E. Albrecht (1998). *Atmospheric Thermodynamics*. Oxford University Press, New York.

Fanning, David W. (2002). *IDL Programming Techniques, Second Edition*. Fanning Press, Ft. Collins, CO, USA.

Gumley, Liam E. (2002). *Practical IDL Programming*. Morgan Kaufman, San Francisco.

Spencer, J. W. (1971). Fourier series representation of the position of the sun. *Search*, 2:172.

Index